Tasting & Grading
WINE

by

Clive Michelsen

JAC International AB

First Edition

JAC International AB
Box 60 220
S-216 09 LIMHAMN Sweden
www.malmo-wine-academy.com
info@malmo-wine-academy.com

© Clive Michelsen, 2005
Original Title: Tasting & Grading WINE ISBN 91-975326-0-6 & EAN 09789197532600
Swedish title: Allt om VINPROVNING ISBN 91-975326-1-4 & EAN 09789197532617
Cover: Jean-Michel van Braak
Layout: Clive Michelsen
Written by: Clive Michelsen
Edited by: Leif Sahlqvist
Printed by: Wallin & Dalholm Boktryckeri AB, Lund, Sweden 2005

ISBN 91-975326-0-6

This book is dedicated to my mother

June Pauline Elizabeth Preston

&

her unconditional love.

**Acknowledgements go to the
following contributors:**

CIVB, Conseil Interprofessionnel du Vin de Bordeaux for use of their pictures.
CIVR, Conseil Interprofessionnel des Vins du Roussillon for use of their pictures.
Dr. Leif Sahlqvist, editor and lecturer at Malmö Wine Academy.
Jean-Michel van Braak, B.A., for his photographs and illustrations.
Bengt Andersson, for his support.
Dr. Nils Stormby, for use of his wine cellar.
Mike Benziger, for some pictures and the introduction to his insectory.
Innovation Skåne, for their support in making this book possible.

Further thanks go to:

Gunilla Larsson, for her continual support
without which this book would not have been possible.

Contents

Chapter 5
Grading Procedures

33

Chapter 6
Wine Marketing, Pricing and Quality

Chapter 7
Grape Varieties, Oak and Additives

Chapter 8
Decanting & Aerating Wine

Appendix

Index

"What pleasures we gain from the anticipation of opening a bottle of fine wine, approaching that first aroma, and savoring its unique character".

Clive Michelsen, 2005

Introduction

Over the last decade I must have scanned through hundreds of bookstores, locally and internationally, for books about wine-tasting and grading. As you might have guessed, there aren't too many available! For this reason, and some nudging from my colleagues, I have put pen to paper to explain what you need to know about wine-tasting and grading.

This book covers the essential aspects for professionals in the trade, wine students, connoisseurs, wine club members and winemakers alike. Beginning in the vineyard and winery I proceed to discuss classical versus modern styles and style- versus fruit-driven wines, picking, the harvest window and various operations within the winery. There is a chapter on identifying defects along with understanding grape, aroma, taste, blend typicities and even pricing ratios in relation to quality.

I trust that you will find this book both interesting and full of helpful information and enjoy reading it as much as I have done in writing it.

Clive Sofus Michelsen

Chapter 1

Principles of Wine

In order for the avid wine enthusiast to taste and grade wine, an intricate partnership between man, machine, science and nature must occur. A cooperation not too easily achieved without dedication, experience, investment and good weather conditions. This requires man to do his work alongside nature, otherwise wine cannot be produced in the quantities and qualities sought by wine connoisseurs today. There are three major steps or processes that need to be discussed so that you can understand more fully what is in your glass and what factors affect what you find there and at what price. These steps are:

- Viticulture
- Vinification
- Marketing, Sales and Distribution

This chapter has been designed to give you a quick overview of the viticulture and vinification aspects associated with grape farming and winemaking. What we taste in the glass is a direct result of what has been done to the wine in the vineyard and cellar. Although winemaking is a science requiring years of study, I will attempt to cover the most important areas as generally as possible.

"Good wine begins in the vineyard". We've all heard that statement thousands of times and as it happens, it is also very true. Without good grapes, you cannot get good wine.

Viticulture

'Terroir', as the French call it, is the composition of location, soil type, mineral makeup and weather conditions (total hours of sunshine and rain with cool evenings, nights and mornings with warm days). The weather conditions directly affect the quality of the grape during the growing season and at harvest time. Too much rain produces diluted grapes, which results in less concentration. Too much sunshine, on the other hand, results in grapes that grow too quickly, producing fruit with excess sugar, less acidity, poor phenolic structure (skin, tannins and color pigments), wines with high alcohol levels, poor length and balance. The key is to produce grapes with the correct balance of sugar, pH, phenolic structure, acidity and good fruit characters (found in the pulp and skins), thus giving the winemaker the best possible prerequisites for the desired wine style.

Fig. 1.1. A vineyard in Bordeaux, France during the winter season.

Soil. Whether from granite, shale or sandstone, there are hundreds of different soil types. The classification of soils becomes quite a daunting task, although they are basically organized according to:

1. Topsoil and subsoil
2. Layers. If layers are present, they are divided into sequences or in order from the surface to the deepest point.
3. Clay content. The amount of clay deposits.
4. Sand content.

The soil makeup therefore directly affects pH levels (acidity /alkaline) and mineral balance, which in turn affect the vine and the grape composition. Soil combinations, such as sandy loam, gravel, clay and other types, need to be carefully considered when matching the vine to the soil. This is an important requirement for good grape quality, vine vigour, production and the vine's health being directly related to this match. Overfertile or rich soils produce too vigorous vines with an excessive amount of bunches as rapid growth produces phenols with loose molecule compactness leading to lesser concentrations. Water retention is another problem. Vines need soils with good water drainage, since they thrive on deep root systems, some of which are known to exceed ten meters in depth, although the average root depth is about 1.5 meters.

The soil's texture is probably the most important property to be considered. It affects the erodibility, water capacity and drainage. The subsoil's grain size is therefore vital and the smaller the grain the better. However, the surface soil helps to conserve moisture, limit erosion and if gravel or large stones (Fig. 1.3) they also reflect light and heat onto the underparts

---

Chemical & Mineral Properties of Soils

pH: is the degree of acidity or alkalinity on a scale 1 (very acid) to 14 (very alkaline). Neutral is 7 and is as natural water but some waters can vary too.

Salinity: is the excess of salts like sodium and magnesium. Too much saltiness restricts root and vine growth.

Potassium (K): provides obvious health benefits but is also responsible for tartrate crystals if not properly cold stabilized.

Calcium (Ca): also provides valuable health benefits but like potassium above it also aids in tartrate crystal formation. Too much lime will result in a high pH and can damage the vine roots.

Other minerals present in the soil include but are not limited to: Iron (Fe), Copper (Cu), Magnesium (Mg), Aluminum (Al).

Fig. 1.2. Typical minerals found in the vineyard's soil

---

of the vine canopy. Naturally, lighter stones reflect and darker ones retain heat.

The surface soil depth is important, as it influences the amount of nutrients supplied to the roots. This supply obviously derives from the minerals in the soil and fertilizers

Fig. 1.3. A gravel soil found in Bordeaux and the Rhône valley of France.

applied. If the nutrients reach the deep sub-soils, 15-35cm, they will normally support vigorous vines.

Weather

Weather conditions are of extreme importance for the vineyard and they can be divided into the following areas:

- Macro-climate conditions covering the district or region

- Meso-climate conditions covering the climate of vineyard blocks. Factors considered are hills, fingers, avenues, trees, altitude, slope of the vineyard, drainage conditions, water retention problems etc.

- Micro-climate conditions are the conditions covering the climate within the vine's canopy. The sun's effect on growth, row direction (north, south, east or west-alignment), trellising systems, pruning and the nature of the soil's surface are all part of the vine's micro-climate. If a vineyard plans to be ecological or organic then micro-climate-management is vital. Annual and seasonal conditions are continually monitored and matched to the vine of choice. For each individual area of the vineyard the annual and seasonal rainfall in millimeters needs to be recorded along with the daily sun exposure, as well as daily temperature variations and slope facing conditions, such as north/south exposure and drainage. Annual pruning and trellising requirements, when needed, are therefore adjusted to meet the changing climatic conditions and the winemaker's need for specific types of fruit. Cool climates need vines that can sustain very low temperatures in the winter and warm climates need vines that can produce under very warm conditions.

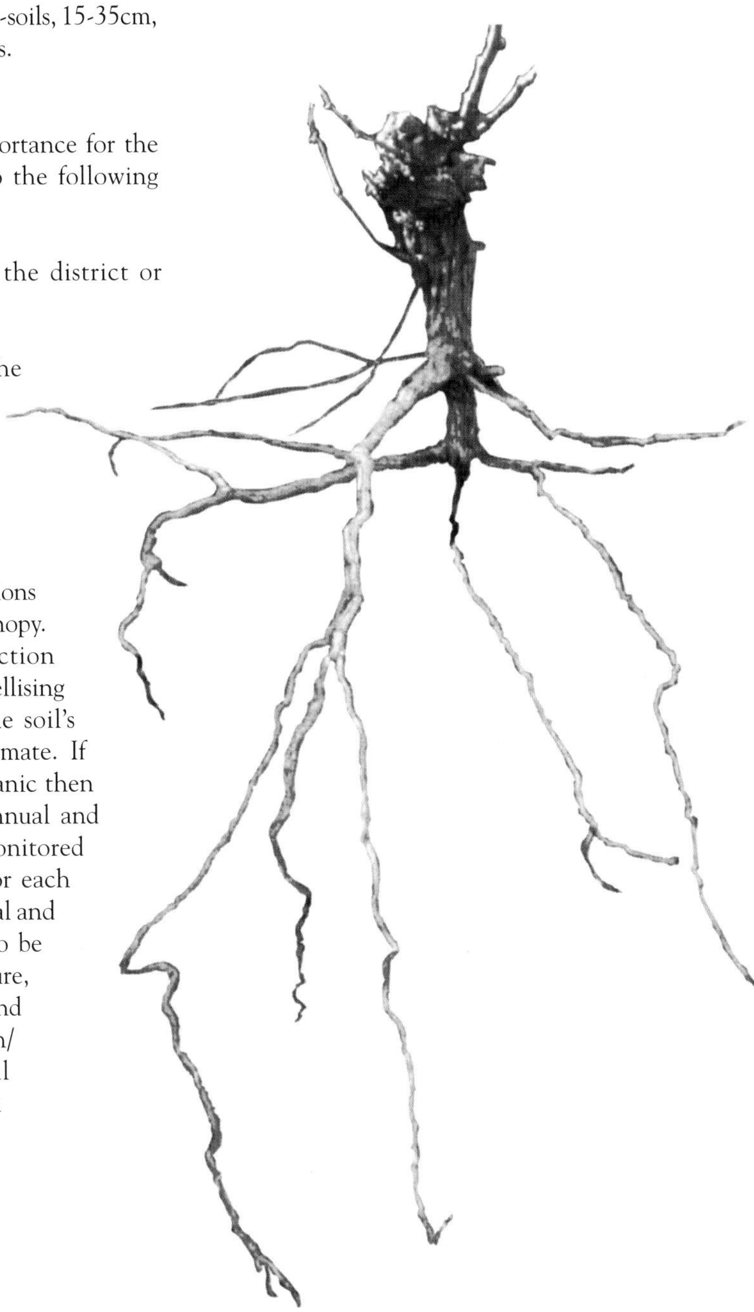

Fig. 1.4. A typical root system. A root system can grow to a depth of over 2 meters with a radius of 1.5 meters. A mature vine can occupy over 18 m³. In dry areas some vines have been known to go to depths of over 10 m in search of water.

The Vine

The selection of the right vine is not as easy as we would like it to be. Meso-climate conditions as stated above need to be considered, along with the soil's pH, mineral composition etc. When these are understood, vine selection can be done. Within the Vitaceae family there are over 3000 vine types, the vast majority of which are wild vines not used in winemaking today. Figure 1.5 illustrates the family tree for our beloved varieties Chardonnay, Cabernet Sauvignon, Merlot and others. We begin with the family name Vitaceae, of whose 11 genera we are only interested in Vitis. The genus Vitis is then broken down into 61 different species. Three species are of interest to winemaking today:

Labrusca, Riparia and Vinifera. Vinifera is the species that dominates the market with hundreds of varieties worldwide. Labrusca and Riparia are native American vines, which can be used in extremely hot and cold climates (-40°C to +40°C). They are also used as root stocks for many European vines today.

Pruning and trellising decisions are directly related to the vineyard's location, meso-climate conditions (sun, rain and wind exposure), drainage, vine type and obviously a balance between the required yield and quality sought.

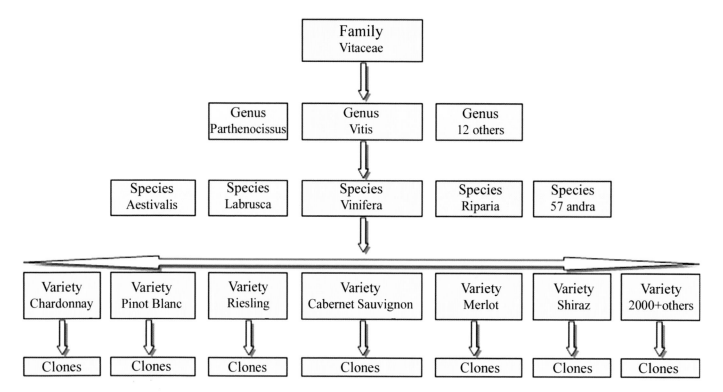

Fig. 1.5. The grape family tree consists of thousands of varieties but for the sake of simplicity only six varieties are shown above.

Procedures during the year of a vineyard

Whether in Coonawarra in South Australia or Napa Valley, every vineyard has its own set of seasonal duties. These duties are divided up into different seasonal responsibilities according to the climatic conditions. Continued vigilence along with good quality control and assurance procedures are required in order to guarantee the winemaker good fruit at harvest time. The following cycle of events is associated with traditional wine growing properties.

Spring

In the spring planting, spraying, soil care and canopy management duties are performed.

- Planting is done in the early spring, as this is the time when everything is starting to warm up and the ground still retains some moisture from the past winter. Too much moisture on the other hand is not good as it will make the roots of the vine rot. The time for planting can vary from region to region and continue well into the early summer.

- Spraying is common in most vineyards today and the first spraying is done in the spring with a so-called Bordeaux mixture (copper-sulfate, a mixture of lime and water) or a lime-sulfur spray that is applied to the buds as they soften. This is done to guard against fungal diseases.

- Tilling or ploughing is also a spring time chore. This is done to aerate the soil primarily in organic vineyards and provide the opportunity for plant growth between the soils, thus attracting the insects to the plants instead of the vine.

Fig. 1.6. A grape bunch at the end stages of flowering. Depending upon the grape variety, it is commonly discussed that there are approximately 100 to 110 days from flowering to picking or harvest time.

Other vineyards would be spraying with herbicides to control weed and grass growth.

- Finally, a canopy management plan would be applied to monitor and limit uncontrollable foliage growth as well as to manage the amount of exposure of the leaves and grapes to the sun.

Summer

The summer is full of vine maintenance in the form of irrigation, spraying and trimming, soil and pest control.

- Irrigation. In some countries irrigation is not allowed, but in warm and dry climates this is essential. A drip system is usually in place to control the exact amount of water needed for each vine.

- Spraying continues in the vineyard with the Bordeaux mixture again. This is usually done in order to prevent a Botrytis cinerea infection, which can occur directly after a humid followed by a dry period. An early Botrytis infection would destroy the crop, as the grapes need to be fully developed prior to such an infection if desired.

- Trimming is a continual process during the growing season. Canes need to be trimmed and the remaining ones tied up to the trellising system, designed for the specific vine type and the climatic exposure of the vineyard.

- Pest control is of major importance. This time is heaven for all the birds, caterpillars, moths and insects, as food is abundant. Here a major difference lies between the organic grower and the farmer who uses pesticides to control this invasion. Vineyards are invaded constantly by insects and pests during the growing season. They want to eat both grapes and leaves. Who blames them? Growing mustard and other plants between the rows is very effective, as many insects prefer mustard to grapes and are therefore drawn towards them instead. So, when you are in a vineyard shop selling its own homemade mustard, buy it, as it served a very good purpose.

Fall

Fall is the time for nervousness in the vineyard. This is when harvest takes place along with post harvest spraying, soil management and vineyard maintenance.

- Most growers in Bordeaux will be praying for the weather to hold, whilst others could be concerned about grape qualities. Harvest is by far the most stressful time in a vineyard and many a wine grower is happy at its completion. The wine style, quality, grape variety and vineyard slope conditions would dictate whether or not the harvest is machine- or hand-picked.

- Spraying is started when about 60% of the leaves have fallen from the vines. This is done to prevent mildew spores from

Fig. 1.7. This is the intermediate stage of development, known as Veraison. Veraison marks the beginning of ripening, where the grape sugars rapidly increase and acidity decreases.

bedding down on the vine for the winter, only awakening in the spring to damage the next year's crop.

- Soil maintenance is done to prepare the soil for next year's crop. The soil is usually fertilized and tilled up to the sides of the vine trunk so as to protect the trunk from the coming winter months.

- Pruning down the canes is also done at the end of the harvest. The pruned ends are either made into chips and included into the soil or simply burnt.

Winter

The winter months seem to be quiet in the vineyard but pruning continues unabated. Trellis repair with overall maintenance of the vineyard and planning for the next year's plantings and/or vine extractions occur. Naturally the winemaker is now full up with fermenting and maturing wine in the cellar.

Red Grapes		White Grapes	
Grape Variety	**Maturing Time**	**Grape Variety**	**Maturing Time**
Barbera	Late	Aligoté	Early midseason
Cabernet Franc	Early late season	Chardonnay	Early midseason
Cabernet Sauvignon	Late	Chenin Blanc	Midseason
Carignan	Midseason	Clairette Blanc	Late
Cinsault	Late midseason	Colombar	Late midseason
Grenache (Noir)	Midseason	Furmint	Late midseason
Malbec (Cot)	Late midseason	Gewürztraminer	Midseason
Merlot	Midseason	Grenache (Blanc)	Midseason
Nebbiolo	Late midseason	Kerner	Early
Pinotage	Early midseason	Marsanne	Late midseason
Pinot Noir	Early midseason	Muscadelle	Early midseason
Pontac	Midseason	Muscat d' Alexandrie	Late midseason
Primitivo	Late midseason	Palomino	Midseason
Sangiovese	Midseason	Pinot Blanc	Early
Shiraz (Syrah)	Late midseason	Pinot Gris (Grigio)	Early
Tempranillo	Midseason	Riesling	Late midseason
Tinta Barocca	Midseason	Sauvignon Blanc	Early midseason
Zinfandel	Midseason	Sémillon	Early midseason
		Sylvaner	Early
		Trebbiano (Ugni Blanc)	Late
		Viognier	Midseason

Fig. 1.8 shows a short list representing the various grape maturing rates in the vineyard. This is of interest, since picking too late or early leaves the winemaker with a number of difficulties. These difficulties cannot always be rectified in the winery, but they can be identified in the glass.

The Growing Season

The growing season varies depending on location, climate conditions within the vineyard and grape variety. Continual vigilance is a must in the vineyard during the growing season, as the grapes ripen at different stages. So do their pH, phenolic structure, acid and sugar levels. All these factors need to be monitored for each variety and block of vineyards in order to yield the required fruit to the winemaker.

Timing of the Harvest

One of the most important questions that a winemaker has to contemplate is the timing of the harvest. What optimum balance (acid, phenolic structure, pH, fruit and sugar) would he/she like to receive during the harvest? This is directly related to the style of wine the winemaker plans to produce. Economic conditions also play a major role in this decision process.

In order to pick optimally, the winemaker would ready the receiving station just prior to harvest. As the grapes are measured on a daily basis, the winemaker prepares himslef for deliveries. The graph (Fig. 1.10) shows the optimal window for harvest. This window is only about three to four days in length (depending on the weather conditions) and cannot be missed if the winemaker wants the fruit balance to be optimal.

Fig. 1.9. Harvest time in the vineyard. In top quality vineyards, this is done by hand and not by machine-picking. Hand harvest insures that the berries are not broken. This eliminates the risk of early degradation through oxygen contact.

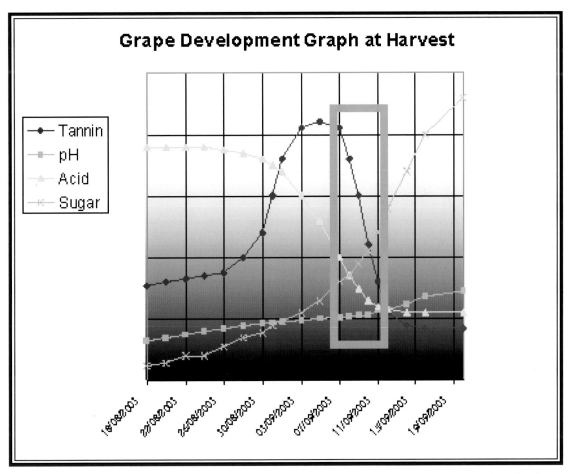

Fig. 1.10. The above graph shows a red-boxed area displaying the optimal window for harvest. This window provides a phenolic (tannin) quality at its peak with a good balance of acids and sugar.

Picking prior to or after this date would require additives such as tannic acid, tartaric acid or even sugar. Both underdeveloped and overripe phenolics produce weak flavonoids and some vineyards use flavor and aroma extracts to increase deficient levels, although the industry explicitly forbids their use. Careful study of the grape's development as well as the desired style of wine is thus very important and a lot of attention to detail is required in the vineyard.

At harvest, sugar levels therefore directly determine the alcohol level after fermentation as shown in the illustration below.

Sugar Content = Alcohol (Must Weight)			
Potential Alcohol (% by volume)	Brix Degrees (USA)	Baume Degrees (France)	Oechsle Degrees (Germany)
15	27.1	15	119
14	25.3	14	110
13	23.5	13	101
12.5	22.6	12.5	97
12	21.7	12	93
11	19.8	11	84
10	18.0	10	75

Fig. 1.11. The sugar content of the grape or must is transformed into alcohol during fermentation by the yeast cells. For example, if you harvest at 23.5 Brix, you should have a 13% wine after the wine is fermented dry, that is to say, with no residual sugar remaining.

Figures 1.12.& 1.12.1. An insectory which is part of the Benziger Estate in Sonoma County, USA. Mr. Mike Benziger, owner of the vineyard stated: "The insectories on our property including the wetland area greatly increased the (bio)diversity of insects and birds and other animals on the property. This diversity over time creates a self-regulating system of predators and prey, eliminating the need for pesticides".

Insectory

An insectory is a sectioned-off insect investigatory area within a vineyard. This area is managed by the vineyard manager or vineyard nursery and its sole purpose is to monitor insect movement from plant to plant. Vineyard insects are studied here and their preferences for food and dislikes noted, which is a very time-consuming and cost-worthy undertaking but extremely beneficial to ecological and organic winemaking.

Understanding vineyard pests, their habitats and food preferences over the vine itself, such as herbs, plants and weeds, will both reduce chemical use and provide sounder, more nutritional grapes in the future. This is why many ecological wineries are establishing insectories to study the insects and their eating behaviors within vineyards today.

As a matter of interest, I have included below a short list of plants that birds, butterflies and other insects like to snack on. Other aspects in regard to ecological and organic vineyards are not discussed here, since this book's major focus is on the grading of wines.

Fig. 1.13 Agastache rupestris

Hummingbird Food Plants:
- Orange Carpet
- Sunset Hyssop (Agastache rupestris)
- Autumn Sage
- Texas Red Yucca
- Malibu Yellow & Red Hot Pepper
- Firecracker and Pineleaf Penstemon
- Mexican Sage

Fig. 1.14. Callirhoe involucrate

Butterfly Food Plants:
- Wine Cups (Callirhoe involucrate)
- Whirling Butterflies
- Yellow Gem
- Kangaroo Paws
- Arctic Summer

Fig. 1.15. Perovskia atriplicifolia

Insect Food Plants:
- Moonshine Yarrow
- Blue Catmint
- Prairie Coneflower
- Russian Sage (Perovskia atriplicifolia)
- Blackeyed Susan
- Purple Coneflower
- Monch

Vinification

Vinification is the process of winemaking, which is accomplished by taking the delivered grapes and turning them into wine or a variety of wine styles, juices and drinks. This is not an easy tasks as many procedures have to be considered from the arrival of the grapes to the finished wine.

The quality of the received grapes is the first and most important decision to be made by a winemaker. These variables of quality include:

- Phenolic (grape skin) ripeness
- Malic and tartaric acid levels
- Sugar level (sucrose & dextrose)
- pH
- Use of stalks and leaves.

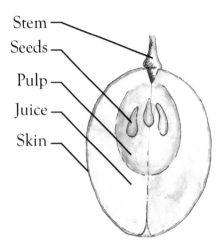

Fig. 1.16. The cross-section of a grape.

Fig. 1.17. Mature grapes just prior to harvest.

In the majority of cases the winemaker is present at the receiving station when the grapes arrive. The final fruit quality has already been determined, and the receiving station is at its busiest receiving the various loads of grapes and testing them prior to destemming. Naturally, complications and hold-ups are common at the receiving station. One of the most important problems is the rapidly rising temperatures of the grapes, as time passes, along with broken skins. Premature fermentations and the presence of bacteria are just a few of the problems facing the winemaker and the quality assurance technician.

The grape quality window, the time when the grapes reach the right consistency, lasts only three to five days if the temperature does not rise significantly. Rising daily temperatures also decreases the picking time. One nightmare

Fig. 1.18. The picture shows a sorting table. Upon arrival to the winery, the grapes are passed along the table and sorted for quality prior to entering the de-stemmer where they are de-stemmed and then crushed before fermentation.

for the vineyard manager is rain just prior to picking. This would cause the grapes to absorb water and dilute the acid sugar balance.

Harvest
The picking usually starts early in the morning to take advantage of the cool weather conditions. This is very important as the warmer midday temperatures play havoc on the grapes' sugar-acid-pH balance. Some vineyards take this so seriously that they even pick at night.

At the receiving station the winemaker receives tractor loads of grapes from different blocks. These have to be organized into the right groups for crushing as quickly as possible, as the lines outside the receiving station continue to grow steadily during the morning hours.

Approval of Bought Grapes
If grapes are being bought from local farmers, they are approved at the receiving station prior to acceptance. These grapes would have to be tested before unloading takes place. In the majority of cases the winemaker lists his quality requirements, for instance the pH, acid, sugar and grape skin values for the grapes to be purchased from the independent growers. Depending on the style and quality of the wine to be produced, the winemaker might also have to adjust the received grapes by either adding or furthering some stalks or leaves during crushing.

Quality Assurance
The larger the winery, the larger the problems. A quality assurance sequence is therefore always necessary to guide the winemaker and to perpetuate the continual flow of grapes. There are legislative and health guidelines the winemaker has to follow that can vary from country to country. The Appellation Controlée (AOC) system in France and the Approved Viticultural Area (AVA) in the US are two examples. Modern winemaking techniques and machines have enhanced this process, ensuring that good quality fruit is crushed as soon as possible after picking.

Winemaking
The next step is to start producing the wine. I have created two flow-charts showing an overview of the winemaking procedures for red and white wines. Not all of the steps are included within the flow-charts; nevertheless, you will attain a good understanding of the process of winemaking.

The use of oak is of vital importance during the fermentation phase. The reason for this is that the tannin and oak flavors from oak vats, staves, chips and powders are best extracted during the fermentation process. The fermenting grapes produce heat, CO_2, alcohols, aromas and other taste characteristics, but it is the heat and CO_2 which aid in oak extraction.

As illustrated in the flow-charts, wine styles can vary depending upon:

1) The quality of the grapes at receipt
2) Grape variety or varieties within the blend
3) Fermentation temperatures and lengths
4) Adjustments made to the must and wine
   (during and after fermentation and prior to bottling)
5) Maturation techniques (types of oak, toasted
   strengths, length in oak, on lees, steel tanks)

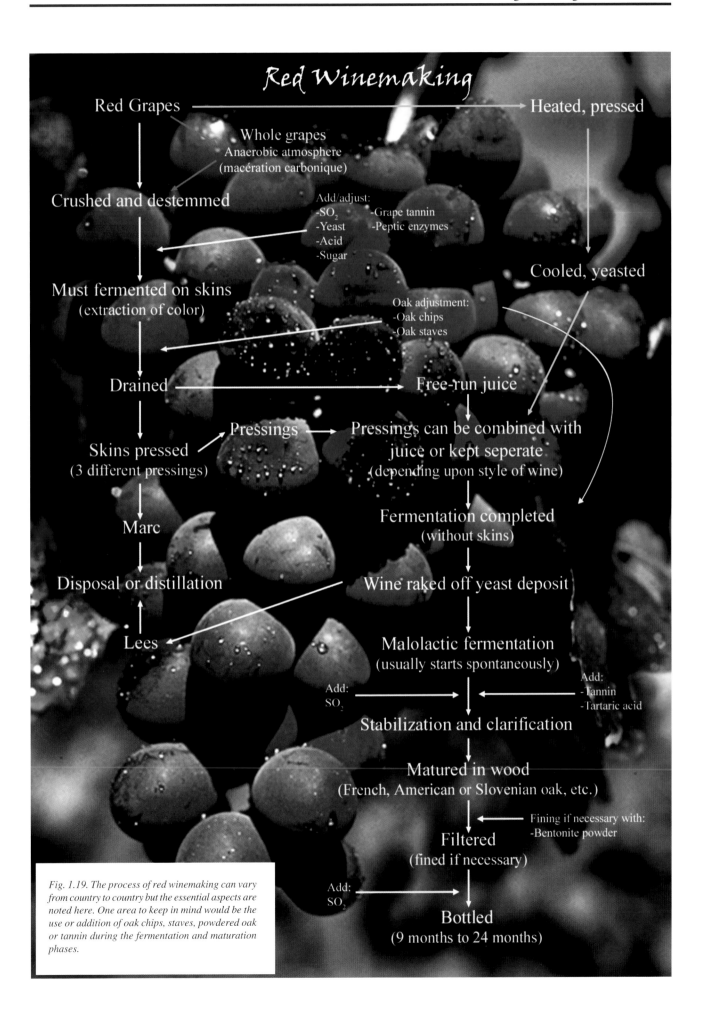

Red Winemaking

Red Grapes ──────────────────────────► Heated, pressed

Whole grapes
Anaerobic atmosphere
(macération carbonique)

Crushed and destemmed

Add/adjust:
-SO₂   -Grape tannin
-Yeast   -Peptic enzymes
-Acid
-Sugar

Cooled, yeasted

Must fermented on skins
(extraction of color)

Oak adjustment:
-Oak chips
-Oak staves

Drained ──────────────────► Free-run juice

Pressings ──► Pressings can be combined with
juice or kept seperate
(depending upon style of wine)

Skins pressed
(3 different pressings)

Fermentation completed
(without skins)

Marc

Disposal or distillation   Wine raked off yeast deposit

Lees   Malolactic fermentation
(usually starts spontaneously)

Add: Add:
SO₂ ──────────────►   ◄────────── -Tannin
                                          -Tartaric acid

Stabilization and clarification

Matured in wood
(French, American or Slovenian oak, etc.)

Fining if necessary with:
-Bentonite powder

Filtered
(fined if necessary)

Add:
SO₂ ──────────────►

Bottled
(9 months to 24 months)

Fig. 1.19. The process of red winemaking can vary
from country to country but the essential aspects are
noted here. One area to keep in mind would be the
use or addition of oak chips, staves, powdered oak
or tannin during the fermentation and maturation
phases.

White Winemaking

White Grapes
↓
Crushed
(may be destemmed with
or without leaves)
↓
Drained
↓
Skins and stems
↓
Pressed
↓
Marc
(disposed of or distilled)
↑
Lees
(expended yeast cells
and pressings)

Add:
-Peptic enzymes
-SO₂
-Tartaric acid

Free-run juice

Pressings

Pressings can be combined with juice
or kept separate
(depending upon style of wine)
↓
Chilled, settled and/or racked
(gives clear juice, can centrifuge or filter)
↓
Ferment dry with cooling
(dry or can be stopped while juice is sweet)
↓
Wine racked off yeast deposit

Add:
-Yeast
-Oak powder or chips

Adjust:
-pH if needed
-fine with Bentonite

Cold-stabilization
(prevent potassium crystals, protein, etc.)

Add:
-Ascorbic acid
-SO₂

Racked and filtered
↓
Tank Storage and/or blending

Fining if needed with:
-Isinglass powder
-Potassium Caseinate powder

Add if needed:
-Ascorbic acid
-Sweetening
-SO₂

Sterile-filtered
↓
Bottled (3 to 9 months old)

Fig. 1.20. The process of white winemaking can, as with red wine, vary from country to country but the essential aspects are noted here. Also as with red wine the use or addition of oak chips, staves, powdered oak or tannin during the fermentation and maturation phases occur.

A Few Stages of the Winemaking Process.

I have included a number of pictures from the cellars of Château Margaux, Lafite-Rothschild and Lynch-Bages in the Bordeaux region to illustrate some of the steps above. All steps shown in figures 1.19 and 1.20 are not included.

The *receiver* and *de-stemmer* receive the grapes as they are tipped into a v-shaped bin with a screw-blade (Fig. 1.21). The grapes converge on a rotating screw-blade at the bottom of the v-shape and are then separated from their stalks as they pass through the de-stemmer via a conveyor belt towards the crusher. The separated stalks are either ground up and used as fertilizers or in some cases even added to the wine must during fermentation. This addition serves to raise tannin and astringency levels.

The *crusher* (Fig 1.22) is used to firmly crush the grapes so that the juice is extracted without damaging or breaking the pips, as broken pips tend to be very bitter, thus raising the bitterness level within the wine. There are a number of different crushing machines on the market today using centrifugal force, which rotates at high speeds, or a cylindrical tube with an inflatable balloon in its center (Fig. 1.21). The inflatable balloon is filled with air, thus reducing the space in the cylindrical tube and uniformly crushing the grapes.

Fig. 1.21. Receiving port with a de-stemmer.

Fig. 1.22. A cylindrical crusher.

A **control panel** (Fig. 1.23) shows the flow of the must and wine from station to station within the cellar. This automation provides the winemaker with an excellent picture of the wine flow in process. Obviously daily monitoring of the wines must be done manually. Continual monitoring of fermentation temperatures and alcohol levels are vital to the success of a good wine.

The **fermentation tanks** (Fig. 1.24) can be steel, oak vats, concrete vats and even oak barrels. Their sizes range from as little as 200 liters to as much as 50,000 liters. The key with most fermenting today is to hold cool, steady temperatures. In Fig. 1.24 you can see horizontal ridges on the sides of each of the tanks. Depending upon the desired temperature of the must an adjustment can be made by pumping either a cold or warm liquid through these pipes. This helps to maintain a steady temperature during fermentation. There are many systems for maintaining temperatures. One of them is a coil system, which is immersed into the must. A cool liquid is pumped through it, which in turn cools the heating must. As already discussed, the fermentation of grape sugars creates CO_2, alcohol and heat. Keeping a stable temperature is therefore very important.

Fermentation (Fig. 1.25) is the process in which yeast breaks down the sugars in the grapes into alcohol. Yeast changes the sugars into the following by-products: alcohol, CO_2 and heat. During fermentation a cap is formed over the fermenting wine, which is caused by the rising CO_2. Since the skins are where the majority of the flavor is, it is important that the cap is frequently punched (broken) and mixed with the rest of the fermenting wine. The 'punching' of the cap and the 'pumping over' of the wine is vital to effective extraction. The use of oak chips, staves and/or tannin powder is more effective during fermentation if extra oak characters and tannin are sought.

Filling the barrels (Fig. 1.26) is important and needs to be done quickly and effectively with the least amount of spill. Here you can see a cellar worker filling the oak barrels with the finished, dry fermented wine. The hole through which he is filling the barrel is called a bung hole. Over an 18-month period the cellar worker will continually have to monitor and top up the barrels of wine from other barrels, as about 10-15 liters are lost through leakage and evaporation. During the maturation process the wine can be stored in a number of different barrels. Some vineyards use new, first and second year barrels at various stages over the 18-month period.

The **maturation** process (Fig. 1.27 and 1.27.1) or ageing of the wine in oak barrels is very important and ranges from as little as three months for some white wines to as much as 18 to 24 months. This naturally depends on the age and quality of the oak barrels, if they are light, medium or heavily toasted barrel, whether or not they are French, American, Slovenian or South American and the quality of the wine to be matured. The wines are matured for an average of 18 months.

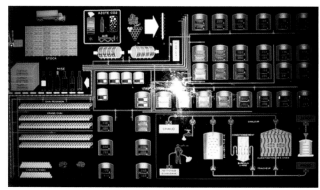
Fig. 1.23. A temperature control and pumping-over station.

Fig. 1.24. Steel fermentation tanks. The horizontal cooling bands fitted with pipes can be seen on the sides of the tanks.

Fig. 1.24.1. French Oak fermentation tanks in Bordeaux, France.

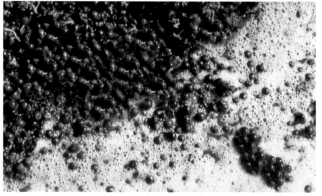
Fig. 1.25. A normal fermentation in process. These are Cabernet Sauvignon grapes.

Fig. 1.26. Filling the barrels with wine for ageing. In the very good châteaux in France this is done three times during the maturation phase. This phase can vary from vineyard to vineyard and ranges anywhere from 1 to 9 months (new French oak) for white wines and 12 to 24 months for red wines. Oak maturation is vital for high quality wines, as it allows the wines to breathe, that is to say, allows for small amounts of oxygen to enter the wine.

They are racked three times during that period and then bottled. Bordeaux Grands Crus unlike any others can be auctioned and sold off whilst still in the barrel (en primeur) and a year prior to bottling. No other wine region has managed to pull off such demand for their product as Bordeaux. A typical Bordeaux cellar is shown in Fig. 1.27.

After the wines have aged sufficiently in oak, they are bottled. This is done in a filling station (Fig 1.28), usually on the premises, but in many remote areas and on small wineries a filling station on wheels is available. The bottles are washed, filled, corked and labeled all on the same line. Classified Bordeaux wines are usually boxed in wooden cases and therefore packed by hand; otherwise, the bottles would be packed by an automatic packer, as is the case in many New World wineries. Maintenance and quality assurance tests are conducted on a continual basis. During washing, bottling, labeling and boxing, cellar workers need to be vigilant, as these machines can fill up to 10,000 bottles per hour. A slight problem holds up production and causes costs to increase.

Fig. 1.27. Oak maturation in process. These barrels are continually monitored and topped up.

Fig. 1.27.1. French oak barrels in Château Lafite-Rothschild in Pauillac, Bordeaux. The wines are aged for 15 to 18 months in medium toasted, new French oak barrels.

Fig. 1.28. A filling, corking and labeling machine at Château Lynch-Bages in Bordeaux.

Testing (Fig 1.29) and quality assurance is of vital importance, so just prior to and after bottling random samples are taken and tested for quality. This is usually conducted at the vineyard, as most wineries have their own laboratories.

All wine products should be tested and evaluated at the winery. A product data sheet or chemical analysis evaluation is, in the majority of cases, conducted on all wines sold.

This evaluation is also available to the end customer (the consumer) if necessary. Your local wine store should have a copy readily available or be able to request it from the distributor.

When conducting a wine-tasting, these evaluation sheets can help you tremendously. Your own impressions could be adjusted, confirmed or refuted when comparing them with the chemical analysis sheet. This will be very helpful to your advancement and enjoyment in wine-tasting.

Finally, the storing of wines is another important issue to consider, as this can dramatically affect the quality and the potential life of the wine. Constant cool temperatures are preferable and naturally warm or light conditions are not good for any wine, as they will hasten the effects of ageing and minimize your potential storage time considerably; moreover, correct humidity levels will prevent the corks from drying out by keeping them moist.

If you are planning on cellaring your wines it is a necessity that you research and prepare your cellar with the correct ambient temperature, humidity and lighting. Your local book store should have a book on how to build or create such a wine cellar.

Fig. 1.29. Testing and quality control.

Fig. 1.30. Storage cages at Château Lafite-Rothschild's cellar. These wines are cellared here for special customers and are up to 20 years old.

Chapter 2

Styles of Wine

Old versus new world, wine technology, adjusting wine styles to suit the customer and classic wine basics. Where on earth do we start? Is there a difference? Countries such as South Africa, Chile and the USA have been producing wines for hundreds of years, so why are these still called New World Wines? In this chapter, I will explain the various styles of wines made today and the differences that might exist, their compositions, alcohol levels and fruit contents among other things.

In order to fully understand the development of wine styles today it can benefit us to recognize the roles, both positive and negative, that business marketing is playing in regard to wine and its style. Market segmentation, the marketing mix (product, price, package…) and volume-driven wines which have become the driving force for the majority of large producers. Typical classic styles are being drowned out by the many 'Coca Cola Wines' full-bodied, overripe, high alcohol wines. Moreover, many of the mediocre wines are now so adjusted with sucrose, glucose, citric and tartaric acid and even tannin that we are find ourselves, more than often, in a quagmire of non-typical wines. On a positive note, their are many advances in wine technology that can help the vineyard manager and winemaker to improve upon quality assurance and control, thus enhancing the overall quality of their wines' typicity.

Fig. 2.2. From another wine-tasting session in Bordeaux. An evaluation of the wine's residual sugar, body, fruitiness and acid content is noted and reflections made on the wine's ability to be cellared.

Fig. 2.1. Old world style wine-tasting. Note the use of the aroma caps.

As discussed earlier in this book, good fruit is of utmost importance if good wine is to be made. Science has intervened, both for the good and the bad. The winemaker, financial director and marketing department all put their heads together and determine the course for each wine made. The location, vineyard, grapes and the climate conditions together determine the basic elements. In addition, the winemaker determines whether the wine produced will be an over-fruity (very ripe / picked late), high alcohol (high sugar level at harvest), full-bodied (extended fermentation with long oak maturation) wine or a more tart (acidic) and flowery with less astringency (tannin). All the above factors have a direct impact on the basic cost structure for each bottle produced and subsequently for the intended target group of customers and volumes expected. Wine after all is business too.

Apart from all of that, there are four major differences in wines produced today: Old World, New World, fruit-driven and style-driven. This does not take fortified, Champagne (sparkling wine) and sweet wines into consideration but mainly focuses on red and white wines.

Old World Style (Classical)

Classical wine styles are not necessarily from winemaking countries in the old world, such as France, Italy and Spain, but wines made in the Old World style, wines which reflect both grape and regional blending characteristics:

Appearance: varied but usually displaying a gradient, clean and viscous. Filtered by either 'racking' or 'filtering'.

Nose (aroma): Typicity depicts the styles and characters from that grape, blend and region. For example: a 'Classic Bordeaux Style' with a pencil-shaving, blackcurrant, plum and French oak character; or a 'Rioja' with the typical buttery vanilla from American oak, dill and red berry characters. These aromas and characteristics are easily recognizable to an avid taster.

Taste: Offering a balance between acidity, tannin and alcohol typically produced by the grape or blend. These characteristics are listed in the chapter 7 of this book. Blended wines are the sum of the varietals. Variables such as estate, appellation and/or regional blends are also considered.

Storage Potential: Classic top-quality wines and styles can be stored for over 25 years and in many cases much longer. Simpler wines in classic style have usually a potential storage time of between 8 to 15 years.

New World Style (Modern)

Modern wine styles are not necessarily from countries like South Africa, USA, Australia, New Zealand, Chile as generally discussed in some wine books but they belong to regions that produce a more fruity alcohol-rich wine, usually with the following characteristics:

Appearance: Deep colors with dark tones and fine filtering or no filtering at all.

Nose (aroma): Very fruity although not very grape-typical in character, as the overripe fruit usually dominates most of the subtle characters. Usually new world wines are divided into two categories of aromas: an overly strong combination of various aromas or a simplistic vinous nose. Not easily identifiable and confused with a number of regional areas.

Taste: 'Power-based wines' as I call them. These are tastes that try to combine a myriad of flavors and sensations into one product. On the other hand, there are those winemakers that over-filter their wines leaving too little.

Storage Potential: Storage potential can range from 6 months to over 12 years depending on the acid, tannin, fruit and alcohol levels.

Old World Style
(Classical)

Style-Driven – Fruit-Driven

New World Style
(Modern)

Style-Driven – Fruit-Driven

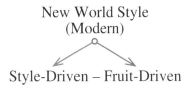

How ripening can affect aroma changes

White Chardonnay Grape	Sugar / ACL. Level (Baumé)
Table Wines	
Fig and dried fruit characters	14°
Tropical fruit, peaches & fig characters	13°
Peach, melon & tropical fruit characters	12°
Melon, peach and citrus characters	11°
Cucumber and citrus characters	10°
Citrus & cucumber characters	9°
Unripe characters	8°

Oak maturation will produce wines with more concentrated and tobacco / oak flavours.

Fig. 2.3. Shows various aromatic changes in the grapes as they ripen. Depending on the style of wine the winemaker can request a certain grape ripeness from the vineyard manager, which provides him with the potential resource materials needed to produce the required character and/or style.

Fruit-Driven

Fruit-driven wine styles are not necessarily connected with New World countries like USA, Australia, Chile but can also include regions in France, Italy and Spain. The common denominator is that they are regions producing wines with usually the following characteristics:

Appearance: Deep to dark tones with a black to blue-red hue when young. Young wines exhibit a very tight gradient from the bowl (center) of the wine to the circumference (1 to 3 mm from the meniscus, a watery colorless band around the rim). Older wines (10 years of storage) usually display a gradual gradient, which extends to about 8 to 10 mm from the rim.

Nose (aroma): An overly ripe, fruit-driven, aroma-packed, high alcohol nose is usually associated with fruit-driven wines. I call these 'Coca-Cola' wines. This type of aroma is usually dominated by one or two major characteristics, such as black currants (dark or red berry characters).

Taste: In the majority of cases they offer high alcohol levels, 13.5% or more and are packed with overripe fruit and additives such as tannic and tartaric acids in an effort to balance the high fruit/alcohol levels with lower acid and phenolic levels.

Length: Can be very long when it comes to fruit and alcohol or in some cases very short.

Balance: Dominated by overripe fruit, high alcohol or too much added tannin.

Storage Potential: Oak-matured wines can usually be stored for as much as 10 to 17 years, while fruit-driven wines, matured in stainless steel tanks, usually have a difficulty passing the 3 year mark.

Style-Driven

Style, grape, region, appellation or vineyard-driven wines are combinations of various winemaking technologies, both new and old. These wines are produced to optimize the grape varietal, blend or specific terroir associated with individual vineyards. For style-driven wines, the grape's characteristics are considered in particular and the desired character balance of the grape maintained as much as possible, as well as its aroma and fruit character, acid, tannin, alcohol, bitterness and oak. These make up the complexities of world class wines, whether New or Old world. Style-driven wines are wines showing the following characteristics:

Appearance: Varies depending on style, region and appellation and in accordance with the appellation's or region's rules. If no requirements are attached to the style, the wine could be vinified under the experimental guidelines that allow vineyards to test various grapes and styles.

Nose (aroma): Typical grape characteristics but with an individual appellation, terroir and/or style.

Taste: Usually good balance in accordance with the grape ratio charts shown for each grape in the grape section.

Length: Consistent with the quality of wine.

Balance: Consistent with the quality of wine produced either in the vineyard to region.

Storage Potential: Consistent with the quality of wine, oak maturation, balance of acid, fruit and tannin.

Wine Acidity Levels

Various Wine Styles	Acidity (grams/liter)
Table Wines	
Sparkling wine	8–12
White dry (light-bodied)	7-9
White dry (full-bodied)	6-8
White semi-sweet	7-9
White sweet (botrytis)	6-9
Red wine (light-bodied)	7-9
Red wine (full-bodied)	5-9
Fortified Styles	
Sherry styles	6-9
Port styles	4-6
Other sweet fortified (Tokay, Muscat, etc.)	4-6

Each group of wine types will have a variety of hues and tones that are associated with them.

Fig. 2.4. The average total acidity for various wine styles.

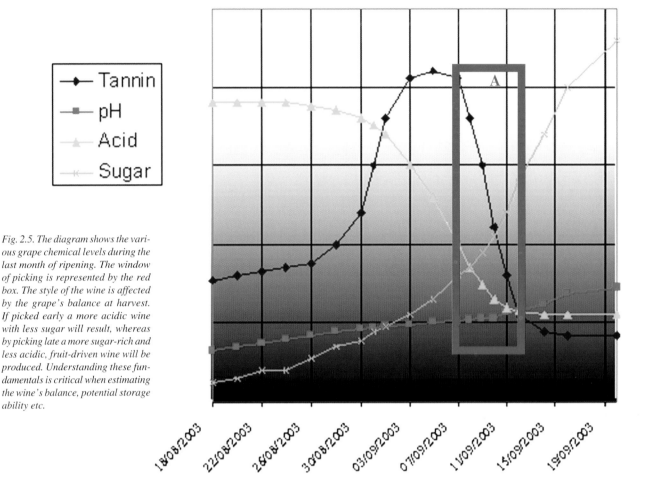

Fig. 2.5. The diagram shows the various grape chemical levels during the last month of ripening. The window of picking is represented by the red box. The style of the wine is affected by the grape's balance at harvest. If picked early a more acidic wine with less sugar will result, whereas by picking late a more sugar-rich and less acidic, fruit-driven wine will be produced. Understanding these fundamentals is critical when estimating the wine's balance, potential storage ability etc.

Harvest and the Style of Wine

The Blue Line (tannin) shows a phenolic development scale from young grapes through maturity. The phenolic structure of a grape includes pigments, tannins, flavor compounds as well as antioxidants and is responsible for the aromas and tannin. In the above example the phenolic quality peeks at around the 3rd until the 7th of September (A). The great chateaux of Bordeaux all take great care in prioritizing picking around the phenolic quality while at the same time balancing it with the sugar, acid and pH content around harvest.

The Yellow Line (malic and tartaric acids) shows how the acid quantity and strength change as the fruit ripens. In unripe fruit malic acid dominates and as the grape ripens the harder, tart malic acid transforms into tartaric acid. The salts found at the bottom of most tanks and bottles as well as acids fuse to pigments, tannin and calcium to produce sediment and other deposits found in wines as they age. Approximately 90 % of the acids found in wine are malic and tartaric. Other minor and volatile acids are found in small concentrations. The fall in acidity is due to dilution and transformation at the same time. Dilution is the water intake and sugar growth. The

acids show a decrease from about 16 g/liter to about 6 g/liter from the 3rd to the 11th of September, a seven day period. The illustration shows typical acidity ranges in grape juice at harvest for a variety of wine styles.

The Light Blue Line (Fig. 2.3; sugar = glucose and fructose, both with the same chemical structure $C_6H_{12}O_6$, the only difference being the molecule shape) shows the sugar content is shown as it is produced through photosynthesis in the leave and also, to a minor extent, the biochemical conversion of malic acid into sugars. The sugars are produced in the leaves and transported to the grapes for storage. The graph shows a gradual increase in the sugar content of the grape. Note the large increase from the 7th to the 19th, which is only a period of 12 days. In this example the sugar content increased from 107 g/liter to over 134 g/liter. Picking too late will produce an overripe fruit with very high concentrations of sugar. Fruit-driven wines usually focus on high sugar content.

The Pink line (pH or Pouvoir Hydrogène = Hydrogen Power) shows the pH level which is important as it affects

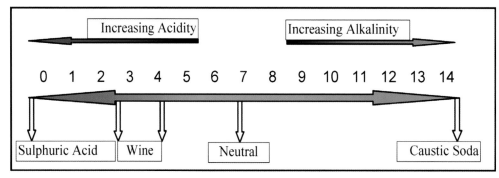

Fig. 2.6. A pH graph showing the scale from 0 to 14. Seven is neutral and wine is between 2.4 to 4.2.

and controls the color of the wine, not to mention the taste. pH is shown on a scale from 0 to 14, where 0 is the most acidic and 14 very alkaline, the neutral point being seven as with pure water. The majority of wines fall between 2.7 to 4.2 with a very acidic white wine, for example a white Riesling from Austria or even a Chenin Blanc from Loire in France, having a pH of 2.8. A soft, fruit-driven Californian red wine has about pH 3.8. It is important to remember that pH is not only an indication of acidity but also indicates the mineral content of the grape.

What style should a winemaker produce?
It all depends upon their customer base and retail price point, economies of scale, distribution channels and saleability. Synergy is therefore of vital importance when creating a production, sales and marketing program for the vineyard.

Quality is the most important issue to be considered. The key is to pick the grape at the precise moment where the phenolic structure is optimal and in balance with the acid, sugar and pH levels, as previously shown by the red box (Fig. 2.5) in the graph. By focusing on this the winemaker achieves the maximum quality possible without having to adjust the must by using a bunch of additives. Achieving this is not as easy as one might think. Grape varieties ripen according to their predestined growth schedule and, obviously, according to the micro-climatic conditions during the growing season.

The answer should lie with regional bodies, winemakers and marketing departments. Nevertheless, I still feel that wineries should be bound by guidelines that adhere to grape and regional typicity.

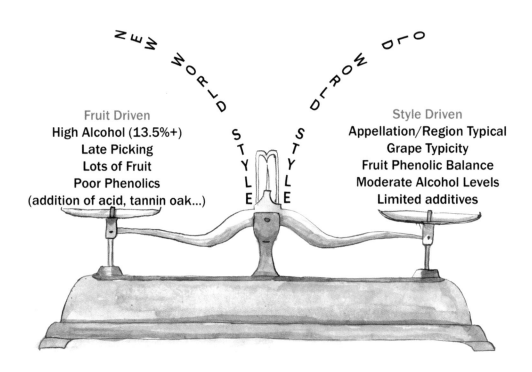

Fig. 2.7. A graphical illustration of Old and New World winemaking styles and methods. Wine-tasters are naturally looking for style-driven wines, which display region and grape typicity more than fruit.

Chapter 3

Wine-Tasting Procedures

Whether you are in Sydney, Cape Town, New York, London or Tokyo there is an accepted way to taste wine. There are tasting norms, including various procedures and steps. They are usually conducted in sequence, so you start with the wine's **Appearance**, move on to **Aroma, Taste** as well as **Current Condition and Storage Potential** and finally create a **Summary**.

In addition to tasting wines, wines can be graded and points assessed to establish a score. Chapter 5 shows you in detail how to grade wines using the 100-point system: moreover, I highly recommend that you follow the grading sheet, included at the back of this book, as you read through this chapter. The more practice you receive in the various stages of tasting the easier the procedures will be to remember.

Variables affecting taste
There are many variables that can affect the taste of a wine. Before we proceed to the tasting procedures I would like to introduce the following basic facts that affect the wine's appearance, aroma, taste, balance and storage potential. They are:

1. Variety of grape

2. The climate and growing conditions within the district
• Soil (mineral content, pH levels, etc.)
• Water levels (irrigation, drainage…)
• Annual and vintage changes in weather conditions

3. Viticulture practices
• Ecological conditions
• Use of pesticides
• Timing of harvest
• Fruit at picking: pH, acidity, sugar and phenolic (grape skin) quality

• Crop size (pruning and trellising practices)
• Diseases within the vineyard (health of the vine)

4. Winery operations and procedures
• Length and temperature of fermentation
• Maturation in steel, oak, etc.
• Filtering techniques
• Adjustments (tannin, tartaric acid, aroma enhancers, micro-oxidation, etc.)
• Varietal grading, selection and blending of both single grape varietals and blends

5. Distribution and storage conditions
• Temperature en route
• Bottle storage conditions (temperature at store, storage standing upright or laying down, in direct sunlight, etc.)

6. Home storage conditions
• Temperature and humidity conditions
• Lighting conditions
• Fluctuations in temperature

7. Wine-serving conditions
• Time of the day
• Temperature of the wine
• Temperature of the room or location in which you are serving the wine
• Environmental conditions (grading conditions, social occasions and whether or not the wine is served with accompanying food or cheese)
• Decanting or aerating (number of times done and how long before tasting)

8. Atmospherics
• Surrounding conditions (comfort zones, people, lighting, equipment etc.)

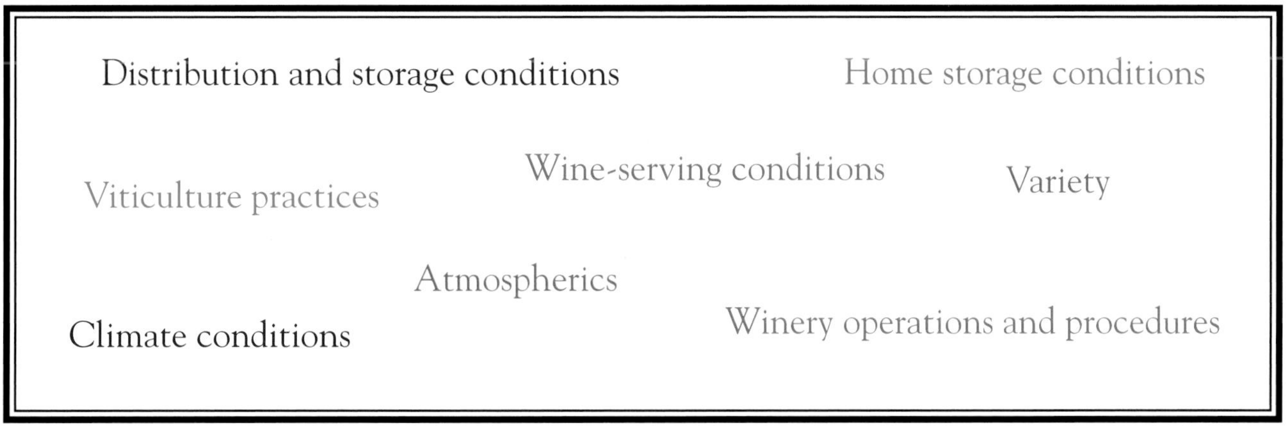

Distribution and storage conditions   Home storage conditions

Viticulture practices   Wine-serving conditions   Variety

Atmospherics

Climate conditions   Winery operations and procedures

Fig. 3.0. Variables affecting aroma and taste.

Appearance and Color

The wine's appearance: color, hue, tone, brightness and viscosity can reveal a lot about its actual condition and age as well as where it might have been made, possible grape types and even some defects.

Procedures for analyzing the Appearance
The following figures illustrate how the appearance of the wine is examined:

1. Vertical position (Fig. 3.1.). Viewing the wine from above, from a vertical position, allows us to analyze the wine's surface brilliance, clarity and depth of color, as well as potential defects such as bubbles (CO_2), protein, etc.

Fig. 3.1. Viewing from above (glass vertical): Look at the wine's surface, its brilliance, depth of color, clarity and any CO_2 or defects.

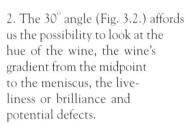

2. The 30° angle (Fig. 3.2.) affords us the possibility to look at the hue of the wine, the wine's gradient from the midpoint to the meniscus, the live-liness or brilliance and potential defects.

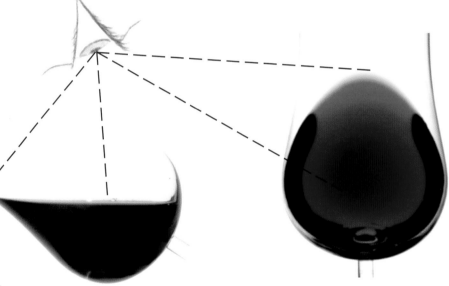

3. Horizontal po-sition (Fig. 3.3.) presents the wine's viscosity by com-paring the legs or arches running down the sides of the glass. To view this you need to swirl the wine rapidly, so that it coats the sides of the glass. The legs then ap-pear after a few seconds. The amount of viscosity depends upon the alcohol and fruit content of the wine. The larger the alcohol and fruit content, the broader and longer the legs.

Fig. 3.2 & 3.2.5. Viewing from above (glass at 30 deg): Look from the center of the wine (bowl) through the rim edge. Look at the wine's color (hue), gra-dient of tone, width and depth of color, clarity and any CO_2 or defects.

Scanning the three views gives you the best possible chance to view both the quality of the wine's appearance and also the possibility of identifying any defects in the most proficient way. The key is to have reflected light from beneath the glass. This shows the best color (hue and tone) in addition to any possible defects.

Natural white blue light is best for viewing wines but not a necessity. A consistent and reflective light source is by far more important when analyzing the wine's appearance. Placing or holding a natural white sheet of paper under the glass and allowing the light to reflect up onto the bottom of the glass will illuminate the wine enough for you to make a good judgement.

Fig. 3.3. Viewing from the side (glass vertical): Look at the wine's legs or arches, its viscosity and any possible signs of defects.

Appearance: Clearness

Clearness is the clarity of the wine. Viewing the wine from all angles, as shown in the previous figures, will help you to categorize the wine's appearance into one or more of the items below.

1. Unclear red and white wines are with major defects.
2. Clear wines (Fig. 3.4.) are free from defects, if red and possibly, if not matured in oak or unfiltered, with some defects, if white.
3. Crystal Clear (Fig. 3.5.) is usually reserved for white, rosé and light red wines which are clear and have no defects.
4. Protein-haze (Fig. 3.6.) is a small, white, flaky sediment and a defect.
5. Salt / Calcium / Tartrate crystals (Fig. 3.7.) are small white, off-white or clear crystals and are considered cosmetic defects.
6. Sediment (Fig. 3.8.) is a normal occurrence caused through ageing, seen as small dark flakes or bits, which can be very fine or coarse and are not defects.

Fig. 3.4. Represents a clear red wine appearance, showing no signs of defects.

Fig. 3.5. Represents a crystal-clear appearance in a white wine, showing no signs of defects.

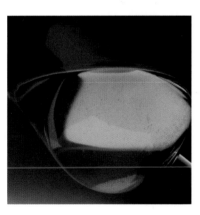

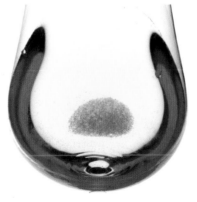

Fig. 3.6. Illustrates a Protein-haze defect within a white wine. The Protein-haze is caused by warmed excess protein within the wine which coagulates to form a haze. This can be prevented through fining with bentonite.

Fig. 3.7. Shows calcium-tartrate crystals in a white wine. This is not a manufacturing defect but more of a cosmetic irritant. It is caused through the attraction of various acids and calcium along with cold storage conditions.

Fig. 3.8. Shows typical sediment that is found in older, heavily macerated and unfiltered wines. This is not a defect and totally normal. It is made up of a combination of acids and phenolic substances (color pigments and tannin). As wines age, their phenolic substances coagulate with the acids to form the sediment. In time this results in a lighter wine with a larger bottle ullage, because the sediment requires less space due to the compactness of its coagulated form.

Appearance: Brightness

Brightness is the liveliness and luster of the wine as seen from all angles. If you've ever seen a pearl with a good luster, you'll know exactly what to look for. As with clearness, the brightness directly relates to the health of the wine. Any indication of dullness suggests that something is not as it should be, whether it has been unduly shaken and the fine sediment stirred up, causing a dull appearance or the wine is with defaults. The lack of brightness is in many cases the first clue to such defaults.

Dull wines (Fig. 3.9.) have no brilliance. They are usually wines spoiled through oxidation, protein haze, yeast contamination, poor racking or filtering techniques producing too much sediment (not vintage port). Although natural sediment is not a manufacturing defect it is more of a cosmetic hindrance to the wine's clarity. In many cases well-made wines have natural sediment as shown in Fig. 3.8. and can easily be remedied through decanting. If a stored wine is raised too quickly and/or shaken during the process of opening, the settled sediment will in most cases diffuse into the wine, causing a murky or dull appearance.

Medium brightness wines (Fig. 3.10.) have a good luster and brilliance with a clear appearance but they are not overly flattering and do not stick out from the rest. They are clear and presentable.

Lively wines (Fig. 3.11.) are bright, brilliant and full of luster presenting a rich and lively appearance. They look fresh, well-made and show a vitality. In contrast to a dull wine a lively wine looks healthy and almost like a living liquid. It shows well when compared to a wine with medium brightness.

Fig. 3.9. Dull brightness

Fig. 3.10. Medium brightness

Fig. 3.11. Lively brightness

Fig. 3.12. Small bubbles typical for a second fermentation in the bottle.

Fig. 3.13. Large bubbles usually created through the addition of CO^2 into already made wine for grape juice.

Appearance: Carbonic Acid

Carbonic Acid (CO_2). This section is used for the analysis of bubbles within the wine.

The Champagne Method is a second fermentation occurring within the bottle and creating about seven atmospheres of pressure. This pressure produces smaller bubbles and finer mousse. It is considered to be the classical and best method of creating carbon acid (CO_2) in superior wines. There are of course other ways to do this, as in the Charmant method, by creating a second fermentation within a large airtight steel tank. The least expensive method is by just adding CO_2 into an already finished wine, thus creating a wine with bubbles as with sodas. There are winemakers who seek to create a slight sparkling or pétillance to their wines, such as Vinho Verde in northern Portugal. If, on the other hand, the intention had been to produce a still wine, this would be considered a defect.

The actual bubbles can say a lot about the production method and the smaller they are the better.

Description of bubbles:

- Small
- Large bubbles, usually 1 to 3 millimeters in diameter, dissipating rapidly, within 5 minutes.
- Few is a description for sparkling and champagne as reflected in the number of bubbles presented, few being less than fifty.
- Many, as in more than a hundred, present in the glass for 5 to 15 minutes.
- Sparkles are represented by a good sparkle with hundreds of bubbles. These bubbles are usually present for 10 to 20 minutes.
- Pearl-like is reserved for the best bubbles, usually those that resemble a string of pearls, rising to the top of the glass. These fine bubbles can continue for at least 20 to 30 minutes.

Fig. 3.14. A second tank fermentation which creates many bubbles with a few larger bubbles.

Fig. 3.15. A depiction of sparkles. These wines are usually made with a second bottle fermentation and the length of maturation is approximately that of good champagne.

Fig. 3.16. A typical champagne method style wine. You can see the 'pearl-like' bubbles rising to the surface. These bubbles last longer and produce a soft velvety mousse.

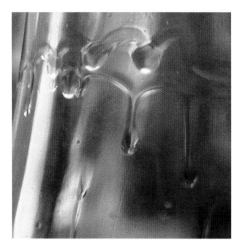

Fig. 3.17. Oily

Fig. 3.18. Thin short legs

Fig. 3.19. Thick long legs

Appearance: Viscosity

Viscosity is the oiliness of the wine's appearance, which can be described in many ways, but legs or arches are the most common. The legs primarily help you to determine the level of alcohol but can indicate the level of fruit or body to an avid wine taster. A watery wine, dissipating rapidly down the sides of the glass, would normally indicate low alcohol and sugar levels. Meniscus is the clear area around the rim.

Legs or arches become visible, as the wine dissipates down the sides of the glass; at the same time, a rapid evaporation of the alcohol within the wine occurs leading to the formation. Therefore, the higher the alcohol the faster rate of evaporation, as alcohol evaporates faster then water, causing the legs to form rather quickly. A number of descriptions can be used, for example:

1. Thin short legs or thin long legs (medium 12.5% abv.)
2. Thick long legs or thick short legs (high 14%+ abv.)

Appearance: Color

Color is broken down into two categories: tone and hue. Tone is related to the climate condition, grape variety and maceration techniques, whilst hue is related to the wine's age, variety and condition.

1. **Tone** is the darkness of the color from 0 = clear or transparent to 100 = opaque or black. Younger red wines are usually darker, getting lighter with time. White wines are usually lighter, turning darker with time.

2. **Hue** is the range in color combinations. Red wines will always have red as their base color (hue) and white wines will have yellow as their base color (hue).

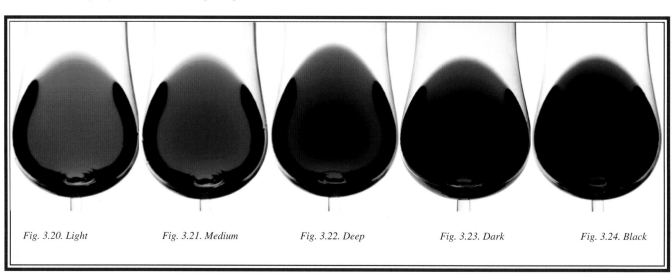

Fig. 3.20. Light   Fig. 3.21. Medium   Fig. 3.22. Deep   Fig. 3.23. Dark   Fig. 3.24. Black

Red Wine Hues

Young red wines always start their life cycle with a blue-red or purple-red hue. These hues change with time, natural chemical reactions within the wine, maturation and with pressure from the climate and environment, such as light and heat. Red wines as opposed to whites usually start their life cycle with a darker tone. As the wine matures, its color lightens and its hue changes to an orange-brick-red color. This change is caused through a reduction by oxygen of the bound anthocyans (tannin pigments) with various acids, found in the wine, by oxygen.

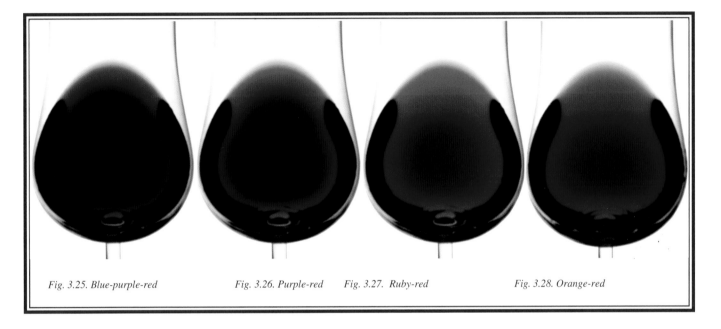

Fig. 3.25. Blue-purple-red   Fig. 3.26. Purple-red   Fig. 3.27. Ruby-red   Fig. 3.28. Orange-red

White Wine Hues

Young white wines nearly always start their life cycle with a greenish yellow tint, progressing to an almost dark amber in very old sweet wines. As time progresses, the already dissolved oxygen reacts with both the acids and tannin pigments. These natural chemical reactions along with the wine's maturation and pressure from the elements such as light and heat cause the wine's color to darken to an almost amber hue. As with red wine, white wines have a richer, darker hue in warmer the climates and if oak-matured.

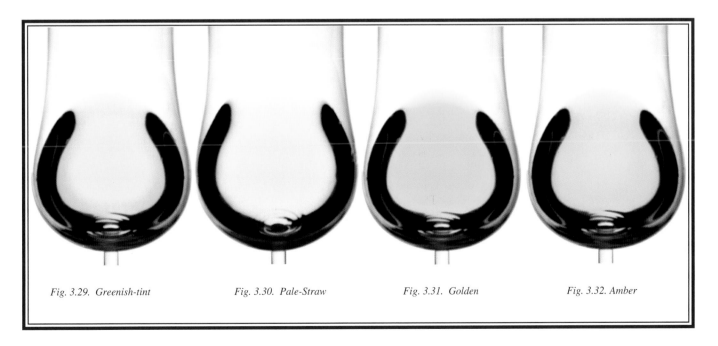

Fig. 3.29. Greenish-tint   Fig. 3.30. Pale-Straw   Fig. 3.31. Golden   Fig. 3.32. Amber

Aroma (Nose)

In the beginning, identifying a bouquet is not as easy as some people may believe. After teaching wine-grading to both beginners and professionals for many years, a number of key factors, required for the wine-taster's success in analyzing the wine's nose or bouquet have emerged. They are patience, practice, aroma samples and learning to combine these with an individual's experiences and associations. All aroma associations that the taster has in regard to his or her background, including cooking experiences, smells as a child and adult and others are all related. Some people's experiences run so deep that just a small hint of a certain aroma is all that is required. The key is to take those and couple them to specific aromas that are found in the wine. One person's leather might be another's wood. Although all of them are relevant in one way or another, one person's association might be more correct than another's.

Over the years I have tried to group character associations together for various styles, grapes and blends. By doing this it becomes a lot easier to couple aromas, unfamiliar to the taster. All you need is practice, samples and examples.

The wine's aroma can also reveal a lot about its current state and/or condition, where it might have been made, possible grape types and the presence of some defects. Areas to consider when analyzing the aroma of a wine are its depth or fullness, grape or blend typicity, age and volatility and negative characters or off-odors. After you have had the opportunity to taste a considerable amount of wines you will be able to see patterns of quality associations. There are two grading sheets that I have developed over the years to describe the complexities of associations and characteristics of an aroma, one advanced and one basic. I will be discussing the advanced grading sheet here.

The Aroma Cap

I designed the Aroma Enhancing Cap® for a number of purposes. Initially, its purpose was to enhance the bouquet by creating a more developed rather than volatile aroma by trapping it within the glass. About twenty minutes is all that is needed for a wine to develop its aroma by reacting with the trapped oxygen. The reduction, or in this case enhancement, serves another purpose too. It is a tool to assist in the comparison of both the still (the trapped aroma) and the volatile (agitated or swirled wine) aromas. The volatile aromas reoccur in the mouth and in the aftertaste via the retro-nasal passage.

After having used the Aroma Cap® for about twenty minutes, enhanced still aromas can be detected when sniffing non-agitated wine. The enhanced, trapped and developed

Fig. 3.33. An Aroma Enhancing Cap®, which traps the aromas within the ullage, the space between the wine and the cap. This produces a more mature and concentrated aroma for evaluation.

wine shows grape typicity and indicates maturing characters. Lastly, the Aroma Cap serves to minimize collateral and collective aromas, emitted through evaporation within the room full of wine-tasters. If you've ever been in a tasting with 30 people and sensed the wine in the air, you'll understand this comment very well.

Procedure for sniffing

1. Remove the Aroma Cap and gently sniff the wine's bouquet. Do not swirl the wine at this stage. If the wine has been in the glass for 15-25 minutes, a more mature, concentrated nose will be evident.

2. Gently sniff the wine, with short to medium breaths while inhaling. Note any characteristics on your sheet. Give your nose a rest while making notes. You don't have to identify all possible aromas during the first sniff. Take your time. Place the Aroma Cap back on the glass each time when you make your notes.

3. Repeat the above steps until you believe that you have identified the characteristics possible.

4. Once you are satisfied with your initial analysis, quickly rotate the glass in small tight circles, which will result in the

Fig. 3.34. Place the Aroma Enhancer Cap on the glass top opening at least 20 minutes prior to a tasting.

Fig. 3.35. Lift the cap gently and take a number of small but evaluating sniffs. Replace the cap directly after sniffing. Repeat the procedure until you are sure that you have identified as many aroma characteristics as possible.

Fig. 3.36. Swirl the wine rapidly in circles, agitating and mixing the wine with the additional oxygen, thus creating a more volatile aroma. Analyze the wine again and compare your notes. Make notes of any additional characteristics.

Fig. 3.37. Repeat until satisfied. Make a note of the difference between the still and volatile aroma characteristics.

wine swirling around the inside of the glass. This movement agitates the wine and creates a volatile solution of oxygen and wine, allowing you to analyze even more aroma characteristics than before. Make notes of these aromas.

5. Note also the difference between the still and the volatile aromas. If there is no difference, this would indicate a young closed, a full-bodied, fruit-driven or alternatively, a tired wine.

Aroma Descriptions

1. Fullness or Depth

At this stage we look at how much boldness, character and depth the wine displays through its aroma, its complexity and fullness. Does the bouquet present us with a variety of characters and does the aroma display depth and balance? Fullness or depth are divided into the following categories:

Dumb. A dumb nose is one without any bouquet both in still and volatile aroma, but most wines today display some characteristics. If a lack of aroma does appear, this is without doubt the result of one or more defects.

Little depth. This is found in a wine showing very few characteristics and with no grape typicity. Simple aromas.

Medium aroma. A medium aroma is a wine displaying a number of characteristics from a variety of fruits. Good distinguishing characters with some grape typicity. An expected aroma but not a surprising one. Some small complex associations may be found too.

Full aroma. To encounter a full aroma the bouquet must present a good variety of fruit characters with a combination of balance and some finesse.

Compound aroma. A compound aroma is a bouquet with many complex associations of fruit, terroir (minerals) and wood (oak characteristics and various bi-characters) in balance with each other. No single aromas should dominate the others but instead present themselves as a compound of balanced aromas.

Elegant. An elegant bouquet is a complex balance of fruit, oak (if used) and typical grape characteristics presented in a balanced finesse. An elegant aroma is reserved for outstanding wines showing this balance. An elegant wine can be soft and gentle on approach with good acidic presence too.

2. Grape or Blend Typicity

This is an essential aspect of grape identification. Without the traditional grape characteristics we will get sameness. Imagine all wines tasting the same with exactly the same acidity, sugar, tannin, oak and character. Life is made up of variety and this is what wine should be too. As we have almost 3000 grape varieties to choose from, all of which have their own characteristics and technical compositions, we must, without abate, insist on winemakers adhering to the accepted and recognized qualities for grapes or blends. Grape and blend typicity is the wine-taster's key in identifying and matching wine with food. Grape or blend typicity is therefore dependent on the grape variety, blend and terroir:

Not at all. No signs of varietal or blend characteristics.

Little. Very few associations can be made. They are present but displayed as half characters.

Good. An aroma showing good grape typicity or blend characteristics. Will show a variety of fruits typically associated with a particular varietal or varietals within a particular blend and style.

Typical. Excellent associations of fruit and terroir with many characteristics of the specific grape or blend present.

3. Age and Volatility

The wine's age and volatility are assessed at the time of drinking. It is important to assess the wine's age and aroma volatility when, you are planning to store your wines for a longer period of time or prior to consumption. Defective wines will show a lot of volatitle aciodity and decantation is highly recommended.

The aroma assessment is also the wine-taster's second indication of the quality condition and storage potential of the wine. The first indication is the wine's appearance (hue and tone) and the last its taste (condition of the acids, tannins and fruit).

Young wine aroma. A young nose is full of fresh fruit and acidity. Typically, when removing the aroma caps, both the still and volatile aromas are the same in heavy, fruit-driven wines, although medium- and light-bodied can differ slightly.

Fig. 3.38. Shows how important the aroma and grape typicity is to the identification process when grading wine. Without this uniqueness all wine becomes the same.

Developing wine aroma. A developing nose is typically softer in character, displaying developing fruit characteristics. When the Aroma Cap is removed, there is a clear difference between the still and volatile aromas in the wineglass.

Mature wine aroma. A mature wine usually has a warmer, less fruity nose and slightly oxidized characters will be present. Acidity levels can either be high or low. When the Aroma Cap is removed, there are usually just a few differences between a volatile and a still nose.

None. No change in the character of the aroma between the volatile and the still liquid.

Little. Small changes in the aroma or bouquet in the wine between the volatile and still state.

Big. Large differences between the volatile and still state of the wine's bouquet.

4. Aroma Characteristics

These are broken down into **Style**, **General**, **Major** and **Minor** characteristics. Aroma characteristics are first sensed in the bouquet, then perceived to be tasted in the mouth while analyzing the wine, since they are actually volatile aromas which travel up the retro-nasal passage (Fig. 3.39.). They are subsequently recognized by the receptors of the olfactory lobe in the upper nose chamber and result in fruit associations of taste rather than smell. To clarify once more, through taste we can only distinguish between acidity, bitterness, salinity and sweetness, so when something tastes like blackcurrants it is actually a smell and not a taste.

The following list is by no means a complete list, as volatile aromas can run into the hundreds. The key is to use your experience to connect your association, whatever it may be, to what the mainstream of tasters list or associate to that particular wine, style or defect. There are patterns of associations and it would be beneficial for you to try to remember them.

Style

Wines should be differentiated according to style, not geographical origin, although they are often called New World and Old World wines. Many New World wine regions have been making wine for more than three hundred years and cherish traditional winemaking skills. Furthermore, advancements in wine technology have emerged in New World regions. At the same time, traditional winemaking procedures originated in the Old World.

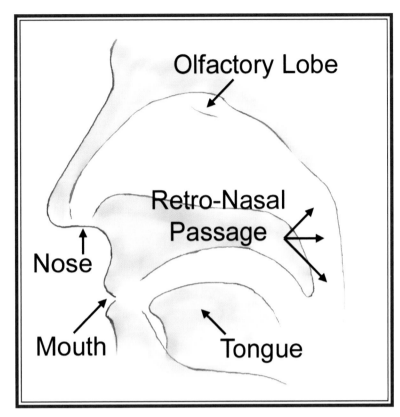

Fig. 3.39. The nose and mouth cavities. The air flows both through the nose and the retro-nasal passage.

New World. The New World style of winemaking is usually associated with fruit-driven (almost overripe fruit) wines and higher alcohol levels.

Old World. The Old World style of winemaking is associated with character-driven maturation and storage (grapes with a structure that would offer the best varietal characteristics over time) producing alcohol levels of around 12,5% (abv) alcohol by volume, some oxidative styles as in some regions in Northern Italy.

General Characteristics

Fruity. Positive aromas of both citrus, dark and light berries, tree fruits and the like. Fruity characters are combinations of the phenolic structure, mineral composition of the earth and obviously the grape varietal.

Vegetative. Vegetative characters are usually compared with cauliflower, broccoli, carrots and even rotten vegetables. These aromas are derived from tannin or the skin's phenolics.

Earthy. Earthiness is a mineral, sandy chalk character, derived from the tannins from both the skins and in the oak used in maturation. Associated to negative aromas such as dusty, basement, mold and garlic. These are usually the result of

---

Positive Aromas

Fruity / Spicy / Floral / Vegetable / Nutty / Caramelized / Woody

Negative Aromas

Chemical / Pungent / Oxidized / Microbiological

Fig. 3.40. These are Major Characteristics and as such usually the initial aromas that the wine-taster recognizes. The aromas are noted and then broken down into more precise categories, so-called Minor characteristics.

hydrogen sulfide (H$_2$S) contamination. This can also be associated to mercaptans, which are a result of H$_2$S degrading. It can be a negative aroma indicating a defective wine, if a moldy association is also present (2-ethyl-fenchol).

Chemical. There are quite a number of associations with chemicals. Sulfur is one example. Used in winemaking to minimize bacterial growth, it occurs in two ways: firstly as an additive to reduce bacterial growth and, secondly, through the toasting of the barrels recognized as a burnt match character.

- **Oxidized.** If a wine smells like sherry, it is oxidized. See oxidized in chapter 4.

- **Wood.** Associated with the wood used in maturation. Can be divided into various types of oak. American oak has a creamy vanilla character, whilst French oak presents a harder burnt vanilla oakiness.

- **Caramelized.** A caramelized character is found in oak-aged wines with a combination of high alcohol, heavily toasted barrels and vanilla characteristics. It can also be similar to Botrytis cinerea in sweet wines and wines that have been oxidized.

- **Microbiological.** In unspoiled wines it is similar to flor-yeast (as in sherry) or lees (as in sur-lie-matured wine in tanks or barrels or a combination of sur-lie and yeast (as in champagne). In negative circumstances it is associated with Sauerkraut, sweaty, mousey and horsy. It is a yeast and bacterial problem caused through poor filtration and/or stabilization procedures within the vineyard.

- **Floral.** Associated with flowers like orange blossom, rose, violets and perpetuated from the grape and its phenolics. A negative floral aroma would be Geranium, as these flowers are associated with a bacterial decomposition of sorbic acid which is an additive to stop yeast fermentation in red wines.

- **Spicy.** Originating from yeast, various grape varieties such as Pinotage, Syrah, Nebbiolo, Merlot, as well as barrel maturation. Recognized as licorice (anise), black pepper, cloves etc. The type of yeast used during fermentation can also develop certain spicy characteristics.

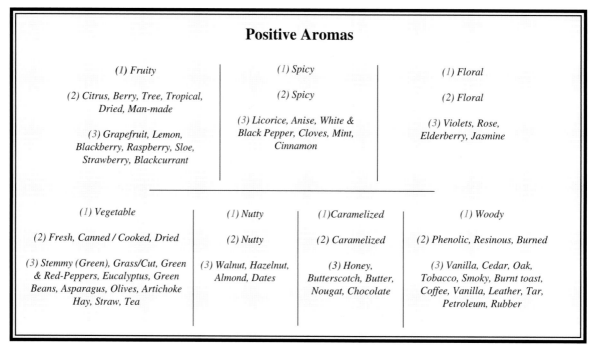

Positive Aromas

(1) Fruity	(1) Spicy	(1) Floral
(2) Citrus, Berry, Tree, Tropical, Dried, Man-made	(2) Spicy	(2) Floral
(3) Grapefruit, Lemon, Blackberry, Raspberry, Sloe, Strawberry, Blackcurrant	(3) Licorice, Anise, White & Black Pepper, Cloves, Mint, Cinnamon	(3) Violets, Rose, Elderberry, Jasmine

(1) Vegetable	(1) Nutty	(1)Caramelized	(1) Woody
(2) Fresh, Canned / Cooked, Dried	(2) Nutty	(2) Caramelized	(2) Phenolic, Resinous, Burned
(3) Stemmy (Green), Grass/Cut, Green & Red-Peppers, Eucalyptus, Green Beans, Asparagus, Olives, Artichoke Hay, Straw, Tea	(3) Walnut, Hazelnut, Almond, Dates	(3) Honey, Butterscotch, Butter, Nougat, Chocolate	(3) Vanilla, Cedar, Oak, Tobacco, Smoky, Burnt toast, Coffee, Vanilla, Leather, Tar, Petroleum, Rubber

Fig. 3.41. Shows Major Characteristics which are best identified by noting and incorporating the identified aromas in sequence. As an example, if I have a fruity aroma (Step 1: General Characteristics), identified by the (1), I would note this and then ask myself what type of fruitiness (Step 2: Major Characteristics), identified by the (2): Citrus, Berry, Tree, etc. Similarly, if Citrus was the answer, I would try to answer what type of Citrus (Step 3: Minor Characteristics): Grapefruit, Lemon orange etc.

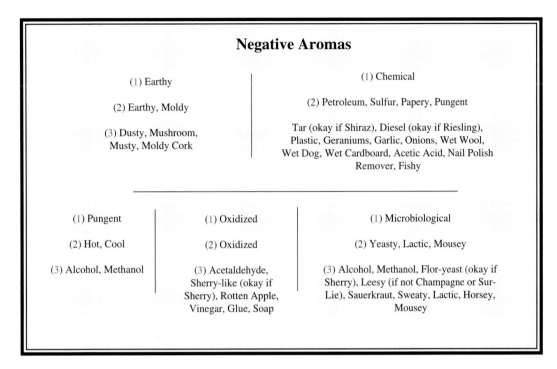

Negative Aromas

(1) Earthy

(2) Earthy, Moldy

(3) Dusty, Mushroom, Musty, Moldy Cork

(1) Chemical

(2) Petroleum, Sulfur, Papery, Pungent

Tar (okay if Shiraz), Diesel (okay if Riesling), Plastic, Geraniums, Garlic, Onions, Wet Wool, Wet Dog, Wet Cardboard, Acetic Acid, Nail Polish Remover, Fishy

(1) Pungent

(2) Hot, Cool

(3) Alcohol, Methanol

(1) Oxidized

(2) Oxidized

(3) Acetaldehyde, Sherry-like (okay if Sherry), Rotten Apple, Vinegar, Glue, Soap

(1) Microbiological

(2) Yeasty, Lactic, Mousey

(3) Alcohol, Methanol, Flor-yeast (okay if Sherry), Leesy (if not Champagne or Sur-Lie), Sauerkraut, Sweaty, Lactic, Horsey, Mousey

Fig. 3.42. Negative aromas found in a wine. As with the positive aromas you should try to break them down from General to Major and Minor characteristics if possible. Note that fortified wines will show high alcohol and Champagne and Sur-lie styles both leesy and yeasty characters so these should not be noted as negatives but as traits.

Major Characteristics

These are broken down from the General Characteristics listed above and can be both positive or negative. As an example, if the wine tastes fruity, the fruitiness needs to be broken down and analyzed. It is important that you ask yourself what, why and how at each step of the tasting as this will help you to arrive at all the answers. What kind of fruit is it? Is it citrus, berry, tropical fruit, dried fruit or man-made?

- **Citrus**. A positive aroma found in white grape wines with good levels of tartaric acid and to a lesser extent those gone through malo-lactic. Naturally, wineries using citric acid as an additive would also enhance these characteristics.

- **Berry**. A positive aroma. A berry aroma can be either dark, light or combination of both types of berries. It is usually associated with red wines and is derived from a fleshy or pulpy fruit and ripe phenolic (skin) structure.

- **Tropical Fruit**. Another positive aroma associated with sweet white wines. It can also be identified with dry white wines with high alcohol levels (fruit-driven styles).

- **Dried Fruit**. A positive character usually associated with heavy tree-fruit and dried fruit. It usually shows on stony type soils. It also provides an association to the heavy use of sulfur.

- **Canned / Cooked**. A negative aroma caused through asphyxia (lack of oxygen) leaving the wine with a stale or 'cooked' smell. Decanting can usually help.

- **Moldy**. A negative character caused by fungi through lack of hygiene in winemaking equipment, barrels and vats.

- **Petroleum**. A positive aroma for maturing Riesling grapes.

- **Mineral**. Mineral characters are positive and are associations to the soil's mineral content.

- **Ester**. Both a positive and a negative aroma. In Amarone, Port, Sherry, Madeira and other fortified wines it is considered a positive aroma but high alcohol aromas in normal table wines are negative.

- **Sulfur**. A negative aroma, as it would indicate too much volatile sulfur present in the wine.

- **Prickly**. A negative aroma. It produces a prickly sensationm, which is caused through volatile acids and/or too much sulfur.

- **Burnt**. Usually a positive aroma, derived from the toasting of the barrels or chips, but it could be negative if caused by excess sulfur use.

- **Yeasty**. Usually a positive aroma if consistent with the style sought. It is present in both unfiltered white and red wines as well as white wines matured on lees.

Minor Characteristics

Minor characteristics are self-explanatory and need not be described in much detail. The most important facts to remember are the interaction of associations between major and minor characteristics and how they relate to the wine. After a number of tastings you will find patterns for various styles, blends and varietal types. These patterns are typical associations for particular styles of wines and an effort should be made to try to memorize them. Remembering these patterns will help you to identify grape variety, region and country. There are both positive and negative characteristics at all levels (Figs. 3.41, 3.42). Diesel and petroleum are not negative if found in a wine containing the Riesling grape variety. Neither is tar or rubber if the Shiraz grape is present.

Defects. Negative aromas are signs that a problem could exist in your wine, which, although, does not necessarily mean that the wine is defective. This will have to be confirmed by tasting the wine. If you have an oxidized nose and this does not belong to an intentional style, it originates from a defective wine. Many identifiable defects can be found in the aroma of a wine (Chapter 4).

Taste

In wine-tasting taste is considered a combination of the taste and the tactile sensations we identify in our mouth and throat when drinking wine. When analyzing wine by taste we discuss various components: tannin, acidity, sweetness, alcohol, fruit quality, weight, length and umami (Fig. 3.48); thereafter, we look for the wine's balance in relation to these

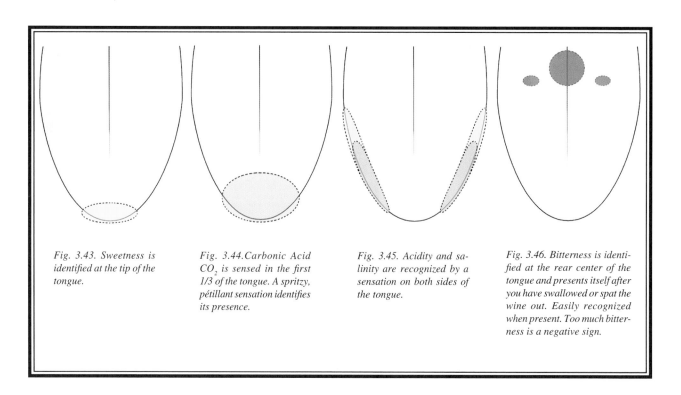

Fig. 3.43. Sweetness is identified at the tip of the tongue.

Fig. 3.44. Carbonic Acid CO_2 is sensed in the first 1/3 of the tongue. A spritzy, pétillant sensation identifies its presence.

Fig. 3.45. Acidity and salinity are recognized by a sensation on both sides of the tongue.

Fig. 3.46. Bitterness is identified at the rear center of the tongue and presents itself after you have swallowed or spat the wine out. Easily recognized when present. Too much bitterness is a negative sign.

components, which are identified in the mouth. Believe it or not, the mouth is a relatively simple instrument with a limited number of functions.

The first lesson in a wine course should cover a number of issues, important for wines, tasting identification and balance as well as their combinations. Within this section (taste), I have included a number of practical exercises that you can use when learning to identify the various sensory areas. These exercises will create the necessary sensation in your mouth and help you identify the areas sensitive to acidity, CO_2, sweetness, bitterness, etc.

The tongue's sensory ability is limited to sweetness, carbonic acid, acidity, salinity and bitterness (Figs. 3.43 - 3.46) which will be highlighted. Naturally, the saliva coating your mouth is also very important. It contains a tasteless liquid made up of salivary and oral mucous gland secretions and the enzyme ptyalin that moistens the walls of your mouth and aids in balance and digestion. Both what we taste and how we taste will be covered within this section.

1. Sweetness

Even though a wine might be called dry, there is a degree of residual sugar in most wines produced today. Sweetness is sensed at the tip of the tongue (Fig. 3.43). In order to sense the various degrees of sweetness you need to purchase a dry white wine, either a Chenin Blanc or a Sauvignon Blanc and 100 g of sucrose, which is better than table sugar as it dissolves better. Pour a small amount, about 20 ml, of the wine into 4 separate containers marked b through e. Add the amount of sucrose (caster sugar), as specified below, into each of the small containers. Mix well and allow the sucrose to dissolve. Once dissolved, pour an additional 80 ml of the dry white wine into the respective containers and stir gently. Next step is to prepare five tasting glasses and pour the mixed solution of Chenin Blanc or Sauvignon Blanc into each of the 5 glasses b-e. The fifth glass will contain the same dry wine unmixed. You should now have 5 different sweetness levels for a white wine to compare. This sweetness tasting exercise can be conducted with sparkling wines too. It is not necessary to do the test on reds, as red wines should always be dry if not a fortified wine like Port or Madeira.

- **Dry** (Select a non-wooded dry
Chenin Blanc or Sauvignon Blanc)
- **Semi-dry** (6-12g/l sucrose)
- **Medium +** (13-34g/l sucrose)
- **Semi-sweet** (35-59g/l sucrose)
- **Sweet** (60-120+g/l sucrose)

2. Carbonic Acid (CO₂)

If a pétillant style wine was not intended, such as a Vinho Verde style, a sparkling wine or Champagne and you still find carbonic acid in it, the wine is defective. CO_2 can be found in all varieties of wines: reds, whites and sweet wines. It is identified by a spritzy prickle on the front of the tongue (Fig. 3.44.). The identification is simple, if a bottle of carbonated natural water is purchased at you local grocery store. Taste the water in the same way as wine but directly after you serve it, as the carbonation decreases rapidly.

Low. A wine exhibiting a slight prickle or pétillance on the tongue, although not so easily recognizable by the amateur. Very small bubbles shown on the surface rim of the wine.

Medium. Recognizable by most tasters as a spritzy, prickly sensation, although not as evident as in Champagne. Small bubbles shown on the surface rim and in the wine itself.

High. No reason to doubt otherwise. Both large and/or small fine bubbles depending on the winemaking style, natural or as an additive. If natural, the ideal appearance would be pearl-like with a smooth, fine, well-balanced pétillant sensation.

3. Acidity

There are a number of acids present in wine, for example: ascorbic acid (vitamin C), sorbic, malic, tartaric and acetic acid (volatile acid). To simplify matters and for the purpose of understanding acidity in general, we will only focus on tartaric acid. Various additives are permitted in winemaking and acid is one of them. The rules are different depending on the country and region of production. Warmer regions usually permit acid additions, while cooler forbid it. The same holds for tannin and sugar. In order to keep the wines balanced, in warm climates or where wines are fruit-driven, there is almost always an adjustment with some type of acid. Without these adjustments hot regions would never be able to produce well-balanced wines with moderate to high alcohol levels, so tartaric acid is one of the major additives.

In our exercise we will, as with the sugar example above, taste the various acidity levels as well. You need to go to your local drug store or pharmacy and purchase 16.5 grams of tartaric acid and a full-bodied bottle of red wine, preferably a Merlot, fruit-driven, 13.5% alcohol by volume. Follow the same procedure as with sugar. An alternative is to use diluted lemon juice in incremental strengths.

- **Little** (1.5-3 g/l)
- **Good** (3-5.5 g/l)
- **High** (6-7 g/l)

Fresh. This is a term used to describe the wine, when it has a good balance of acidity to tannin, in red and acidity, sweetness and body in white wines. A good acid level keeps the wine fresh but does not overpower the overall fruit, character and taste.

Marked. This is usually reserved for wines with too much acid, when the volatile acids overwhelm the wine's fruit, character and style.

Alcohol	Weight	Length	Fruitiness	Umami
Alcohol is felt by the degree of warmness, weight and sensitivity at the rear-sides of the tongue. For more information, see page 40.	Weight is sensed by the heaviness and body of the wine. It is a tactile wholeness of weight felt throughout the mouth (cf. p. 41).	Length is felt by all sensory areas of the mouth including the throat. Excellent wines will have a lingering aftertaste, balanced and showing the wine's characteristics. The longer the after-taste, the better. (cf. p. 42).	Fruitiness is measured by a combination of grape sweetness, fruitiness and acidity (cf. p. 41).	Umami is an overall metallic sensation left in the mouth after tasting full-bodied red wines. Originates from Monosodium L-glutamate (MSG).

Fig. 3.48. Other items detectible in the mouth.

4. Bitterness

Some small amounts of bitterness can be found in most wine styles and colors, red, white, sparkling and sweet. Identifying bitterness is very easy. All you need to do, if not allergic to nuts, is to purchase some bitter almonds and chew on one. One is sufficient. If you would rather abstain from chewing on a bitter almond, which gives the best example of bitterness, there is another alternative. Boil some water and add in about ten (10) tea-bags in the boiled water. Let stand until cool. Remove the tea-bags and taste the tea. You will find the same result but with some tannin. A clear sensation will be noticed after about 10 seconds at the rear center of the tongue.

Low. A slight bitterness in the length, offering a well-balanced wine but not affecting the wine's overall taste negatively.

Medium. A little too much bitterness present in the wine but not enough to be defective. It dominates the wine's aftertaste, fruit and length. Usually the result from too many stalks and leaves present during winemaking.

High. If high bitterness is present, as when you tasted the bitter almonds, the wine is unbalanced and defective. A bacterial growth has caused this unpleasant aftertaste, which dominates the wine totally. Return the wine.

5. Tannin (Phenolics)

Tannin (fine, coarse and added varieties) is sensed around your gums, palate and even teeth. It is identified as dryness or a dried-out, leathery, woody feeling of astringency.

Astringency. Astringency is the total grouping of polyphenols. Polyphenols are also known as flavonoids which are all antioxidants and include anthocyanins (color pigments) and tannins. These are all grouped together and for the purpose of tasting called tannin or the wine's astringency. Tannin has a life span, which is illustrated in Fig. 3.50. A complex compound, whose structure affects the life and stability of the wine itself, it is extracted from the stems, pips, leaves, grape's skin and the oak barrels used for maturation.

These tannins together with the acid makeup and fruit give us the balance required for good wines with storage potential. The tannin to acid and fruit ratio is therefore extremely important and directly reflects the quality of the wine. Later in this book you'll find a number of typical grape ratios for both red and white wines. All wines have some tannin in their structure, but obviously red wines using colored grapes receive more contact with the grape juice during maceration and fermentation, where color and tannins are extracted.

The tannin's complex structure begins its life cycle in wine as a young, tough, cloying compound, connecting itself to the saliva in the mouth. This is why red wines with a lot of tannin feel dry. The tannin is bound to the saliva molecule, leaving the mouth without lubrication, hence dry. The life cycle of tannin includes the following sequence:

During the initial stages of maturation, the tannin has a tactile sensation of being rough and very dry. This is indicated by the steep upward curve as seen in the diagram. I call the tannin of this stage *'Young Tannin'*.

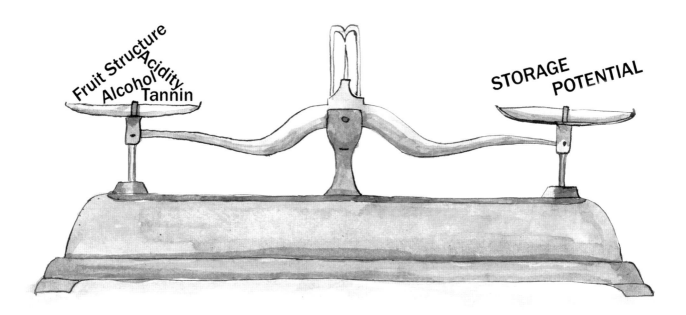

Fig. 3.49. The various entities necessary for cellaring a wine.

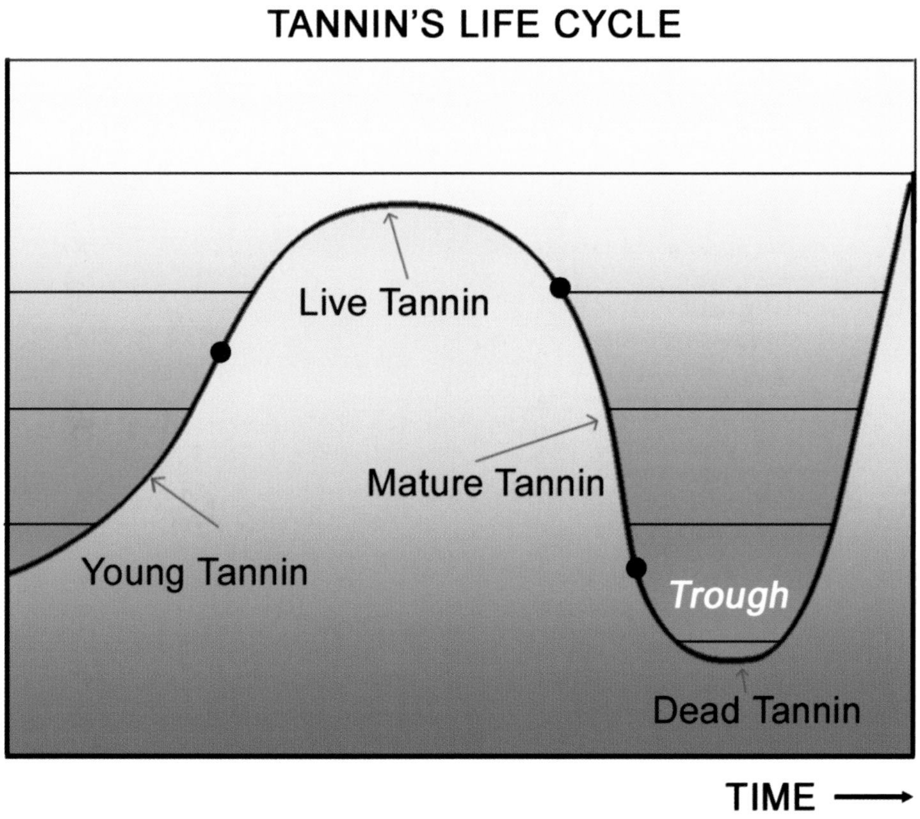

TANNIN'S LIFE CYCLE

Fig. 3.50. The tannin's life cycle shows what the taster can expect from tannin quality over time. The quality of the tannin is directly related to the phenolic quality at the time of harvest; moreover, winemaking techniques such as extraction time, use of enzymes, length of fermentation, temperature and the use of oak, oak powder and other additives. The mouth is not able to detect these additives but it can recognize the size, fine to coarse, soft, hard, harsh and whether or not they are living or dead tannins.

The tannin's peak (Fig. 3.50) shows tannin at its best balance. Through the interaction with acids and oxygen tannin breaks down into a mature, rounder structure, thus giving the wine a smooth tactile sensation. Although still dry the wine is now more balanced. This peak can continue to exist for a number of years depending on the style of wine. French Grands Crus Classés from Bordeaux are typically produced to reach their optimum balance at eight to fifteen years of age. This tannin development reaches maturity considerably earlier for fruit-driven wines. I call this stage '**Live Tannin**'.

As the wine ages past the tannin's peak and progresses down the curve, the tannin's ability to attach to the saliva in the mouth reduces and balance therefore declines. This reduction enhances the wine's acid content and remaining fruit, a stage which is called '**Mature Tannin**'.

As the tannin approaches the trough of the life cycle curve, this reduction is very noticeable and the wine tastes and feels without structure and body. As always, there is an exception to the rule. Tannin which has been added, usually during

fermentation or maturation, does not have the same life cycle as described here. Tannin of this kind does not produce the same results as natural grape tannin. It remains hard and coarse, which can be noticed in older wines, as the tannin levels are as '**Young tannins**'.

When reaching the trough the tannins become very dry, hardened and produce bitterness in the aftertaste. At this stage the tannin's life cycle degenerates considerably and proceeds rapidly up the back end of the curve. I call the tannins of this stage '**Dead Tannin**'.

A tannin tasting exercise is very simple, but unfortunately only two sensory levels can be demonstrated. As with bitterness ten tea bags are used, immersed into one liter of boiling water. Leave them for about ten minutes. Let cool and taste as you would taste wine. You will feel the tannin drying out your mouth by attaching to the saliva molecules. This level is usually soft tannin. Another test would be to find some red grapes from your local store. Taste one before purchasing them, as many grapes sold through grocery stores have low

Adjustment needed to taste alcohol difference			
From Original Wine	40%	96%	Adjusted Wine
12	1.250	0.521	12.5
12	2.500	1.042	13
12	3.750	1.562	13.5
12	5.000	2.083	14
12	6.250	2.604	14.5

Fig. 3.51 An alcohol adjustment chart for increasing alcohol levels for educational purposes. The measurements above would represent the use of either 40% or 96% of ethyl alcohol in milliliters (ml) added to 100 ml of red and/or white wine.

phenolic (tannin) structures. If the tannin is good, you may use them for a tasting exercise. Break the grape with your teeth separating the pulp from the pips and skin. Swallow the pulp. Chew on the remaining pips and skin. You will notice the tannins beginning to interact with your gums by binding themselves to your saliva. Some bitterness will also be present from the pips.

Defining Tannin Strength

Soft. Soft tannin perceived to be round and light in its tactile form.

Dry. Dry tannin is associated with typical Rioja and Burgundy style wines. They have a smooth feel with a medium weight sensation.

Hard. Hard tannin feels firm and structured.

Harsh. Harsh tannin has an abundance of tannin and its presence requires a lot of fruit and acid along with high alcohol levels. A good example is a Northern Rhône or Piedmont.

Defining Tannin Structure and Quality

Fine. Fine tannins are very smooth, 'satin and velvety-like' in perception and balance extremely well with the wine.

Coarse. Coarse tannins are rough and larger in perception, normally edgy and not well balanced with other components of the wine.

Dead Tannin. Dead tannins are hard, very dry and overwhelm the wine. They are the dominating factor in relation to balance and do not serve the wine's purpose.

6. Alcohol

The alcohol is the total amount of alcohols present in the wine. This is a tactile assessment and feels warm, gives the wine weight and creates a slight sensitivity (to some) around the gums and the extra sensitive area of the tongue. Assessing the differences in alcohol levels, especially if in small

increments of half a degree, is one of the more difficult things to do in wine-tasting and takes some practice. I have therefore included an exercise for tasting alcohol too.

Purchase a 12% abv red wine at your local store along with a neutral grain spirits mixer (96%, ethanol or ethyl alcohol) if available in your area. If not available, a vodka of 40% but as neutral as possible is acceptable.

By making these additions according to the table (Fig. 3.51.) you would be able to compare the various tactile sensations between the original 12% in one glass with the other strengths in the remaining glasses. Areas to pay attention to when analyzing the effects from the various strengths would be warmth, weight, sensitivity, nose characteristics and viscosity. It is important here to recommend the use of neutral grain spirits, as they contain no additional peaks on the gas chromatograph and are therefore clean from other aromas and associations as well.

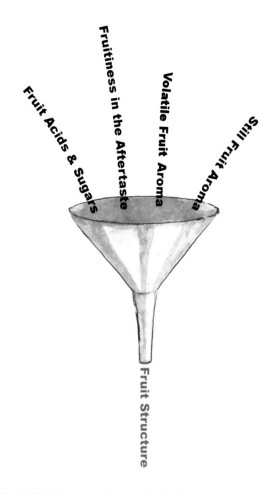

Fig. 3.52. Fruit structure is one of the hardest items to recognize when tasting. This is because it is a combination of the still and volatile aromas, grape acids and sugars.

Warmth. As the amount of alcohol increases within the solutions prepared you will be able to sense a warmer feeling throughout the mouth.

Weight. As the wine increases in alcohol, so does the weight and fullness perception.

Sensitivity. The sensitive areas on both sides at the rear of the tongue also produce a tactile sensitivity to higher alcohol levels.

Nose. Ethyl alcohol produces a more distinct prickly sensation in the nose the higher the alcohol level.

Viscosity. The wine's arches and oiliness are more evident and emerge faster, the higher the alcohol levels. The reason for this is that alcohol evaporates more rapidly in higher concentrations.

7. Fruit Structure

Fruit structure requires many tastings to understand. Unfortunately, most tasters are not too sure of what to look for and very few people in the world have been taught the how and what of identifying the fruit quality of a wine.

The Aroma Cap is recommended to identify the volatile aromas and volatile fruit aromas in the mouth. These two aroma characteristics are combined and the fruit quality evaluated. The Aroma Cap provides us with the ability to identify and compare the quality level of the wine's bouquet in both still (developed) aromas and volatile state. A comparison of grape quality and finesse is then made. A very good volatile aroma in the nose will also be a volatile aroma or fruit aftertaste with the same character or characters within the mouth.

It should be noted that fruit-driven wines have a more pronounced fruit structure than style- or terroir-driven wines. Although the fruit structure in non-fruit-driven wines are not as evident as those in the fruit-driven, the fruit is still present, although in a more subtle form.

Thin. Very little fruit present in the wine. Poor volatile fruit characters within the bouquet and aftertaste.

Medium. Good fruit characters displayed in both the bouquet, retro-nasal aroma and the aftertaste. No fruit dominations.

Compound. Excellent fruit with very well defined fruit in both the volatile bouquet, retro-nasal aroma and the aftertaste. Often encountered in fruit-driven wines.

Elegant. Finesse and gentle fruit characters in both volatile bouquet, retro-nasal and the aftertaste. Well-balanced with other elements and no dominating single character but good blending of all components.

Fig. 3.53. A full-bodied, sweet, white wine from Bordeaux.

8. Body

The overall weight impression one has on the wine tasted is a combination of alcohol, fruit complexity and tannin in red wines. In white, fortified or Amarone style wines there is also residual sugar content.

Thin. Light in consistency. The wine would usually have low alcohol and high acidity levels.

Light. Light to medium-bodied. Usually reminiscent of Beaujolais style or (carbonic maceration) fruitiness with high acidity, low tannin and alcohol levels.

Medium. Medium-bodied wines are usually around 12 to 12.5% alcohol. They have good fruit characters and are balanced in weight with alcohol, acidity and tannin.

Full. Full-bodied wines are usually oak-matured with alcohol levels of 12.5% to 13.5 %. They display compound fruit characters and have adequate amounts of tannin.

Powerful. Heavily oak-matured wines with lots of fruit-driven characters. Adequate amounts of tannin with high alcohol levels of between 13 to 14.5%.

9. Length

Length or aftertaste is one of the overall quality characteristics looked for in well-made wines. Wines without length are usually short, flabby, cloying and simple. Length is attributed to a combination of acids, phenols and fruit present in red wines and acids, residual sugars, fruit and phenols, if oak-matured, in white wines. Quality wines will have very long length, offering lingering sensations and characteristics reminiscent of the wine just tasted. The longer the aftertaste the better the wine, as long as the wine remains in balance with its style, blend and grape characteristics. Length is an important factor in quality wines and especially for the sommelier at a restaurant when matching wines with foods.

Wines with over-dominating aftertaste sensations, for example too much bitterness or too much alcohol are not considered to have positive lengths, even though they can be sensed long after the wine has been tasted. These dominating characteristics do not enhance the enjoyment of the wine and should therefore be considered negative if not in balance.

Measurement of Length. Length is measured in time by the number of seconds the sensorial characteristics remain within the mouth and throat.

Short. Once swallowed all sensorial characteristics of the wine tasted disappear rapidly (within 10 to 15 seconds) leaving no evidence of grape typicity, balance or style.

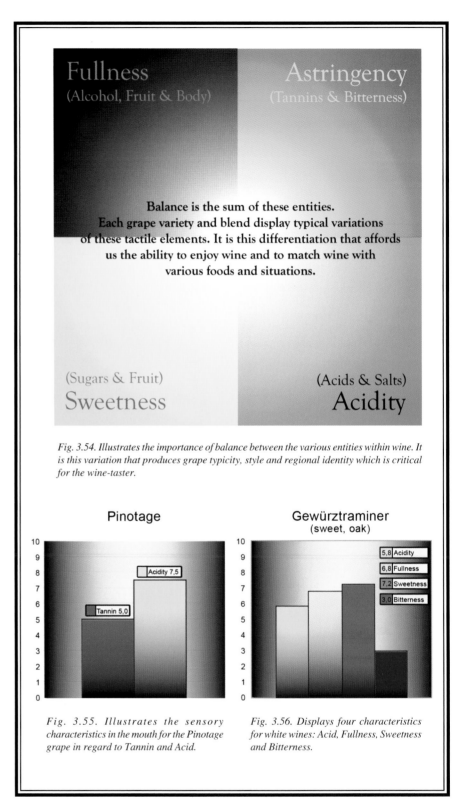

Fig. 3.54. Illustrates the importance of balance between the various entities within wine. It is this variation that produces grape typicity, style and regional identity which is critical for the wine-taster.

Fig. 3.55. Illustrates the sensory characteristics in the mouth for the Pinotage grape in regard to Tannin and Acid.

Fig. 3.56. Displays four characteristics for white wines: Acid, Fullness, Sweetness and Bitterness.

Medium. A medium length will provide the taster with at least 15 to 30 seconds of characteristic sensation.

Long. Long aftertastes offer balanced lengths of between 30 to 45 seconds, leaving the taster with very good and lasting impressions of the wine.

Very Long. Excellent length offering grape and style typicity lasting for more than 45 seconds. Some wines have been known to last for up to two minutes.

If you think what has been said so far is a lot to remember then you're in for another surprise.

10. Taste Balance

Balance is the combination of all of the above sensorial characteristics. Moreover, there is one major additional factor to consider. Is the wine's taste in balance for that specific variety, blend, style or region? These integral combinations of balance are vital not only to the longevity of the wine, but to the wine's terroir (mineral make-up) and style. The overall balance, in accordance with its varietal or blend characteristics, region, style and length is important when matching wine with food. In chapter 7 I describe traditional grape varieties and their balance ratios for acidity/tannin in red wine and acidity/residual sugar/fullness and bitterness if present for white wine varietals (Figs. 3.55 - 3.56).

Measurement of Balance. Is the quality of the individual tactile and sensory stimuli and their sum in accordance with specific grape varieties, blends and regional styles. Balance takes into consideration fullness, astringency, sweetness, acidity and umami (MSG).

Unbalanced. This is usually a wine that has a dominating factor of one or two characteristics that simply overwhelms the wine and drowns out other characters.

Balanced. A balanced wine has all the major sensorial objectives required for that variety or style of wine and is in balance with itself. No dominating characteristics.

Well-balanced. A well-balanced wine offers very good balance between all major sensorial areas of the mouth. The wine displays good length and is typical for that region, style, grape and/or blend.

Very well-balanced. Very well-balanced wines are wines with finesse. Near perfect balance between all sensorial areas and offering very long length. Only the world's very best made wines can achieve this balance of terroir, acid, phenol, residual sugar, fruit and length.

Potential Storage and Current Condition

What requirements are necessary in order to store a wine and

Fig. 3.57. Another illustration showing the importance of grape and regional identity.

how long can it be stored? Are temperatures and humidity important? In this section I will attempt to explain what we need to take into consideration when looking at all the above questions.

1. White wines

Adequate acidity, residual sugar, fruit and alcohol are required in white wines in order to store them for longer periods. The most important of these are acidity and fruit content, without which the wine cannot be stored. A wine has passed its maturity if it lacks these elements. Obviously good characteristics

Fig. 3.58. The author, analyzing a white sweet wine from Sauternes in his friend Nils Stormby's wine cellar. His enormous collection of at least 100 different vintages of Chateau d'Yquem ranges from 1804 to the present.

is a foregone conclusion. Due to good acid levels very good, dry, white wines from for example Germany, Burgundy in France and the NW USA have the ability to last for between 20 to 30 years.

2. Red wines

A good tannin structure along with acid and fruit is what is required for red wines. A red wine without acid is flabby and flat and will not taste good or will not last. Low tannin can be acceptable, as long as there is adequate acid and fruit. Storage for 30 years is not uncommon for very good Bordeaux, Napa Valley wines and a few others.

3. Sweet wines

Sweet wines or, dessert wines, as some people say incorrectly, are dependant on their residual sugar and acid levels for longevity. Good acidity levels are extremely important for sweet wines, as it maintains the balance in taste and also acts as a preservative. Some exceptionally good sweet wines have the ability to exceed 50 and even 100 years.

4. Fortified wines

Fortified wines are wines with grape alcohol added to the natural wine or wine must either after fermentation, as with Sherries or during fermentation, as with Port or Madeira. These wines are high in alcohol and range from 15.5% to 17.5% for various Sherry types and from 18% to 20.5% for various Ports and Madeiras. The preserving factor in these wines is the alcohol, after which come residual sugar, acid and fruit. Very good fortified wines have the ability to last 75 to 100 years or more.

5. Champagne / Sparkling Wines

Acid, fruit, lees and carbonation are key ingredients to the successful longevity of bubbly. Lees consist of expended yeast cells along with phenols (tannin) and these are excellent preservatives; in addition, CO_2 and the usually high acid content of the grapes used in Champagnes or sparkling wines made in the 'Champagne Méthode' have a very good potential for ageing. Unfortunately, most consumers are under the impression that these wines cannot be stored. Good Champagnes or sparkling wines made in the Champagne Méthode are good for a minimum of 10 years and many excellent Champagnes can last as long as 25 to 30 years.

Fig. 3.59. Another view of Nils Stormby's impressive wine cellar.

Fig. 3.60. The author tasting a wine in Nils Stormby's wine cellar, whilst trying to contemplate on how to get his friend Nils to open a 1961 Petrus.

Current Condition

Noting the current condition of the wine is extremely important for future reference. Naturally, the appearance, nose and taste would indicate this condition, but I find it very useful to include a short note about my overall impression, while estimating the current and potential storage of the wine.

Measurement of Current Condition. This is an assessment summary of the wine's individual active elements as well as its characteristic vitality.

Young. Young wines are lively, full of adolescent fruit with their highest acid, tannin and residual sugar levels. They are wines offering fresh fruit but usually need to settle for a number of years if they are full-bodied wines.

Developing. Developing wines are wines that have all their attributes showing well but still in need of ageing. Can usually be paired properly with food and enjoyed in various situations.

Mature. Mature wines have reached their peaks. These are wines that need to be drunk, as they will not improve with time. They are perfectly in balance with all elements in the wine and complement both food and social situation.

Summary

The summary is broken down into the following sections: Balance, Quality and Value for money. It usually creates the greatest amount of discussion in wine-tastings, as tasters invariably try to argue their point of view with much tenacity, which can create a lot of fun. With enough information gathered in your tasting sheet you are able to discuss your wine for either 10 seconds or 20 minutes. The key is to have the information at hand if necessary. All the sections above are covered in the grading sheet; moreover, direct examples are given of how to apply points to the various sections, when grading your wine. Once the wine has been analyzed, graded for balance and quality and points assessed, the next item to address is the matter of price-setting.

Fig. 3.61. Chateau d'Yquem 1900 and 1928.

Good. A well-balanced wine will have no dominating characteristics. The wine can be appreciated and matched with different kinds of foods. Not all sections (Appearance, Nose, Taste) are in balance but no defects are present or noticeable.

Very Good. A wine has a 'Very Good' balance when all its constituents are balanced with each other. The wine should display a number of typical characteristics and should also have very good length. A very good taste ratio for the grape variety, blend and/or style of wine should be expected.

Excellent Balance. A wine with an 'Excellent Balance' displays superior grape characteristics with near perfect taste ratios for the grape variety, blend and/or style of wine recognized from that producer and region. Very long aftertaste with lingering characteristics.

1. Overall Balance

Overall balance is measured from the wine's appearance, nose, acidity, sugar, fruit, body, alcohol, tannin if red and length. Balance for taste is measured by ratios between tannin and acidity in red wines and acidity, fullness and sweetness for white wines and fortified wines. These ratios are shown in chapter 7 and in the appendix.

- **Unbalanced**. An unbalanced wine has a dominating characteristic which overwhelms the rest of the wine. This domination prevents the wine from showing true grape characteristics, the blend and/or style. It detracts the tasters from appreciating the wine as it should be intended. This can be the result of defects within the wine or just poor wine making.

- **Fair balance**. A fairly balanced wine will have some dominating characteristics but one can still, to an extent, appreciate the wine without difficulty. Not all sections (Appearance, Nose, Taste) are in balance but no defects are present or noticeable.

Aggressive, aromatic, astringent, attenuated, attractive, austere, backward, balanced, beefy, big, bitter, bland, botrytis, cat's pee (blackcurrant bush), clean, cloying, coarse, common, complex, cooked, corked, corky, creamy, crisp, delicate, deep, delicate, developed, distinguished, dry, dull, dumb, dusty, earthy, elegant, estery, fat, feminine, fine, finesse, firm, flabby, flat, fleshy, flinty, flowery, forceful, forward, foxy, fragrant, fresh, fruity, gamey, gentle, graceful, green (raw, young and stalky), hard, harsh, heady, heavy, herbaceous, hollow, leathery, light, limpid, little, lively, long, luscious, maderized, mature, meaty, medium-body, medium-dry, medium-sweet, mellow, metallic, milky, moldy, mousey, musky, musty, neutral, nuance, nutty ordinary, oxidized, perfume, plummy, poor, positive, powerful, prickly, puckering, pungent, racy, refreshing, rich, ripe, robust, rough, round, rubbery, rugged, salty, savory, scented, sensuous, severe, sharp, short, silky, simple, smoky, smooth, soft, spicy, stalky, steely, stewed, strong, subtle, superficial, supple, sweaty, tangy, tart, thin, tough, unbalanced, unripe, vanilla, varietal, vegetal, velvety, vigorous, watery, weak, well-balanced, yeasty, zest, zestful, zing, etc.

Fig. 3.62. A number of commonly used descriptives in wine-tasting.

2. Quality

Quality is the descriptive summary of the wine tasted, using both the analytical values assessed plus various descriptive words to portray the wine's quality, style, terroir and how it can be matched to situations, food and the like. A wine's quality is usually expressed in summary form. Summaries are important, since they are usually the only reference many wine-buyers see prior to purchasing the wine. Some descriptive terms to be used are found in Fig. 3.62.

3. Value

After all the tasting, analyzing, grading as well as the discussions have ended, the next aspect to be discussed is usually whether or not the wine is price-worthy. I have taken the liberty of including in chapter 6 a number of price ratio scales for red, white, Champagne, Port and sweet wines used by myself when consulting in the trade. These price ratios have been used to educate importers and wine salesmen on

price and price-setting techniques and are very useful when estimating if a wine is of value or not. Chapter 6 covers the US, U. K., European continent (France, Italy, Spain and Germany) and the Swedish monopoly market.

The vast majority of wine-drinkers want to feel assured that they have purchased a product within or better than the considered price level for a wine of that variety, blend, style and from that region and/or country. Some people might argue that you can never compare a Chilean wine to a South African or American or French wine but I disagree totally. The science of winemaking is studied world-over today and there are no secrets. Winemakers know how to use enzymes, what type of yeasts they prefer and the style that they want to create etc. The value of the wine tasted should be based upon the quality in relation to grape typicity, region, appellation and style. Some consistent brands on the other hand have the ability to demand more for their products, as they offer consistency, quality and long term tradition.

Fig. 3.63. Some more wine in Nils Stormby's cellar. The storage conditions are perfect with the correct humidity and temperature.

Chapter 4

Defects

Defects can be divided into two categories. The first includes manufacturing defects, harmful to the wine and results in both an unbalanced product and, in some cases, headaches. The second category represents more visual (cosmetic) defects, which do not affect consumers.

Manufacturing defects

Manufacturing defects are problems such as post-fermentation, oxidation, corked wine, trichloranisole (TCA), sulfur etc.

1. **Post-fermentation** or second fermentation occurs when a still wine contains fermentable sugars in small quantities. If fermentable yeast is present in the wine, fermentation will start. Today many modern fruit-driven wines are picked late and not fermented totally dry. A second fermentation can therefore recommence within the bottle if there is yeast left. Sugar and yeast together ferment, creating alcohol and carbon dioxide, as shown below. Poor filtering is usually the reason for a second fermentation.

Post-fermentation All Wines

Appearance:
The bottle cork could be raised slightly due to pressure from carbonic acid. The wine can show small bubbles around the rim edge of the wine. It can also be a cloudy wine with a sandy flake deposit.

Aroma:
Not detectable in most still wines, but in extremely poor cases the wine could smell of yeast and/or baked bread.

Taste:
A slight petulant sensation on the tip of the tongue.

Fig. 4.1. What can be found in a wine, if post-fermentation takes place.

$$\text{Yeast} + \text{Sugar} = \text{Alcohol} + \text{Carbon Dioxide}$$

$$C_6H_{12}O_6 \qquad 2C_2H_5OH \qquad 2CO_2$$
$$\text{Glucose} \qquad \text{Ethanol} \qquad \text{Carbon Dioxide}$$

Fig. 4.2. The fermentation process by which yeast transforms sugar into alcohol and carbon dioxide.

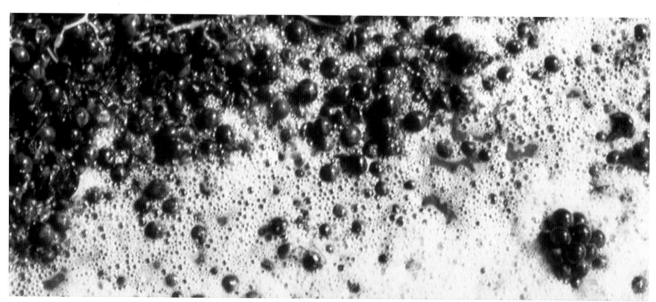

Fig. 4.3. A normal fermentation underway.

2. Oxidation is the result of wine in contact with oxygen, which directly increases the rate of natural decomposition, resulting in an oxidized wine. Under normal circumstances all wine will deteriorate with time.

The wine's style together with its composition of components: fruit, acids, tannin, etc., determine the longevity and storage potential of the wine.

There are a number of wines produced today which show oxidative or madeirized characteristics and these winemaking practices have been followed for hundreds of years. Examples of these fortified wines are: Sherry, Port, Madeira, Rancio and other fortified wines, which should therefore not be considered defective.

There are also 'old style' winemakers, producing wines in a slight oxidative style such as with some Barolos from Piemonte in Italy. These wines are exempted from negative associations as this is their style. Please note that there are both modern and traditional winemakers in Piemonte with different manufacturing styles. There is also a modern winemaking practice of micro-oxygenating the wine, while the wine is still in the tanks, which is intentional and thus not a defect.

Oxidized Wines

<u>White Wines</u>
Appearance:
From a pale yellow to a dull, brownish, golden straw color.

Aroma:
Losing grape and varietal characteristics and fruitiness, becoming tired and smelling of caramel.

Taste: Loss of fruit, marked volatile acidity with potential for bitterness.

<u>Rosé Wines</u>
Appearance:
From a clear, brownish-pink to a dull pink color.

Aroma: Losing grape and varietal characteristics and fruitiness, becoming tired and smelling of caramel.

Taste:
Loss of fruit, marked volatile acidity with potential for bitterness. Lack of tannin but in some rare cases hardened tannins.

<u>Red Wines</u>
Appearance:
From a pale, brownish-red to an orange-brown hue.

Aroma:
Losing grape and varietal characteristics and fruitiness, becoming tired and smelling of caramel.

Taste:
Loss of fruit, marked volatile acidity with potential for bitterness. Lack of tannin quality could be very low or even hardened.

Fig. 4.4. What wines look like if oxidized.

Fig. 4.5. The best type of cork is supple and elastic, which allows very small amounts of oxygen to pass. This prevents suffocation of the wine.

3. Corked or Trichloro-2, 4, 6-anisole (TCA)
is the result of a chemical reaction between the
penicillium mold, found in natural cork crevices
and the chemicals used to sterilize the corks prior
to use.

The reactive chemical used is chlorine-based.
About 4% of all wines using natural corks can become tainted with a TCA as a result of treatment
(sterilized) with a chlorine-based chemical.

In 1996 the European Cork Federation recommended a number of improvements, such as
changing the chlorine-based chemicals to perox-
ide-based instead. Further recommendations to
enhance storage conditions, hence reducing mold
growth and improving harvesting procedures, have
also been implemented. These recommendations
should decrease the number of corked wines.

TCA is also found in oak barrels, staves, chips and
other wood products treated with chlorophenol,
so it is not just limited to corks as most people
assume.

Corked Wines

Appearance:
No evidence.

Aroma:
There are five levels of strength. This defect smells
like new cork, musty, moldy like fungi or rotting veg-
etation. If you are not sure, smell the cork before the
wine and if the wine smells like the cork, you have a
corked wine. Once you identify this smell for the first
time, you will never forget it.

Taste:
It can have a flat and stagnant tactile sensation but
shows more of a volatile aroma confirming what was
smelt earlier.

---

*Fig. 4.7. Corked or trichloro-2,4,6-anisole (TCA) characteristics found in wines. Ap-
proximately 4% of wines using natural corks and oak are usually affected by TCA.*

Fig. 4.6. Oak barrels at Château Lafite-Rothschild in Bordeaux.

Fig. 4.8. A standard wine-tasting. Due to the concentrated aroma in the ullage of the glass, the Aroma Cap helps to identify many defects.

6. Volatile Acidity. All wines have some volatile acidity, acetic acid ($CH_3CO OH$). The problem arises when there is too much bacteria and oxygen in the wine and a shortage of sulfur dioxide (SO_2). The bacteria convert the alcohol to acetic acid (wine vinegar), where, in turn, ethyl acetate (cf. above) forms. Left untreated the wine becomes undrinkable.

7. Hydrogen Sulfide (H_2S). If allowed to react with ethanol this reactive gas smells like rotten eggs, ethyl mercaptans, onions, garlic and other organic sulfides. Hydrogen sulfide can come from a number of sources during the winemaking process. The key is to remove it with blue copper-sulfate crystals as soon as detected. It becomes almost impossible to do so later, since it has a very high boiling point.

4. Ethyl acetate ($CH_3COOCH_2CH_3$) is a volatile acid, produced when acetic acid (CH_3COOH) reacts with ethanol ($HOCH_2CH_3$) and bacteria start production of ethyl acetate and water. This defect is usually explained from poor filtration in young wines. These esters in turn are broken down by water into alcohols and acids producing additional esters and hundreds of compounds, which, in aged wines, help to produce many of the excellent aromas identified toady. It is responsible for a piquant smell similar to that of glue or sealer.

8. Yeast Spoilage usually occurs through poor filtration and presents itself by making the wine unclear with a fine flaky or sandy deposit, which disperses into a cloudy haze when shaken. If fermentable yeast and some sugar is present in the wine, fermentation is possible. In some cases bag-in-boxes have been found to resemble a football shape due to the gas pressure buildup. In worst cases the yeast spores can be recognized under a microscope. Yeast spoilage usually occurs only in white wines (cf. post-fermentation above).

| Ethanol | + | Acetic acid | = | Water | + | Ethyl acetate |
| $H OCH_2CH_3$ | + | $CH_3CO OH$ | = | H_2O | + | $CH_3COOCH_2CH_3$ |

Fig. 4.9. How ethyl acetate forms in wine. It is usually due to poor filtration.

9. Mousiness is yet another defect, more evident in poor sweet and dry white wines from past years but seldom apparent in today's modern wineries. It is a microbiological and yeast spoilage resulting from poor sanitation practices within the vineyard. An undesirable off-odor and taste of mice or rodents can be identified. Very hard to detect even for the avid tasters, it is one of the most serious bacterial or lactic acid bacteria spoilages. Prevention of mousiness is accomplished through proper sanitation practices and correct use of sulfur dioxide (SO_2) levels in reference to pH levels.

5. Sulfur Dioxide (SO_2) in a wine acts as an antioxidant and an inhibitor of microbiological growth. It has been used for hundreds of years and will continue to be in use until a better solution can be found. If the levels are too high, it can be detected. Smelling like a struck match, it is sensed as a prickling feeling at the back of the throat and tip of the nose. Since sulfur dioxide reacts with oxygen, decanting the wine will dissipate the majority of the detectable amounts. Some people are allergic to SO_2, so sensitivity varies dramatically.

10. Geraniums (crushed geranium petals) is the smell associated with a bacterial decomposition of sorbic acid in red wines. This contamination occurs when lactic bacteria metabolize sorbic acid into 2-ethoxy hexa-3, 5-diene, an unsaturated compound.

Cosmetic Defects

Cosmetic Defects such as tartrate crystals, sediment, protein, iron casse, copper casse and cork are also found in wines but these are not harmful and do not affect the quality of the wine.

1. Tartrate Crystals are formed from either calcium tartrate or potassium bi-tartrate (cream of tartar) which originate from the soil and grape itself. These tartrates usually combine with tartaric acid and fall as deposits. They are not dangerous but usually form through a poor stabilization process or by the presence of protective colloids within the wines. These colloids prevent the crystals from depositing themselves during cooling and later denature themselves.

Fig. 4.10. Tartrate crystals in a bottle of Château d'Yquem.

Tartrate Crystals in Wines

Appearance:
Do not affect color. They are small 'crystal-like' clear to white deposits at the bottom of the bottle.

Aroma:
No effect.

Taste:
No taste.

N.B. Consumers usually suspect broken glass or added undissolved sugar, which is not the case. Broken glass is usually a lot larger and not in crystal form. Sugar would not remain undissolved either.

Fig. 4.11. Tartrate crystals in wines.

Sediment in Red Wines

Appearance:
Small dark sludge.

Aroma:
None.

Taste:
No wine taste. If tasted, the sediment usually has a dry taste.

N.B. When present decant the wine very carefully so as not to disturb the sediment. If you are serving a very old wine, let the wine stand up a couple of days prior to serving it.

Fig. 4.12. Sediment in red wines.

Fig. 4.13. Second year barrels at Château Latour in Bordeaux.

3. Protein Haze is a cosmetic defect. It is related to copper casse (cf. below) and usually forms in warm climates where, the grapes achieve higher protein content. Consisting of small, white, very light pieces, which are easily disturbed. This defect is not harmful. Decant gently.

4. Cork is not the same thing as corked. If you have some pieces of cork floating in your wine, there is no reason to be alarmed. Pick them out with either a spoon, serviette or your finger if nothing else is available.

5. Iron and Copper Casse. Iron Casse is dissolved iron within a wine and is usually more noticeable in white wines. Iron casse presents itself as a fine white deposit at the bottom of the bottle. It is not harmful and can be simply furthered by decanting. Copper casse, on the other hand, is seen as a brown haze formed in anaerobic conditions (without oxygen present) between proteins and cuprous ions. Once the bottle is opened and the wine aerated, these elements oxidize and dissipate, which results in a clear wine without haziness. This is not harmful unless totally discolored.

6. Botrytis Cinerea or noble rot as it is also known, is a fungal disease, occurring most commonly in conditions where humidity is about 90% and temperatures between 16°C to 19°C / 60°F to 66°F. In most cases this fungus can produce excellent concentrations of sugar and acid. If undesired, it causes a huge problem for the vineyard manager. Some of the world's most expensive wines are made from Botrytis-infected grapes.

Fig. 4.14. Tartrate crystals in a bottle of Château d'Yquem.

2. Sediment is nothing more than various components of a wine formed in a normal reaction. The sediment found at the bottom of the bottle after storage is usually a compound made up of phenolics (the grape's pigments and tannin) and acidity in the wine. During the ageing process these elements gain weight by combining and fall to the bottom of the bottle. This is another explanation for the color change and reduction in the ullage.

Fig. 4.15. Botrytis-infected grapes.

Chapter 5

Grading Procedures

The following chapter will explain how to grade or score wines in a consistent way while using the 100-point system. There is another system, the 20-point grading scale, which will be briefly addressed at the end of the chapter.

As discussed in chapter 3, there is a norm for tasting and grading. These procedures are usually conducted in the following sequence: **Appearance** first, then **Aroma and Taste, Current Condition and Storage Potential** and finally a **Summary**.

Variables Affecting a Wine's Grade

The following variables should be considered when grading or scoring a wine:

1. Grape variety, typicity and style.

2. Climate conditions, affecting the wine's balance and fruit quality.

Fig. 5.0. An advanced class at the Wine Academy.

3. Growing conditions that could affect a grade are as follows:

- **Soil** (mineral content, pH levels, etc.) affects the acidity and storage potential.

- **Water levels** in regard to irrigation, drainage and rain fall, prior to picking, affect the quality of the fruit by changing the acid/tannin balance of the grape, which can result in poor berry growth.

- **Viticulture practices** in relation to pruning, the use of pesticides and the timing of the harvest all directly relate to the fruit quality and balance. Fruit structure at picking is decisive for pH, acidity, sugar and phenolic (grape skin) quality. Poor canopy management can create uneven ripeness in berry bunches or the other extreme, where too much sun exposure can burn the grapes thus damaging the phenolic structure.

4. Winery operations and procedures directly influence the wine's quality, for example correct selection of enzymes (used to aid in extraction) and yeast strains (strains can be bought to enhance various characteristics) to be used during fermentation. Furthermore, the length of the extraction period as well as fermentation temperatures are vital.

5. The use of **oak barrels or steel tanks** during fermentation and the maturation stages of wine production affect the quality of the product and the potential storage time. Wines matured in oak and/or receiving some kind of oak treatment all benefit from tannin and tannin extract enhancement.

6. Filtering techniques affect quality too. Exaggerated and over-filtering (smaller than 4 microns) reduces the amount of flavor compounds, thus weakening the character and balance of the wine. The decision whether to filter, rack or both would be dictated by the style of wine desired.

7. Adjustments to the wine during fermentation and after directly affect the quality of the aroma, balance and length of the wine. Additions of tannin, tartaric acid, aroma enhancers, micro-oxidation amongst others all play major roles in character and quality.

8. Varietal grading, selection and blending affect the end product in regard to character, balance and grape typicity.

9. Distribution and storage conditions, such as temperatures, humidity and light exposure, play a significant role for the potential storage time of the wine.

10. Wine serving conditions (atmospherics) are important for how the wine is perceived and appreciated.

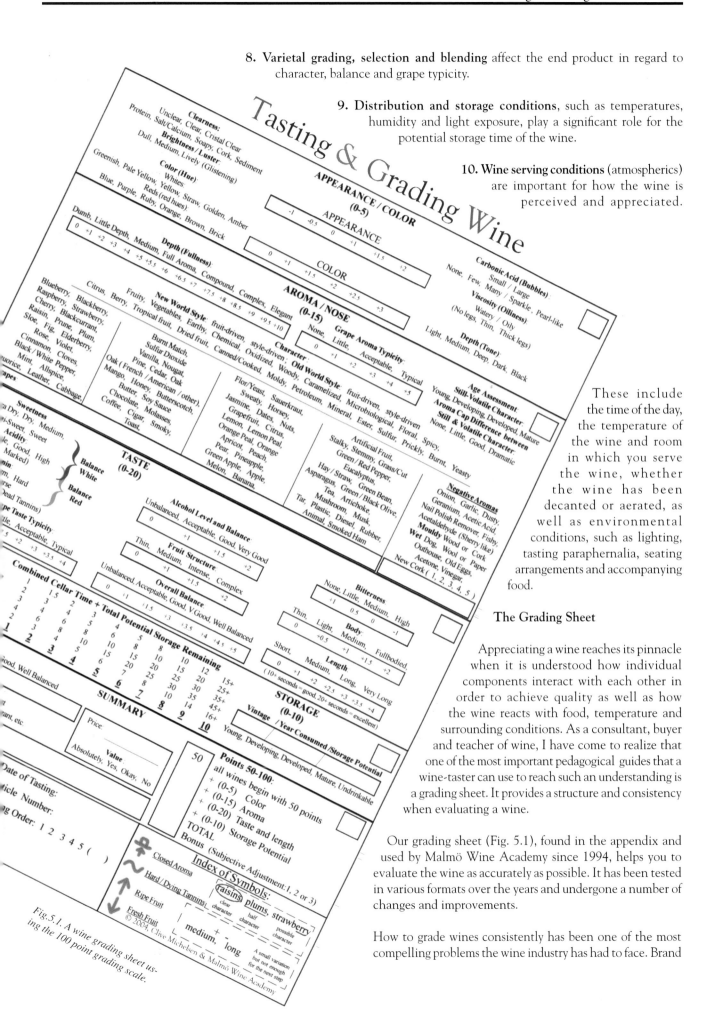

Fig. 5.1. A wine grading sheet using the 100 point grading scale.

These include the time of the day, the temperature of the wine and room in which you serve the wine, whether the wine has been decanted or aerated, as well as environmental conditions, such as lighting, tasting paraphernalia, seating arrangements and accompanying food.

The Grading Sheet

Appreciating a wine reaches its pinnacle when it is understood how individual components interact with each other in order to achieve quality as well as how the wine reacts with food, temperature and surrounding conditions. As a consultant, buyer and teacher of wine, I have come to realize that one of the most important pedagogical guides that a wine-taster can use to reach such an understanding is a grading sheet. It provides a structure and consistency when evaluating a wine.

Our grading sheet (Fig. 5.1), found in the appendix and used by Malmö Wine Academy since 1994, helps you to evaluate the wine as accurately as possible. It has been tested in various formats over the years and undergone a number of changes and improvements.

How to grade wines consistently has been one of the most compelling problems the wine industry has had to face. Brand names should not play a role in this process. The grading sheet used here provides the grader with a consistent manual to follow. The methodical sequence of steps allows the taster to judge wines upon their quality as well as to keep the variation of points scored, by a group of tasters, to a maximum of 3 points from each other for the graded wines.

This chapter explains and guides you through the process of setting points to this grading sheet and discusses how we arrive at established points for each section.

These explanations together with those in chapter 3 should enable you to conduct your own tasting. Each of the following sections will begin with a basic point summary (within the boxes) along with an extract of the section, followed by an explanation in detail with each part highlighted for easy recognition.

In order to get started, the first step is to fill in the details of the wine to be tasted in the box at the bottom of the sheet (Fig. 5.2.).

Fig. 5.1. Mr. Peter Nordenström is completing a grading sheet. Wine judges grade many wines during the course of a tasting, so it is necessary to document correctly.

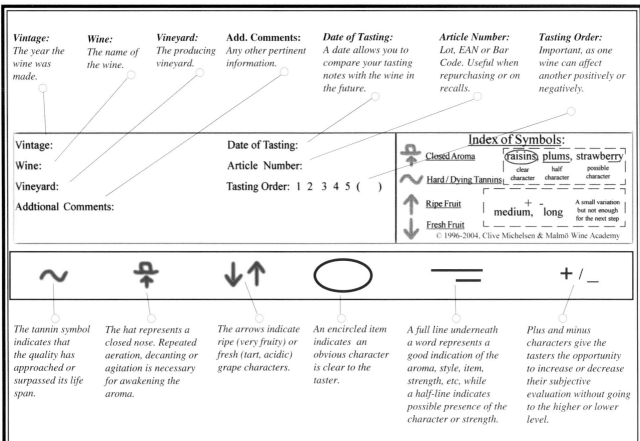

Fig. 5.2. Information section of the wine grading sheet.

Grading the Wine's Appearance and Color

The wine's Appearance and Color (chapter 3) reveal a lot about its present state and condition, where it could have been made, possible grape varieties and the potential presence of defects.

There is a total of five points awarded. Appearance receiving from -1 to 2 points and Color from 0 to 3 points. Champagnes and Sparkling wines are an exception, where Appearance and Color receive a maximum of (3) three points, moreover Color and Depth a maximum of (2) two points.

The following terms are used for describing the surface areas of the wine:

Rim Edge
The rim edge or meniscus is the outermost part of the wine. It is water-like and colorless.

Rim Proper (Age / Readiness / Color)
The rim proper is where the wine's color begins.

Rim Width (Age / Readiness / Color / Clarity)
The rim width is a band of color, ranging in width from 1 mm to 20 mm. It is instrumental when grading color in relation to age, the older the wine the wider the rim width. When the pigments combine with acids and tannin, the wine becomes lighter and the rim width wider.

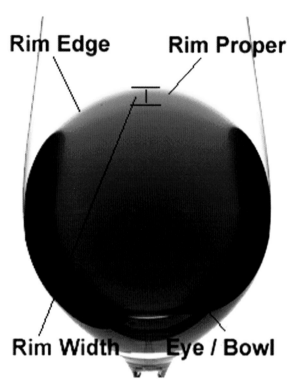

Fig.5.3.5. Explains the various components of the wine's gradient.

Eye or Bowl (Hue, Depth, Clarity)
The eye or bowl is important when analyzing the wine's age, gradient (from bowl to rim proper) and clarity. Sediment of most types would be noticeable here.

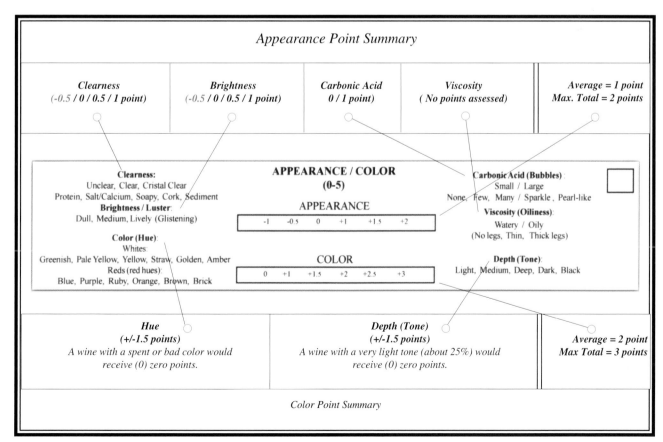

Fig. 5.3. Appearance and Color point summaries.

Appearance

The Appearance section, including *Clearness* and *Brightness*, contains a maximum of (2) two points, the average wine receiving just (1) one point. When grading *Carbonic Acid* an extra (1) point is assessed, so the grade is for a total of three (3) points instead of the usual two (2) points. Please note: There are no points given for viscosity, but a deduction is possible if the wine is not viscous.

Clearness

Red wines are always graded as Clear and white wines as Crystal Clear, unless dull or showing defects (chapter 6). Note that cosmetic defects are not manufacturing defects. An Unclear wine would be graded minus one (-1) in clearness, whereas a Clear or Crystal clear wine is given a maximum of one (1) point.

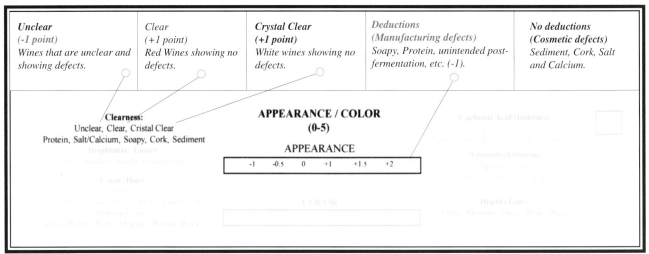

Fig. 5.4. Appearance – Clearness point assessment section.

Brightness

Brightness is the liveliness and luster of the wine as seen from all angles: top, side and tilted at 30 degrees. It tells us if we have a living wine, a wine with vigor and acidity. It reflects the 'health or vibrancy' of the wine. A sick or defective wine has no liveliness.

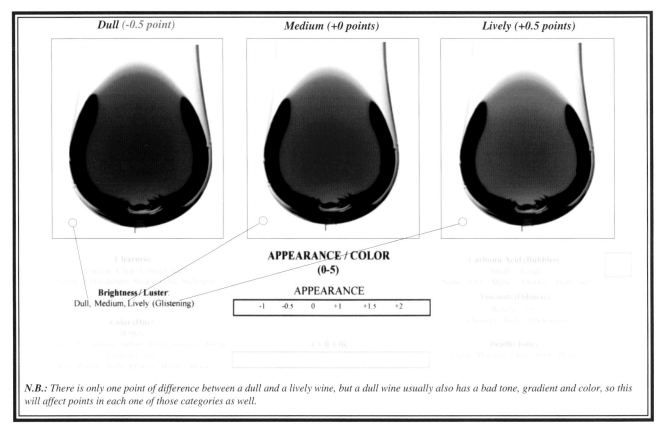

N.B.: *There is only one point of difference between a dull and a lively wine, but a dull wine usually also has a bad tone, gradient and color, so this will affect points in each one of those categories as well.*

Fig. 5.5. Appearance – Clearness point assessment section.

Carbonic Acid (CO_2)

Wines with bubbles! The more small, pearl-like bubbles the better for appearance, quality and length. When grading CO_2 you do not need to consider viscosity. Carbonic Acid is graded out of 1 point. Half a point should be for the size of the bubbles and another half a point for pearl-like strings, since both color and depth are graded out of 1 point. These points are added to the wine's Clearness and Brightness. Together they can make up a maximum allowable points for Appearance. Keep in mind that this only occurs in Champagne and sparkling wines.

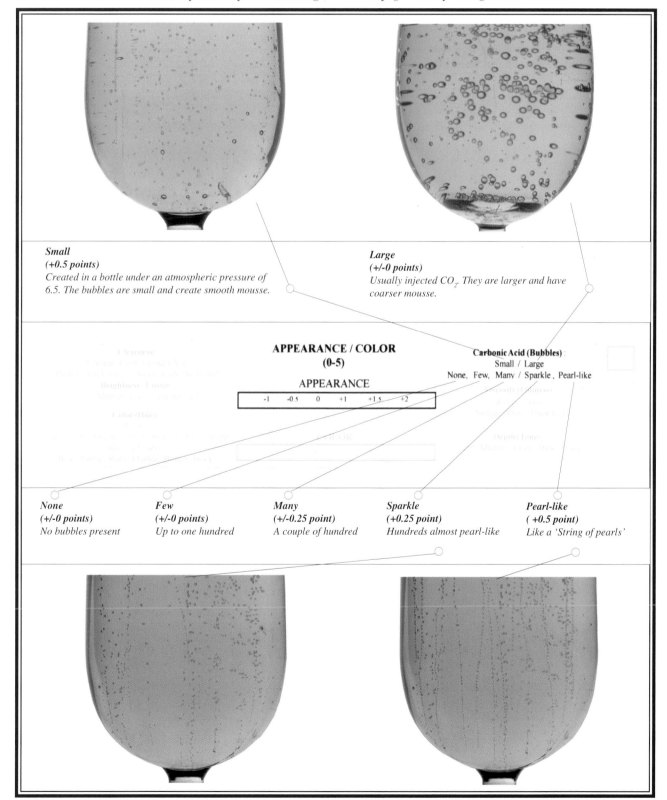

Small
(+0.5 points)
Created in a bottle under an atmospheric pressure of 6.5. The bubbles are small and create smooth mousse.

Large
(+/-0 points)
Usually injected CO_2. They are larger and have coarser mousse.

APPEARANCE / COLOR
(0-5)

APPEARANCE

| -1 | -0.5 | 0 | +1 | +1.5 | +2 |

Carbonic Acid (Bubbles) :
Small / Large
None, Few, Many / Sparkle , Pearl-like

None
(+/-0 points)
No bubbles present

Few
(+/-0 points)
Up to one hundred

Many
(+/-0.25 point)
A couple of hundred

Sparkle
(+0.25 point)
Hundreds almost pearl-like

Pearl-like
(+0.5 point)
Like a 'String of pearls'

Fig. 5.6. Appearance – Carbonic Acid point assessment section.

Viscosity

Viscosity is the oiliness of the wine's appearance, also known as 'tears' or 'legs'. The legs can help to determine the levels of alcohol and body to be expected from the wine. High viscous tension on the rim of the glass represents high alcohol and sugar contents. In most cases, wines with high alcohol has long slender legs and those with high sugar take longer to appear and have thicker or fuller legs. Alcohol evaporates quicker than water and other solubles in the wine, thus causing the legs to appear. Normally, long legs would be the most desirable, since they usually offer good balance between sugar and alcohol. Viscous tension is not assessed for Champagnes or sparkling wines, as agitating the wine causes loss of carbonic acid (bubbles).

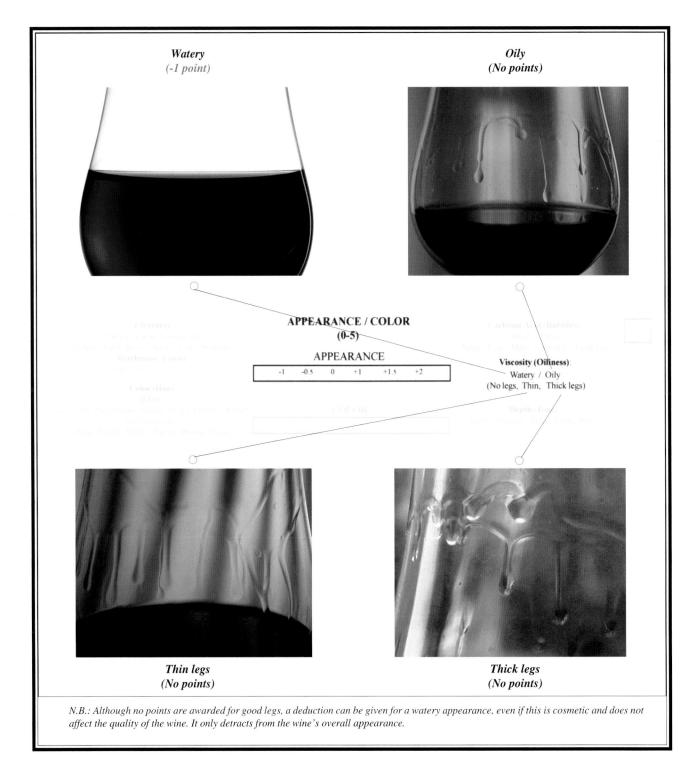

Fig. 5.7. Appearance – Viscosity point assessment section.

Color

Color and Depth receive their points simultaneously in a single package. They represent the result of a number of strategically important decisions in grading. The wine's color is affected by a number of variables such as oxygen exposure, the age of the wine, the winemaking style, climate conditions and the grape variety. Color is divided into the two major categories Hue and Tone, but Gradient is possible to add as a third. For our purposes, we consider Tone and Gradient together as one entity. A total of three points are given for Hue and Tone.

Hue

A good hue in relation to the age of the wine is very important. Wines with good hues/colors for their age can receive from 0 up to 1.5 points with an average of 1. For example, if a wine turns hue (starts to change color) already within its second year, it is not good and will receive poor points. The longer the wine can hold its hue the better, but wines of age (8 years plus) receive good points if they have good hues for their age. Naturally, variety, tannin quality (Anthocyans) and the use of enzymes during extraction are instrumental in color development. See Chapter 7 for more details.

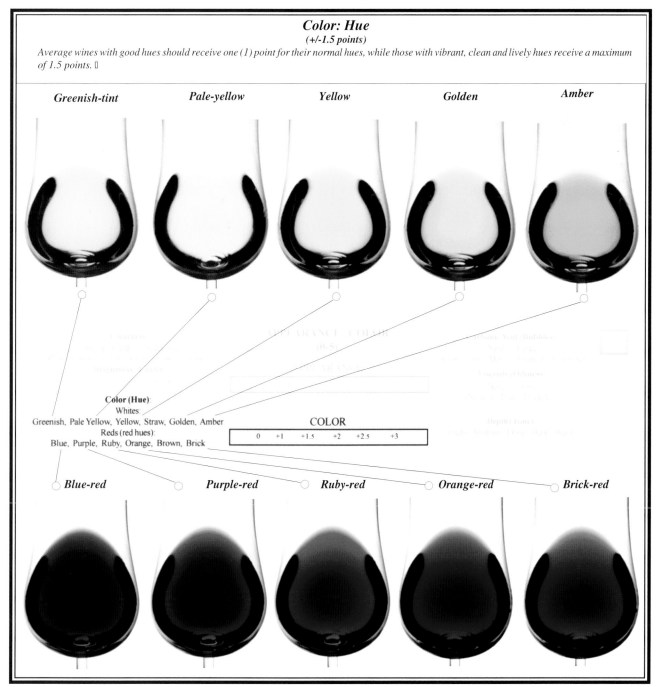

Fig. 5.8. Appearance – Hue point assessment section.

Depth

Depth or Tone is the darkness and gradient of the color hue from 0 = transparent to 100 = opaque or dark-black. The gradient of the wine varies depending on climate conditions, use of enzymes for maximal color extraction, fermentation temperatures, maceration times, age of the wine, oxygen contact and grape variety. Tighter gradients, the gradient of darkness from the center or bowl to the rim of the wine,

seen as black in Fig. 5.9 indicates good sunny conditions, long maceration periods and grape variety with a thick skin. As the color changes, so does the tone.

Wines with good depth for their age usually receive one point with a maximum of 1.5 points.

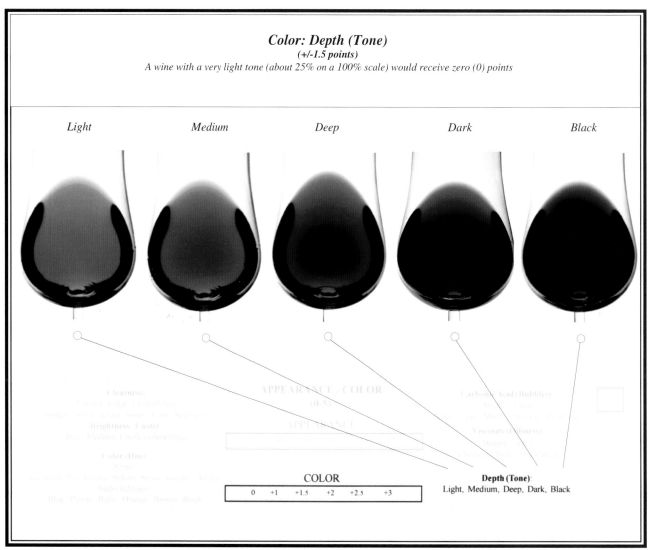

Fig. 5.9. Appearance and Tone point summaries.

Fig. 5.10. The Grape variety, climate conditions, the phenolic quality, the use of enzymes and naturally maceration length and temperatures all affect the 'Appearance and Tone' of the wine to be tasted.

Phenolic quality is measured in mg/l and will at its peak consist of between 300 to 375 mg/l. At the final stages of maturity, the grape sugars increase, while the acids decrease rapidly. The phenolic components (tannins and pigments) also diminish slightly just prior to picking. Well-grown grapes are usually picked with a phenolic weight of about 250 to 300 mg/l.

Aroma (Nose)

Identifying a bouquet or aroma in a wine is not the easiest thing to do and grading the wine's nose is even more difficult. The key to understanding the basics when grading aroma is to establish your own references and aroma associations as soon as possible. Once you have established these references and their associations you can adjust them over time.

There are a number of aroma samples available on the market that can help you. I have a set of 40 aromas (10 white, red, oak and defect aromas), which are used at the Wine Academy. In chapter 3 it was mentioned how you could make your own set of aroma samples. This is critical, since it allows you to associate and compare a sample with a wine, if and when in doubt. A set of aroma samples can be ordered from www.malmo-wine-academy.com if necessary. Try to identify a number of key characters, break them down and analyze them separately. This usually gives you the best possible understanding of how to grade depth and grape typicity.

Fig. 5.11.5. Bengt Andersson analyzing a wine's aroma.

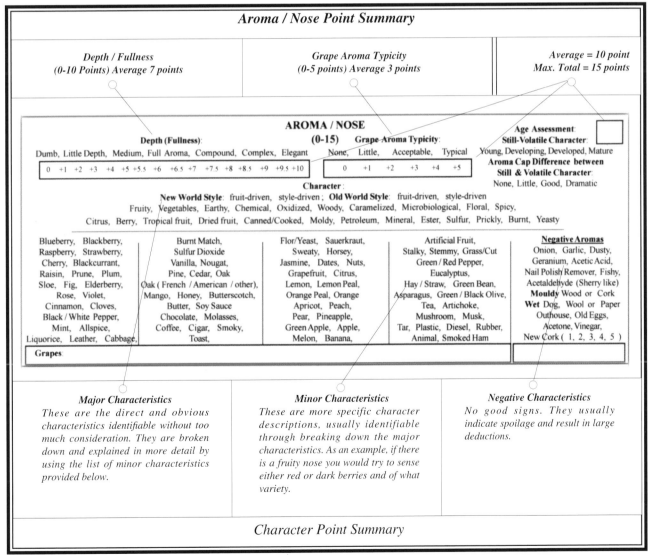
Fig. 5.11. Aroma point summaries.

Depth or Fullness.

Assessing points to the aroma table is not as difficult as it looks. The depth and quality of the aroma is the key. High quality is not necessarily lots of fruit but rather harmony of finesse and character, revealing the winemaking style, region and grapes. This fullness or depth of aroma is vital for high points. The parameters associated to each of the grapes will be discussed.

Depth or fullness is graded out of 10 points. An average of around 7 points should be given to a wine displaying a full aroma, while deductions are made for lesser wines or wines displaying negative aromas. Wines of good depth receive higher points. For example, a 90 point plus wine usually represents an elegant wine and in most cases receives 8 or 9 points out the ten for depth or fullness.

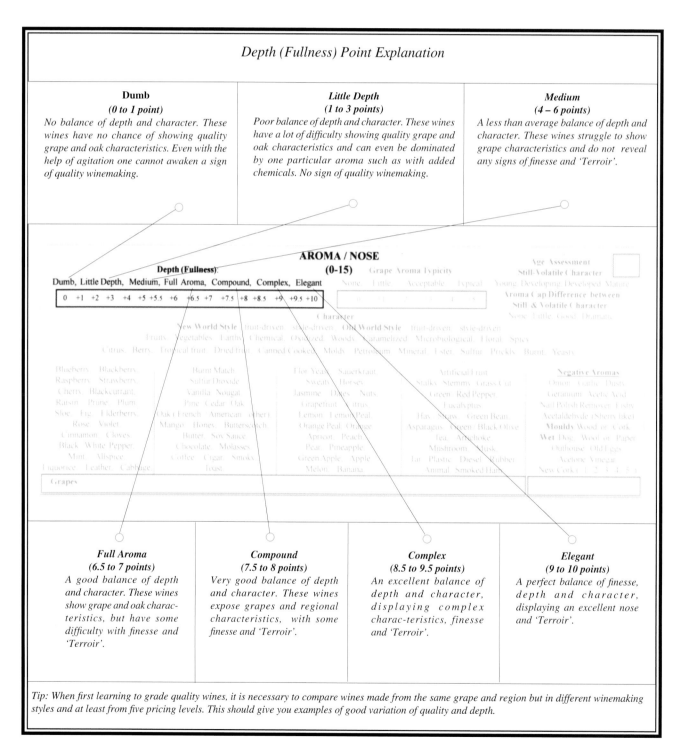

Fig. 5.12. Aroma depth and quality point assessment summaries.

Grape or Blend Typicity

Without varietal or regional characteristics, there is just sameness. Imagine all wines with the same aroma, with the same fruit-driven, high alcohol, heavy dark berry fruit characters. How do we then match wine with food, climate and situation?

This Grape and Blend Typicity grading section affords us the opportunity to identify these varietal qualities. There are five grading points for the typicity and these are of vital importance not just for the winemaker but the consumer too, as they constitute the base for variety, blend, terroir and region.

Grape and Blend Typicity defined in Fig 5.13 has an average point assessment of three (3) out of a possible five (5) points. Well-made wines, showing typical varietal characteristics for their grapes and blend, should receive full points. For example, Château Lafite-Rothschild, a 1st growth from Pauillac, Bordeaux, takes great care during their vinification and maturation phases to insure that grape typicity is evident in their wines. When you taste a Lafite you know it is a Lafite, as it shows unmistakable grape typicity and regional (appellation) identity.

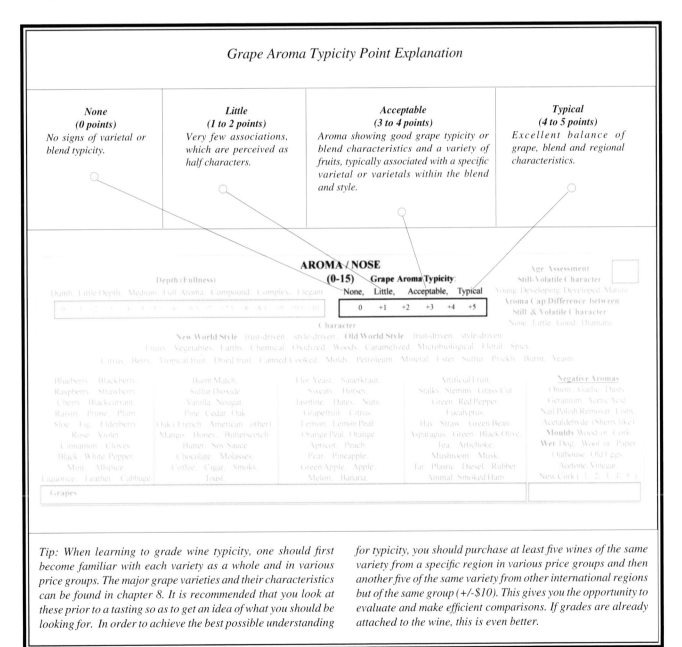

Tip: When learning to grade wine typicity, one should first become familiar with each variety as a whole and in various price groups. The major grape varieties and their characteristics can be found in chapter 8. It is recommended that you look at these prior to a tasting so as to get an idea of what you should be looking for. In order to achieve the best possible understanding for typicity, you should purchase at least five wines of the same variety from a specific region in various price groups and then another five of the same variety from other international regions but of the same group (+/-$10). This gives you the opportunity to evaluate and make efficient comparisons. If grades are already attached to the wine, this is even better.

Fig.5.13. Grape Aroma Typicity measures how typical a grape's aroma is to its variety and/or blend.

Age and Volatility.

The wine's age and volatility are measured at the time of drinking. No points are given for these assessed values.

This is the wine-taster's second indication of the quality condition and storage potential of the wine. The first indication was the wine's appearance (hue and tone) and the last will be its taste (condition of acids, tannins and fruit). The age will then be conclusively considered, when grading the wine's storage potential at the bottom.

Fig. 5.14.5. Storage conditions will affect the maturation, age and volatility of the wine.

Age and Volatility Assessment

Young
A young nose is very fresh, full of 'volatile fruit' and acidity. Typically, when removing the aroma caps, both the still and volatile aromas are the same in heavily fruit-driven wines but medium- and light-bodied wines can differ slightly.

Developing
A developing nose is typically softer in character, displaying rounder, more mellow fruit characteristics.

Developed
A slightly oxidized character from ageing might be noticeable, but the wine is more likely to have a well-balanced nose, offering many characteristics and some finesse.

Mature
A mature nose, is usually warmer, less fruity and slightly oxidized. Acidity levels can be high or low.

AROMA / NOSE
(0-15)

Depth (Fullness)   Grape Aroma Typicity

Dumb Little Depth Medium Full Aroma Compound Complex Elegant   None Little Acceptable Typical

Age Assessment:
Still-Volatile Character:
Young, Developing, Developed, Mature
Aroma Cap Difference between
Still & Volatile Character
None Little Good Dramatic

Character
New World Style fruit-driven style-driven **Old World Style** fruit-driven style-driven
Fruity Vegetables Earthy Chemical Oxidized Woods Caramelized Microbiological Floral Spicy
Citrus Berry Tropical fruit Dried fruit Canned Cooked Moldy Petroleum Mineral Ester Sulfur Prickly Burnt Yeasty

Blueberry Blackberry,	Burnt Match,	Flor-Yeast, Sauerkraut,	Artificial Fruit,	**Negative Aromas**
Raspberry Strawberry	Sulfur Dioxide	Sweaty Horsey	Stalky Stemmy Grass/Cut	Onion Garlic Dusty
Cherry Blackcurrant,	Vanilla Nougat,	Jasmine Dates Nuts	Green / Red Pepper,	Geranium Acetic Acid
Raisin Prune Plum,	Pine Cedar Oak	Grapefruit Citrus	Eucalyptus	Nail Polish Remover, Fishy
Sloe Fig Elderberry,	Oak (French American other)	Lemon Lemon Peel,	Hay Straw Green Bean,	Acetaldehyde (Sherry like)
Rose Violet	Mango Honey Butterscotch,	Orange Peal Orange	Asparagus Green Black Olive,	**Mouldy** Wood or Cork
Cinnamon Cloves,	Butter Soy Sauce	Apricot Peach	Tea Artichoke	**Wet** Dog Wool or Paper
Black White Pepper,	Chocolate Molasses,	Pear Pineapple,	Mushroom Musk,	Outhouse Old Eggs
Mint Allspice,	Coffee Cigar Smoky,	Green Apple Apple	Tar Plastic Diesel Rubber	Acetone Vinegar
Liquorice Leather Cabbage	Toast	Melon Banana	Animal Smoked Ham	New Cork 1 2 3 4 5
Grapes				

Tip: The wine should be poured into the glass at least twenty minutes prior to analysis. Once this has been done, an Aroma Cap® should be placed over the glass opening. This traps the aroma characters within the ullage of the glass, thus allowing the air (oxygen) to break down the volatile elements and produce a more prolonged aged wine. Firstly it affords us the possibility to estimate the ageing potential by using one more tool and, secondly, it provides us with the volatile characteristics associated with a retro-nasal aroma. Lastly, it keeps the room somewhat less vinous, especially if you are a large group tasting five wines.

Fig. 5.14. Aroma – Age and Volatility Assessment

Aroma Cap Differential (*Still versus Volatile*).

The wine's general quality condition can be assessed from the wine's aroma. The Aroma Cap helps to concentrate these aromas, thus enhancing your ability to detect both volatile and mature characteristics.

Although no points are given for these assessed values, an assessment of the wine's condition and development can be made by evaluating the differential between the still and the volatile aroma (in an agitated state). The identified characteristics are then confirmed in the retro-nasal aroma and in the aftertaste.

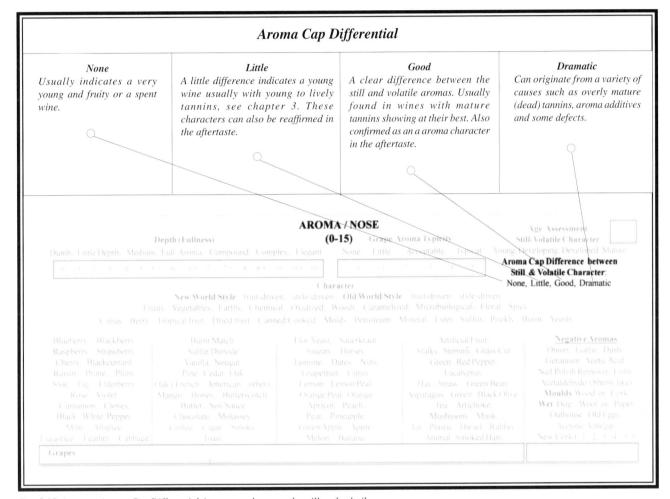

Aroma Cap Differential

None	*Little*	*Good*	*Dramatic*
Usually indicates a very young and fruity or a spent wine.	A little difference indicates a young wine usually with young to lively tannins, see chapter 3. These characters can also be reaffirmed in the aftertaste.	A clear difference between the still and volatile aromas. Usually found in wines with mature tannins showing at their best. Also confirmed as an a aroma character in the aftertaste.	Can originate from a variety of causes such as overly mature (dead) tannins, aroma additives and some defects.

Fig. 5.15. Aroma – Aroma Cap Differential Assessment between the still and volatile aromas.

Fig. 5.15.5. Evaluating the aroma using the Aroma Cap, which helps to enhance the wine's characteristics.

Characters & Major Character Assessment

Assessing the wine's major and minor characteristics is of vital importance, as this justifies the points established for depth and grape/blend typicity. It is therefore critical that all associations are filled in, whether directly evident or only suspected. With the aid of the index symbols shown at the beginning of this chapter you can circle, underline (full or half) or use plus and minus, thus indicating all your associations so as to establish as accurate an analysis as possible.

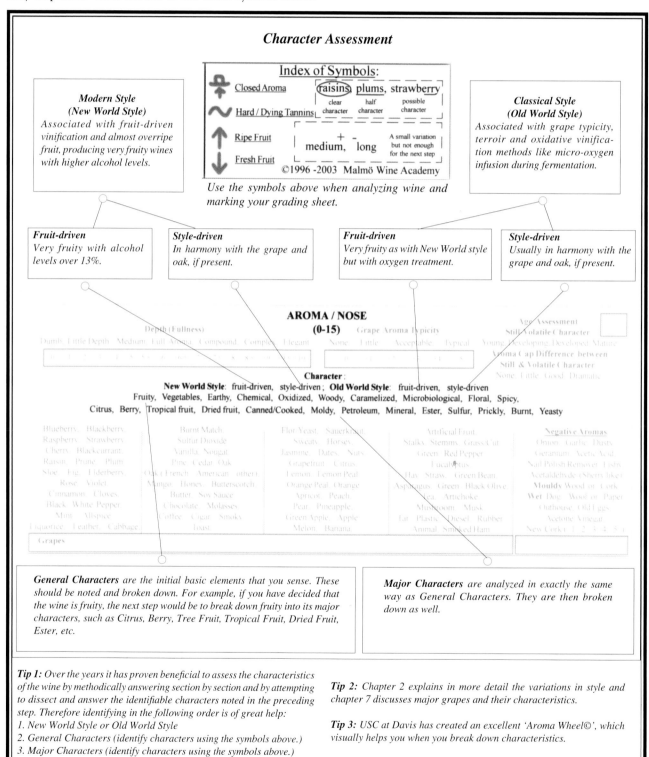

Fig. 5.16. Aroma – Character Assessment.

Minor Characters shown below are representative for most of the vinifera species, although you might still find additional ones that you want to use in your description of the wine. This is entirely acceptable and a box called Grape is provided for this at the bottom of the Aroma section in the grading sheet. There are patterns that usually follow grape varieties and styles, so it is quite important that you study chapter seven and familiarize yourself with them.

Negative aromas are noted and points deducted for each. Some of them, such as Diesel and Petroleum are not negative if found in a wine containing the Riesling grape. Tar and Rubber are not negative if Shiraz, Cabernet Sauvignon or Merlot grapes are present. Cork taint (TCA) comes in five grades with one (1) being the least detectable and five (5) being the dominating TCA aroma. If a wine is given two (2) points or more for being corked, you should not continue grading it. You simply indicate the grade of cork, replace the cork and return the wine to the store for replacement. If you purchase more than one bottle, try another one, which will hopefully be fine, although it has happened that entire batches have been affected.

Fig. 5.17.5.

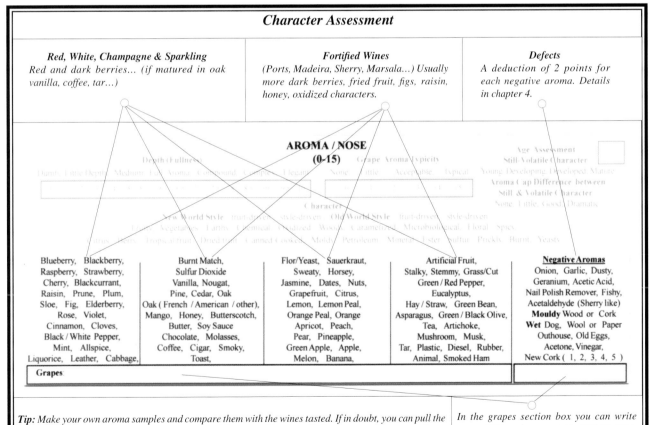

Character Assessment

| **Red, White, Champagne & Sparkling**
Red and dark berries... (if matured in oak vanilla, coffee, tar...) | **Fortified Wines**
(Ports, Madeira, Sherry, Marsala...) Usually more dark berries, fried fruit, figs, raisin, honey, oxidized characters. | **Defects**
A deduction of 2 points for each negative aroma. Details in chapter 4. |

AROMA / NOSE (0-15)

| Blueberry, Blackberry, Raspberry, Strawberry, Cherry, Blackcurrant, Raisin, Prune, Plum, Sloe, Fig, Elderberry, Rose, Violet, Cinnamon, Cloves, Black / White Pepper, Mint, Allspice, Liquorice, Leather, Cabbage, | Burnt Match, Sulfur Dioxide Vanilla, Nougat, Pine, Cedar, Oak Oak (French / American / other), Mango, Honey, Butterscotch, Butter, Soy Sauce Chocolate, Molasses, Coffee, Cigar, Smoky, Toast, | Flor/Yeast, Sauerkraut, Sweaty, Horsey, Jasmine, Dates, Nuts, Grapefruit, Citrus, Lemon, Lemon Peel, Orange Peal, Orange Apricot, Peach, Pear, Pineapple, Green Apple, Apple, Melon, Banana, | Artificial Fruit, Stalky, Stemmy, Grass/Cut Green / Red Pepper, Eucalyptus, Hay / Straw, Green Bean, Asparagus, Green / Black Olive, Tea, Artichoke, Mushroom, Musk, Tar, Plastic, Diesel, Rubber, Animal, Smoked Ham | **Negative Aromas**
Onion, Garlic, Dusty, Geranium, Acetic Acid, Nail Polish Remover, Fishy, Acetaldehyde (Sherry like) **Mouldy** Wood or Cork **Wet** Dog, Wool or Paper Outhouse, Old Eggs, Acetone, Vinegar, New Cork (1, 2, 3, 4, 5) |

Grapes

Tip: Make your own aroma samples and compare them with the wines tasted. If in doubt, you can pull the aroma sample and compare with it, which will build your confidence and help you to readjust some of your pre-determined associations. In chapter 3 you will find some examples of how to create your own samples from household supplies. Otherwise you can purchase them from www.malmo-wine-academy.com.

In the grapes section box you can write any additional comments, variety type, blends and/or other associations or aroma characters that you sense.

Fig. 5.17. Aroma – Minor and Negative Characters.

Taste

Taste is the total balance of the taste and tactile sensations we assess in our throats and mouths. The aftertaste when the wine has been tasted is also called length (chapter 3). When analyzing wine by taste we consider various components (tannin, acidity, sweetness, alcohol, fruit structure, weight, length and umami (chapter 3), after which we look for the wine's balance in relation to all them. This is done through taste and tactile sensory recognition in the mouth. Identifying fruit structure is an exception as you utilize aroma, taste and tactile sensations together to arrive at your analysis.

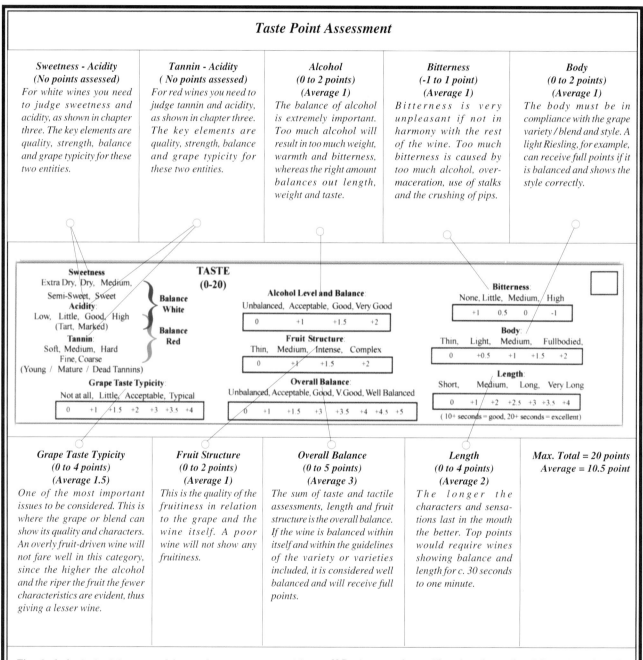

Taste Point Assessment

Sweetness - Acidity
(No points assessed)
For white wines you need to judge sweetness and acidity, as shown in chapter three. The key elements are quality, strength, balance and grape typicity for these two entities.

Tannin - Acidity
(No points assessed)
For red wines you need to judge tannin and acidity, as shown in chapter three. The key elements are quality, strength, balance and grape typicity for these two entities.

Alcohol
(0 to 2 points)
(Average 1)
The balance of alcohol is extremely important. Too much alcohol will result in too much weight, warmth and bitterness, whereas the right amount balances out length, weight and taste.

Bitterness
(-1 to 1 point)
(Average 1)
Bitterness is very unpleasant if not in harmony with the rest of the wine. Too much bitterness is caused by too much alcohol, over-maceration, use of stalks and the crushing of pips.

Body
(0 to 2 points)
(Average 1)
The body must be in compliance with the grape variety / blend and style. A light Riesling, for example, can receive full points if it is balanced and shows the style correctly.

Grape Taste Typicity
(0 to 4 points)
(Average 1.5)
One of the most important issues to be considered. This is where the grape or blend can show its quality and characters. An overly fruit-driven wine will not fare well in this category, since the higher the alcohol and the riper the fruit the fewer characteristics are evident, thus giving a lesser wine.

Fruit Structure
(0 to 2 points)
(Average 1)
This is the quality of the fruitiness in relation to the grape and the wine itself. A poor wine will not show any fruitiness.

Overall Balance
(0 to 5 points)
(Average 3)
The sum of taste and tactile assessments, length and fruit structure is the overall balance. If the wine is balanced within itself and within the guidelines of the variety or varieties included, it is considered well balanced and will receive full points.

Length
(0 to 4 points)
(Average 2)
The longer the characters and sensations last in the mouth the better. Top points would require wines showing balance and length for c. 30 seconds to one minute.

Max. Total = 20 points
Average = 10.5 point

Tips: *In the beginning it is suggested that you focus on one aspect of the tasting at a time, for example, you take a sip of the wine and analyze it for acid and note the results. Once this has been completed, you take another sip and analyze the tannin, then alcohol and so on. Once you have mastered the tasting analysis section, you will after some exercise be able to complete the majority of these assessments with just one sip. It is just a matter of training.*

N.B.: *Aroma and taste. There have been a lot of discussions about this and the most important aspect to remember is that an aroma which passes through the mouth up to the retro-nasal passage is sensed by the olfactory lobe in the upper nasal passage (chapter three). Thus, the mouth has no sense of smell but the characters sensed via the retro-nasal passage can be considered a 'Volatile Aroma'. This aroma is initially detected in the 'Aroma/Nose' section, while comparing the difference between a still and volatile aroma using the Aroma Cap.*

Fig. 5.18. Taste – Point Assessment Summary.

Sweetness, Acidity and Balance

The strength and quality levels of acidity, tannin and sweetness as well as their balance are the factors to be considered within this grading section. The illustrations (Fig. 5.19.) show how these entities balance each other. It is therefore important to focus on the individual strengths and qualities of each element and grade them accordingly, as they can be masked by one another.

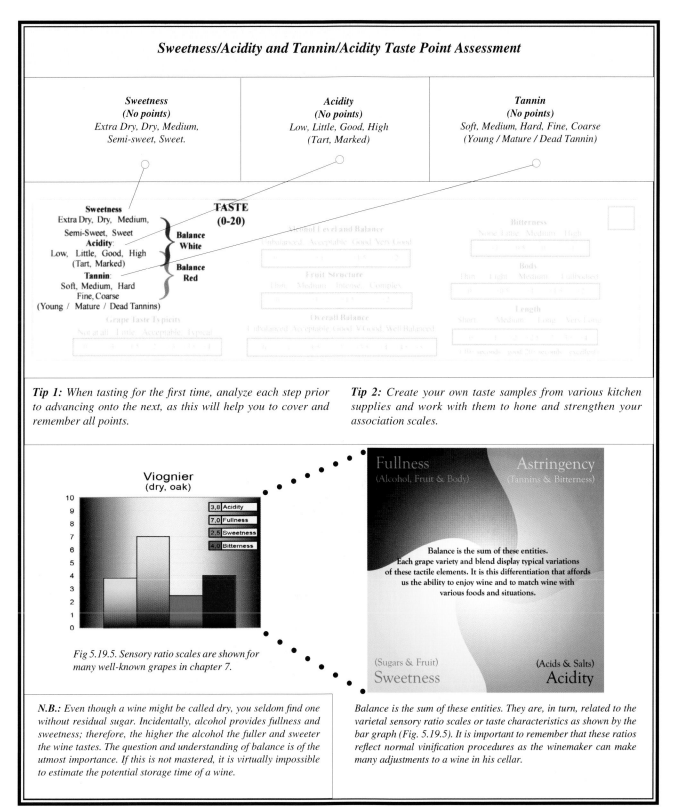

Sweetness/Acidity and Tannin/Acidity Taste Point Assessment

Sweetness
(No points)
Extra Dry, Dry, Medium, Semi-sweet, Sweet.

Acidity
(No points)
Low, Little, Good, High (Tart, Marked)

Tannin
(No points)
Soft, Medium, Hard, Fine, Coarse (Young / Mature / Dead Tannin)

Tip 1: When tasting for the first time, analyze each step prior to advancing onto the next, as this will help you to cover and remember all points.

Tip 2: Create your own taste samples from various kitchen supplies and work with them to hone and strengthen your association scales.

Fig 5.19.5. Sensory ratio scales are shown for many well-known grapes in chapter 7.

Fullness (Alcohol, Fruit & Body) **Astringency** (Tannins & Bitterness)

Balance is the sum of these entities. Each grape variety and blend display typical variations of these tactile elements. It is this differentiation that affords us the ability to enjoy wine and to match wine with various foods and situations.

(Sugars & Fruit) **Sweetness** (Acids & Salts) **Acidity**

N.B.: Even though a wine might be called dry, you seldom find one without residual sugar. Incidentally, alcohol provides fullness and sweetness; therefore, the higher the alcohol the fuller and sweeter the wine tastes. The question and understanding of balance is of the utmost importance. If this is not mastered, it is virtually impossible to estimate the potential storage time of a wine.

Balance is the sum of these entities. They are, in turn, related to the varietal sensory ratio scales or taste characteristics as shown by the bar graph (Fig. 5.19.5). It is important to remember that these ratios reflect normal vinification procedures as the winemaker can make many adjustments to a wine in his cellar.

Fig. 5.19. Taste – Sweetness, Acidity, Tannin and balance.

Alcohol Level and Balance

Apart from creating a warmer, sensory feeling alcohol is responsible for additional weight, sensitivity, aroma, viscosity, bitterness and storage length. Nevertheless, a good balance is of the utmost importance. Too much alcohol will dominate the wine's aroma and taste. Too little reduces the overall storage potential and limits volatile characteristics.

As the alcohol content increases, it usually affects the body of the wine by making it taste more full-bodied or weighty, warm and powerful. In wines with too much alcohol a hot or burning sensation is also sensed.

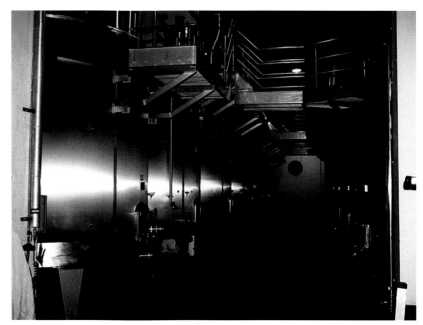

Fig. 5.22. Fermentation tanks in Bordeaux.

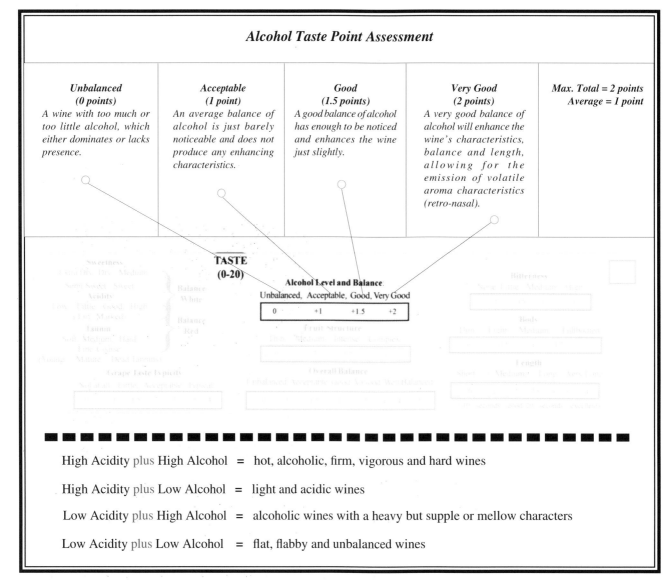

Alcohol Taste Point Assessment

Unbalanced (0 points)	Acceptable (1 point)	Good (1.5 points)	Very Good (2 points)	Max. Total = 2 points Average = 1 point
A wine with too much or too little alcohol, which either dominates or lacks presence.	An average balance of alcohol is just barely noticeable and does not produce any enhancing characteristics.	A good balance of alcohol has enough to be noticed and enhances the wine just slightly.	A very good balance of alcohol will enhance the wine's characteristics, balance and length, allowing for the emission of volatile aroma characteristics (retro-nasal).	

TASTE (0-20)

Alcohol Level and Balance
Unbalanced, Acceptable, Good, Very Good

0	+1	+1.5	+2

High Acidity plus High Alcohol = hot, alcoholic, firm, vigorous and hard wines

High Acidity plus Low Alcohol = light and acidic wines

Low Acidity plus High Alcohol = alcoholic wines with a heavy but supple or mellow characters

Low Acidity plus Low Alcohol = flat, flabby and unbalanced wines

Fig. 5.23. Taste – Alcohol Point Assessment describes the balance of alcohol (above) and alcohol plus acidity levels (below).

Fig. 5.24. Grapes being crushed. Too much crushing can cause the seeds to be broken, thus causing a slight bitterness in taste.

Bitterness

Originating from the phenol family of tannins, bitterness is usually caused by crushed pips in the fermentation and/or the use of stalks, for strengthening of the tannins and the use of pharmaceutical tannin or the tannin derived from the oak barrels. Bitterness along with acidity is used as one of the elements to balance sweet wines. A small amount of bitterness helps to extend the length of the wine. Too much, on the other hand, is dominating and negative.

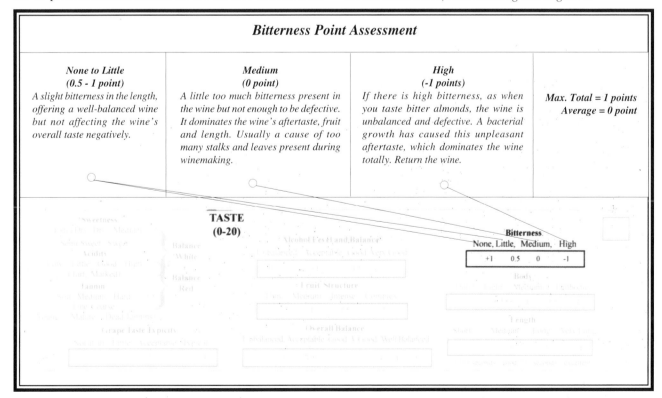

Bitterness Point Assessment

None to Little (0.5 - 1 point)	Medium (0 point)	High (-1 points)	
A slight bitterness in the length, offering a well-balanced wine but not affecting the wine's overall taste negatively.	A little too much bitterness present in the wine but not enough to be defective. It dominates the wine's aftertaste, fruit and length. Usually a cause of too many stalks and leaves present during winemaking.	If there is high bitterness, as when you taste bitter almonds, the wine is unbalanced and defective. A bacterial growth has caused this unpleasant aftertaste, which dominates the wine totally. Return the wine.	Max. Total = 1 points Average = 0 point

Fig. 5.25. Bitterness Point Assessment.

Fruit Structure

This is one of the hardest of the tasting sections to complete. When identifying fruit structure and quality you should glance over some of the aroma characteristics to confirm the volatile aromas. In the aroma section you used the 'aroma cap' to identify the volatile aromas, which can also be confirmed in the mouth via the retro-nasal passage. These aromas are compared for fruit quality and finesse.

A very good volatile aroma, not volatile acids which is a defect, will be reproduced retro-nasally and exposed as an aftertaste with the same fruity characters as in the mouth. Fruit-driven wines obviously have a more pronounced fruit structure than classical, style-driven. Although the fruit structure in a classical fruit-driven wine is not as evident as in a modern, fruit-driven, it is still present but in a more subtle form.

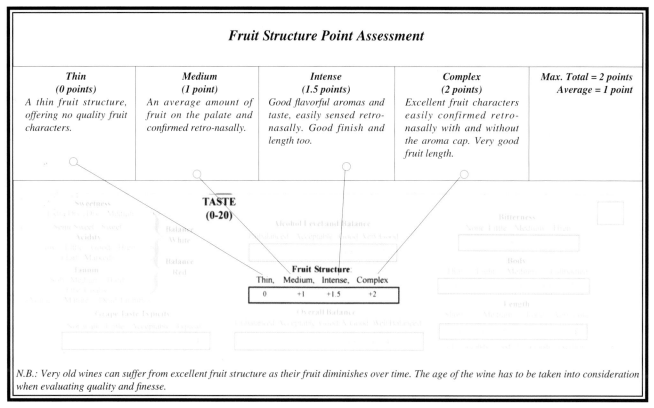

Fruit Structure Point Assessment

Thin (0 points)	Medium (1 point)	Intense (1.5 points)	Complex (2 points)	Max. Total = 2 points Average = 1 point
A thin fruit structure, offering no quality fruit characters.	An average amount of fruit on the palate and confirmed retro-nasally.	Good flavorful aromas and taste, easily sensed retro-nasally. Good finish and length too.	Excellent fruit characters easily confirmed retro-nasally with and without the aroma cap. Very good fruit length.	

N.B.: Very old wines can suffer from excellent fruit structure as their fruit diminishes over time. The age of the wine has to be taken into consideration when evaluating quality and finesse.

Fig. 5.26. Taste – Fruit Structure Assessment.

Fig. 5.27. The quality of the fruit depends upon many factors but good trellising is one of them. A balance between exposure, vigor, variety and micro-climate conditions is vital.

Body

This is the overall weight impression one has of the wine tasted for that varietal or regional style. It is a combination of alcohol, fruit structure and tannin in red wines, plus residual sugar content, if white, fortified or Amarone style. I have also, on a number of occasions, heard tasters incorrectly referring to the body as the compactness of the wine.

For example, a Pinot Noir from Burgundy does not receive less points for body when compared to a full-bodied Cabernet Sauvignon from Napa Valley. Varietal and regional characteristics determine whether or not for that style of wine it is full-, medium-, light- or thin-bodied (cf chapter 7).

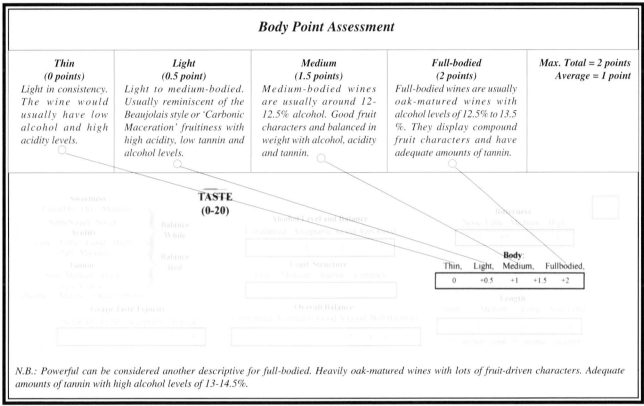

Body Point Assessment

Thin (0 points)	Light (0.5 point)	Medium (1.5 points)	Full-bodied (2 points)	Max. Total = 2 points Average = 1 point
Light in consistency. The wine would usually have low alcohol and high acidity levels.	Light to medium-bodied. Usually reminiscent of the Beaujolais style or 'Carbonic Maceration' fruitiness with high acidity, low tannin and alcohol levels.	Medium-bodied wines are usually around 12-12.5% alcohol. Good fruit characters and balanced in weight with alcohol, acidity and tannin.	Full-bodied wines are usually oak-matured wines with alcohol levels of 12.5% to 13.5 %. They display compound fruit characters and have adequate amounts of tannin.	

N.B.: *Powerful can be considered another descriptive for full-bodied. Heavily oak-matured wines with lots of fruit-driven characters. Adequate amounts of tannin with high alcohol levels of 13-14.5%.*

Fig. 5.28. Taste – Body Assessment.

Fig. 5.29. A vineyard in Roussillon, France.

Grape Taste Typicity

In short, grape typicity is assessed individually for each grape and as a blend. This is one of the most important points that distinguishes the 'birds from the bees'. Truly talented wine-makers can match grape typical characteristics to their style of wine. A Cabernet Sauvignon should taste and have a balance like a Cabernet Sauvignon and a Pinot Noir like a Pinot Noir. Although grape typicity can vary between grapes, styles and regions, the similarities in varietal and varietal clones are basically the same. Grape typicity requires that the wine's taste is in balance with the specific variety, blend or style (cf chapter 7). Naturally additives can change this by creating well-balanced wines that are not taste-typical. Instead wines that display sameness instead. The 'Grape Taste Typicity' score therefore rewards wine-makers that preserve varietal taste characteristics.

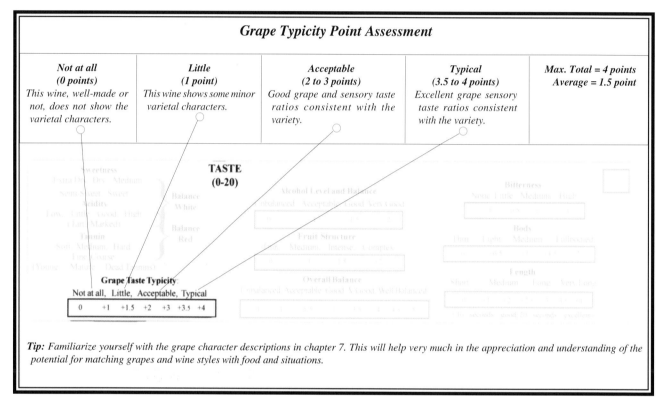

Fig. 5.30. Taste – Grape Typicity.

Fig. 5.31. Grape typicity can be found primarily in the world's classic wine regions.

Overall Balance

Overall balance is the combination of all of the above sensorial characteristics of taste for both varietal and blended wines, for example grape typicity, length and fruit structure

See chapter 7 for varietal characteristics, in which I discuss traditional ratios for Acidity-Tannin for red wine and Acidity-Residual Sugar-Fullness for white wine varietals.

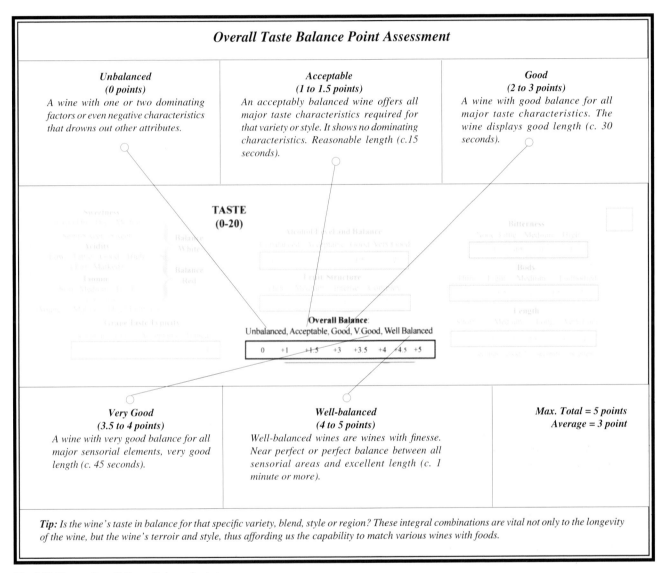

Overall Taste Balance Point Assessment

Unbalanced
(0 points)
A wine with one or two dominating factors or even negative characteristics that drowns out other attributes.

Acceptable
(1 to 1.5 points)
An acceptably balanced wine offers all major taste characteristics required for that variety or style. It shows no dominating characteristics. Reasonable length (c.15 seconds).

Good
(2 to 3 points)
A wine with good balance for all major taste characteristics. The wine displays good length (c. 30 seconds).

**TASTE
(0-20)**

Overall Balance:
Unbalanced, Acceptable, Good, V.Good, Well Balanced

| 0 | +1 | +1.5 | +3 | +3.5 | +4 | +4.5 | +5 |

Very Good
(3.5 to 4 points)
A wine with very good balance for all major sensorial elements, very good length (c. 45 seconds).

Well-balanced
(4 to 5 points)
Well-balanced wines are wines with finesse. Near perfect or perfect balance between all sensorial areas and excellent length (c. 1 minute or more).

Max. Total = 5 points
Average = 3 point

Tip: Is the wine's taste in balance for that specific variety, blend, style or region? These integral combinations are vital not only to the longevity of the wine, but the wine's terroir and style, thus affording us the capability to match various wines with foods.

Fig. 5.32. Taste – Overall Grape Balance for taste.

Fig. 5.33. As the seesaw illustrates, quality is directly related to the combination of these elements. If one of them is excluded, this affects balance.

Length.

Length is the aftertaste of the wine or the lingering sensations of aroma and taste, once you have either swallowed or spat. The longer the sensations remain the better. Length is attributed to a combination of acids, phenols and fruit present in red wines. For white wines acids, residual sugars and fruit are considered. These combinations are the primary cause for length. Length is measured in the number of seconds the tactile sensations remain within the mouth and throat.

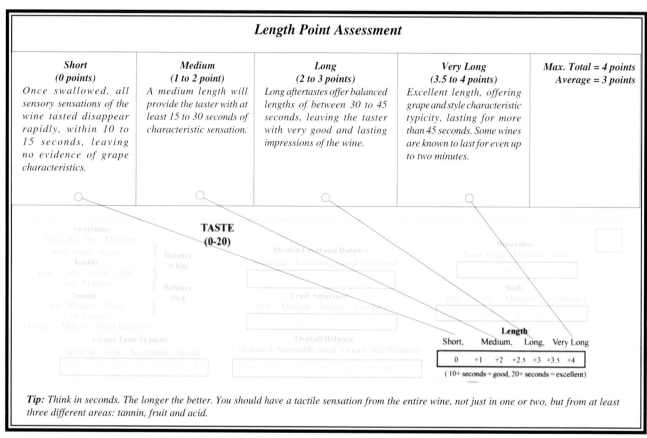

Length Point Assessment				
Short **(0 points)** *Once swallowed, all sensory sensations of the wine tasted disappear rapidly, within 10 to 15 seconds, leaving no evidence of grape characteristics.*	**Medium** **(1 to 2 point)** *A medium length will provide the taster with at least 15 to 30 seconds of characteristic sensation.*	**Long** **(2 to 3 points)** *Long aftertastes offer balanced lengths of between 30 to 45 seconds, leaving the taster with very good and lasting impressions of the wine.*	**Very Long** **(3.5 to 4 points)** *Excellent length, offering grape and style characteristic typicity, lasting for more than 45 seconds. Some wines are known to last for even up to two minutes.*	**Max. Total = 4 points** **Average = 3 points**

TASTE (0-20)

Length:
Short,   Medium,   Long,   Very Long

| 0 | +1 | +2 | +2.5 | +3 | +3.5 | +4 |

(10+ seconds = good, 20+ seconds = excellent)

Tip: Think in seconds. The longer the better. You should have a tactile sensation from the entire wine, not just in one or two, but from at least three different areas: tannin, fruit and acid.

Fig. 5.34. Taste – Length Point Assessment.

Total Current and Potential Storage

This section is based on the current and potential storage (longevity) of wines. When evaluating a wine, we need to take into consideration its age at the time of tasting. This is done by crediting the wine for the time already cellared. If, at the current age and time of tasting, the wine has still another 5 or 10 years remaining before losing its appeal, the wine should receive credit for that time as well.

Assessing storage potential has great relevance, since good wine is a vintage product which requires long maturation and can be stored and used for celebrations, such as social happenings. Below there is a table chart, giving you the credits for various wine types, their combined cellar times and total potential storage remaining as well as descriptions of how to use the table.

Fig. 5.35. Illustrates various Bordeaux vintages with good storage potential.

The Storage Point Assessment

Max. Total = 10 points
Average = 5 points

White wines
Adequate acidity, residual sugar, fruit and even alcohol are required in white wines in order to store them for longer periods. The most important of these constituents are acidity and fruit content, without which the wine cannot be stored. A wine has passed its maturity if it lacks these elements. Due to good acid levels very good dry white wines from Germany, Burgundy in France and the NW USA have the ability to last for between 20 to 30 years.

Red wines
A good tannin structure along with acid and fruit is required for red wines. A red wine without acid is flabby and flat and will not taste good or last. Low tannin can be acceptable, as long as there is adequate acid and fruit. Alcohol is obviously a preserving entity and is always present, unless the alcohol level is too low. Storage for 30 years is not uncommon for very good Bordeaux and Napa Valley wines as well as a few others.

Sweet wines
Sweet wines are dependant upon their residual sugar and acid levels for longevity. Good acidity levels are extremely important for sweet wines as, they maintain the balance in taste and also act as preservatives. Some exceptionally good sweet wines have the ability to exceed 50 and even 100 years.

Fortified wines
Fortified wines are wines which have had grape alcohol added to the natural wine or wine must either after fermentation has finished, as with Sherries or during fermentation, as with Port or Madeira. These wines are high in alcohol and range from 15.5% to 17.5 for various Sherry types and from 18% to 20.5% for Ports and Madeiras. The preserving factor in these wines is alcohol, after which comes residual sugar or acid and fruit. Very good fortified wines have the ability to last 75 to 100 years or more.

Champagne/Sparkling Wines
Acid, fruit, lees and carbonation are key ingredients to the successful longevity of bubbly. Lees consists of expended yeast cells along with phenols (tannin), which are excellent preservatives; in addition, CO_2 and the usually high acid content of the grapes used in Champagnes or sparkling wines made according to the Champagne Méthode provide a very good potential for ageing. Unfortunately, most consumers are under the impression that these wines cannot be stored. Good Champagnes or sparkling wines made according to the Champagne Méthode are good for a minimum of 10 years and many excellent Champagnes can last as long as 25 to 30 years.

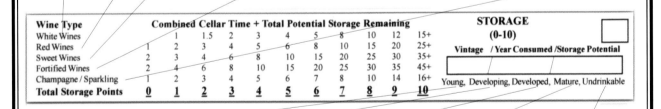

Wine Type	Combined Cellar Time + Total Potential Storage Remaining										STORAGE (0-10)
White Wines		1	1.5	2	3	4	5	8	10	12	15+
Red Wines	1	2	3	4	5	6	8	10	15	20	25+
Sweet Wines	2	3	4	6	8	10	15	20	25	30	35+
Fortified Wines	2	4	6	8	10	15	20	25	30	35	45+
Champagne / Sparkling	1	2	3	4	5	6	7	8	10	14	16+
Total Storage Points	**0**	**1**	**2**	**3**	**4**	**5**	**6**	**7**	**8**	**9**	**10**

STORAGE (0-10)

Vintage / Year Consumed /Storage Potential

Young, Developing, Developed, Mature, Undrinkable

Young
Young wines are lively, full of adolescent fruit with their highest acid, tannin and residual sugar levels. They are wines which offer fresh fruit and usually need to settle for a number of years, if they are full-bodied wines, in order for us to appreciate their true balance.

Developing
Developing wines are wines that have all their attributes showing well but are still in need of ageing. Can usually be paired properly with food and enjoyed in various situations.

Developed
A developed wine is a wine at its best. These wines perform very well and continue to do so for a few more years. They are in harmony with themselves and at their most desirable stage of consumption.

Mature
Mature wines are wines at their peaks. These are wines that need to be drunk, as they will not improve with time. They are perfectly in balance with their constituents and complement both food and social situation.

Undrinkable
An undrinkable wine is a wine with defects or a wine that has passed its maturity stage, a wine with either extremely hard or 'dead' tannins or a cloying wine lacking in acidity.

Tip: When considering the storage potential and grade for wine keep in mind the current condition of the wine, how much fruit, acid, sugar, tannin and the wine's balance.

Fig. 5.36. Total Potential Storage Point Assessment.

The Storage Point Assessment

The charts in Fig. 5.37 to 5.39 display various wine types, represented by numbers on their right. These numbers are relative to the type of wine and the credit each one receives, based on their current age and the potential for additional storage or cellaring time. In order to explain the table correctly I have included an example to be followed.

We have tasted a dry white wine (Fig. 5.37) that is four years old and concluded that it is almost mature now but has enough acid, fruit and balance to continue for another 4 years at which time it would have passed its preferred drinkability. In order to arrive at a credit we ought to do the following:

The example wine is currently 4 years old. Select the white wine category, as it is a white wine that we will be crediting. Move along the horizontal axis to the corresponding number for white wines representing the current age of the wine. This is noted on your sheet. If the wine can be cellared or stored longer, another point will be added to this, otherwise the combined cellar time and potential storage time would just be five (5) as listed vertically in the last horizontal 'Total Storage Points' row.

Wine Type	Combined Cellar Time + Total Potential Storage Remaining										
White Wines		1	1,5	2	3	4	5	8	10	12	15+
Red Wines	1	2	3	4	5	6	8	10	15	20	25+
Sweet Wines	2	3	4	6	8	10	15	20	25	30	35+
Fortified Wines	2	4	6	8	10	15	20	25	30	35	45+
Champagne / Sparkling	1	2	3	4	5	6	7	8	10	14	16+
Total Storage Points	**0**	**1**	**2**	**3**	**4**	**5**	**6**	**7**	**8**	**9**	**10**

Fig. 5.37. Storage Grading White Wine

Wine Type	Combined Cellar Time + Total Potential Storage Remaining										
White Wines		1	1,5	2	3	4	5	8	10	12	15+
Red Wines	1	2	3	4	5	6	8	10	15	20	25+
Sweet Wines	2	3	4	6	8	10	15	20	25	30	35+
Fortified Wines	2	4	6	8	10	15	20	25	30	35	45+
Champagne / Sparkling	1	2	3	4	5	6	7	8	10	14	16+
Total Storage Points	**0**	**1**	**2**	**3**	**4**	**5**	**6**	**7**	**8**	**9**	**10**

Fig. 5.37.5. Storage Grading White Wine

Wine Type	Combined Cellar Time + Total Potential Storage Remaining										
White Wines		1	1,5	2	3	4	5	8	10	12	15+
Red Wines	1	2	3	4	5	6	8	10	15	20	25+
Sweet Wines	2	3	4	6	8	10	15	20	25	30	35+
Fortified Wines	2	4	6	8	10	15	20	25	30	35	45+
Champagne / Sparkling	1	2	3	4	5	6	7	8	10	14	16+
Total Storage Points	**0**	**1**	**2**	**3**	**4**	**5**	**6**	**7**	**8**	**9**	**10**

Fig. 5.38. Storage Grading White Wine

Wine Type	Combined Cellar Time + Total Potential Storage Remaining										
White Wines		1	1,5	2	3	4	5	8	10	12	15+
Red Wines	1	2	3	4	5	6	8	10	15	20	25+
Sweet Wines	2	3	4	6	8	10	15	20	25	30	35+
Fortified Wines	2	4	6	8	10	15	20	25	30	35	45+
Champagne / Sparkling	1	2	3	4	5	6	7	8	10	14	16+
Total Storage Points	**0**	**1**	**2**	**3**	**4**	**5**	**6**	**(7)**	**8**	**9**	**10**

Fig. 5.39. Storage Grading White Wine

The next step requires that you add the remaining potential time for storage, if any, but in this example, another 4 years to the already current age (Fig. 5.38). Move horizontally along the row, then add an additional 4 years to the already 4-year aged wine thus giving 8 years of potential storage time.

This estimation is obviously based on the quality of the wine at the time of evaluation plus the amount of acid, fruit and overall balance of the wine being evaluated. Once the grade for the current age of the wine plus the potential remaining life span has been established and noted on the scale, you should move vertically down from that point (Fig. 5.39) to the Total Storage Points. The result for the above example being seven (7) points. Seven therefore represents the actual credits received for the total potential storage time.

When is a wine too old

At what condition is a wine considered to be too old? This is one of the more important and complicated questions posed to wine professionals and this intricate problem has naturally a number of variables.
Mature wines develop a gentle subtleness of fruit, acid, tannin and finesse. In red wines color changes occur as their tannins and fruit acids combine to form fine black sediment and fall to the bottom of the bottle. White wines have tannin too,

especially if they have been oak-aged, but less concentrated than in red wines. This tannin comes from the skins, pips and oak and it can also form a clear sediment as reds but to a much lesser extent.

Oxygen, from the wine's ullage, between the cork and wine, also reduces the wine through long-term oxidation and the wine's youthful character naturally dissipates, leaving a balance of fruit, alcohol, acids and body in white wines and fruit, tannin, acid, alcohol and body in red wines. When these entities become unbalanced, in relation to their styles and grape characteristics, the wine becomes too old.

In red wines the tannin is usually the first to show this by becoming overly hard, dead tannin as in the trough of the tannin's life cycle (Fig. 3.50). This causes the wine to become unbalanced as the hardened, 'dead' tannins dominate the wine's taste and length. This cannot be identified in the aroma or appearance of the wine.

In wines with less tannin and in white wines a dominating caramel-butterscotch-coumarine aroma character, reminiscent of mercaptans or mousiness-like characters (see page 51) can be identified. Taste can either become dominated by existing volatile acids and high alcohol or flat and flabby wines with no acidity.

Fig. 5.40.

Summary Section

The summary should disclose the findings of the analysis and tasting and give a good, short description of the wine. Any aspects in relation to the wine's attack, its initial presentation or adjustment of the various points can be settled within this section. It should be used to describe the wine in the shortest and most accurate manner possible.

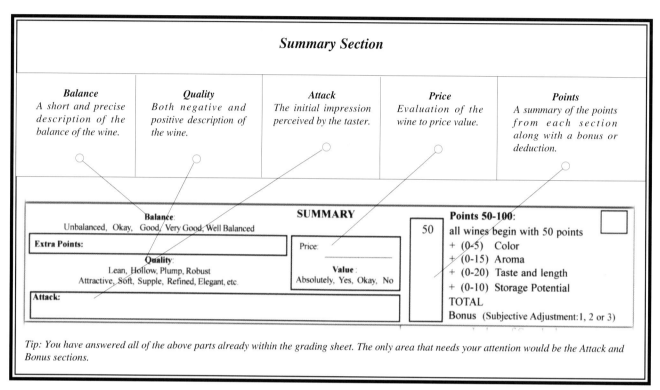

Fig. 5.41. Summary Assessment.

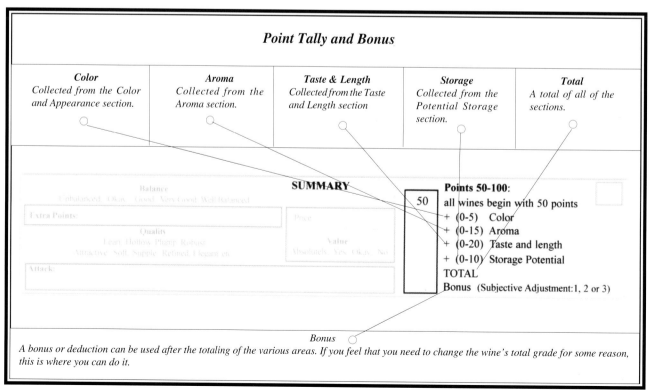

Fig. 5.42. Point Tally and Bonus.

Total Wine Balance

Total balance is the final evaluation that measures the wine's Appearance, Nose, Acidity, Sugar, Fruit, Body, Alcohol, Tannin and Length. *Overall Balance for Taste* is measured by ratios between tannin and acidity in red wines and acidity, fullness and sweetness in white wines and fortified wines. These ratios are depicted in chapter seven.

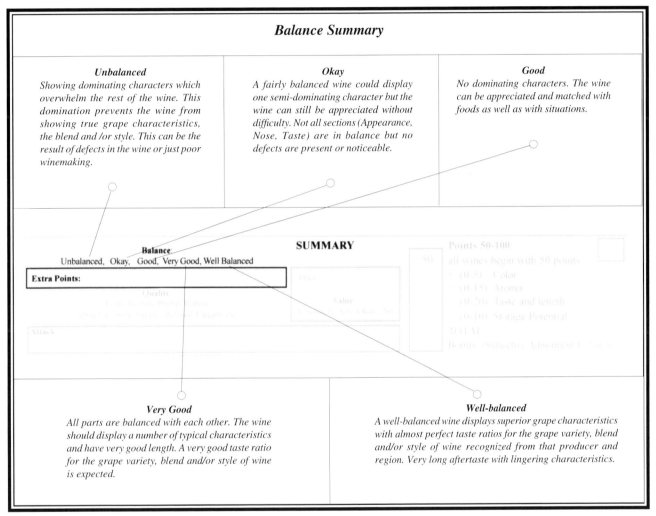

Balance Summary

Unbalanced
Showing dominating characters which overwhelm the rest of the wine. This domination prevents the wine from showing true grape characteristics, the blend and /or style. This can be the result of defects in the wine or just poor winemaking.

Okay
A fairly balanced wine could display one semi-dominating character but the wine can still be appreciated without difficulty. Not all sections (Appearance, Nose, Taste) are in balance but no defects are present or noticeable.

Good
No dominating characters. The wine can be appreciated and matched with foods as well as with situations.

Balance
Unbalanced, Okay, Good, Very Good, Well Balanced

Extra Points:

SUMMARY

Very Good
All parts are balanced with each other. The wine should display a number of typical characteristics and have very good length. A very good taste ratio for the grape variety, blend and/or style of wine is expected.

Well-balanced
A well-balanced wine displays superior grape characteristics with almost perfect taste ratios for the grape variety, blend and/or style of wine recognized from that producer and region. Very long aftertaste with lingering characteristics.

Fig. 5.43. Balance Summary.

Fig. 5.44. The wine cellar at Château Lafite-Rothschild in Bordeaux.

Quality

Quality is the summary of the wine tasted. Here we use descriptive words to portray the wine's quality and style as well as how it can be matched to situations, food and the like. Summaries are important as they are usually the only reference many wine buyers see prior to purchasing the wine.

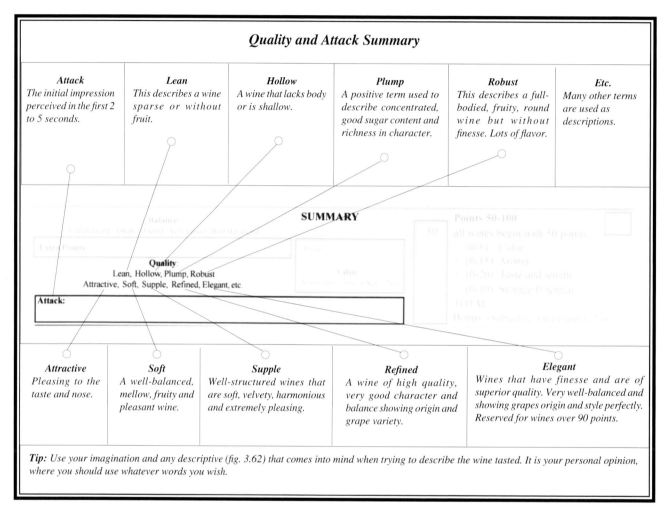

Fig. 5.45. Summary – Quality and Attack

Value

Price-worthy or not, that's the question. In chapter 6 the pricing and quality points are discussed in a graph, called 'Price to Wine Ratio Chart'. After many years of research and from my own experience as an importer and consultant, I have created a pricing scale based on quality and price. This section is very useful when it comes to buying a price-worthy wine. No one likes to realize that a wine was a total waste of money. On the other hand, if you drink one that is of good value, you feel very satisfied. After a number of tastings you will feel familiar with the price-setting and quality levels and the benefits of this will become evident.

At this point you hopefully begin to understand how to grade wines by using the 100-point system. Once you have had

the chance to use this grading sheet consistently, you will develop your own database, enabling you to express yourself comfortably on issues concerning different types and styles of wines, both professionally and for your own pleasure. You will be able to present a wine in 10 seconds or 10 minutes, depending on how much of the information you would like to use.

The 20-Point System

The 20-point system is not as widespread as the 100-point system but in use internationally and also present at judging shows. There are a number of 20-point scales, but the most famous one is called the Davis Score Card and comes from the Department of Viticulture and Enology at the University of California at Davis. A list of the points is shown below. The 20-point system is a good and quick system, although consistency and reliability are not as good as with the 100-point system. Comparative experiments at Malmö Wine Academy have shown that the 20-point system usually has a variance of some 6.5% while the 100-point system could maintain a 3.1% variance.

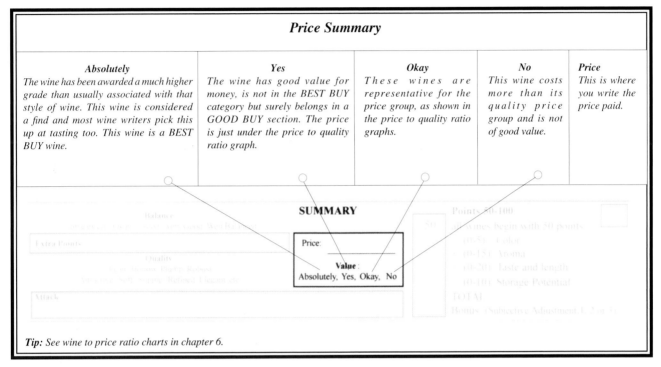

Fig. 5.47. Summary – Price worthiness section.

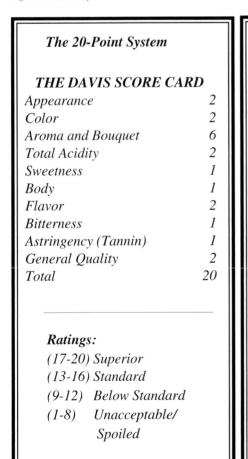

The 20-Point System

THE DAVIS SCORE CARD

Appearance	2
Color	2
Aroma and Bouquet	6
Total Acidity	2
Sweetness	1
Body	1
Flavor	2
Bitterness	1
Astringency (Tannin)	1
General Quality	2
Total	20

Ratings:

(17-20) Superior

(13-16) Standard

(9-12) Below Standard

(1-8)   Unacceptable/
        Spoiled

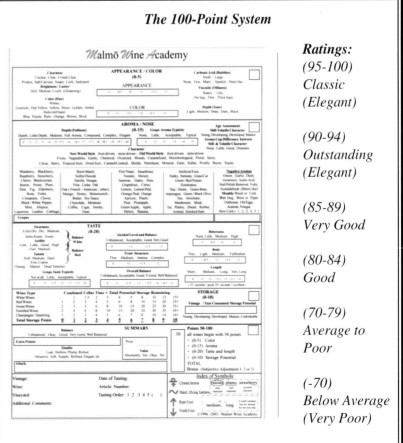

The 100-Point System

Ratings:

(95-100)
Classic
(Elegant)

(90-94)
Outstanding
(Elegant)

(85-89)
Very Good

(80-84)
Good

(70-79)
Average to
Poor

(-70)
Below Average
(Very Poor)

Chapter 6

Wine Marketing, Pricing and Quality

Marketing, Sales and Distribution

Marketing is widely used throughout the beverage industry. Beverages more than most rely on the ability to categorize and price according to quality and to market to customers based upon demographic segmentations in relation to food, occasion (situation), disposable income and many other strategies.

Variations in distribution and logistics are so dramatic that the creation of regional strategies is becoming important for each segmented group or category. Therefore, the sales organization has to take into consideration the regulations and restrictions controlling the products, in regard to retail (on- and off-trade, wine clubs), wholesale (distributors, sales agents and wine schools) and the fast-growing direct marketing channel. The export market is also guided by these rules, although the delivery system and distribution channels vary dramatically from country to country.

The chain of events from vineyard to consumer may differ slightly from country to country because of legal restrictions, but the procedures are the same, there's just a lot more of them. Understanding product, price, place, promotion and the marketing mix in the country of operation is the initial and most important step, prior to production. Grasping what the vineyard can produce and what the end users (customers) eat and drink is another first step.

Marketing Principles for Beverages

Marketing of wines is a process and this process is the single most important aspect for any producer, wholesaler and retailer within the beverage industry. Critical strategic decisions in planning, market strategy, sales, production, product or brand development and even finance, are affected by this process.

1. Marketing Analysis and Planning
Wine marketing is responsible for a complete analysis of both internal and external factors as well as all relevant environmental influences that could affect wines, brands and quality. Furthermore, marketing provides each operational and functional area of the winery or wholesaler with its analysis and how this analysis affects their area-specific tasks. For instance, a pricing analysis could indicate potential strengths, weaknesses, opportunities and/or threats (SWOT) within the current or potential market. Therefore, the analysis can sometimes require radical or even unpopular decisions to be made in relation to the wine's price and quality in order to maximize the brand or wine's position.

Fig. 6.1. One of Systembolaget's retail stores in Sweden.

2. Selecting Target Markets
Once the marketing analysis is complete and analyzed correctly, selecting a target group, market or markets for specific brands or wines is accomplished by matching identified strengths and weaknesses to particular target markets and production.

3. Marketing Implementation
Putting plans, words and production into action is the next step and this is coordinated and launched with realistic logistical and distribution channel support. Marketers must make sure that the plan has synergy and that it can be translated and transplanted into concrete actions and tasks. Otherwise the plan is doomed for failure.

Fig. 6.2. A Systembolaget retail store in Sweden.

4. Marketing Control

Controls are important, as they allow you to measure and assess, on a continual basis, the efficacy of the marketing plan. There should be a reporting system that enables you to monitor and evaluate performance throughout the chain of events, thereby insuring synergy effects and a successful implementation of the plan from production to consumer.

Targeting Agents, Distributors, Retailers and Consumers

1. Demand Measurement and Forecasting

Current and future market size and market segments need to be estimated and calculated. Such market size estimations require looking at competing products and estimating their current level of sales. In Canada, the Control Board like Systembolaget in Sweden, Alko in Finland and other state-controlled entities can all provide you with valuable statistical reports in relation to price, volume, region, etc. The rates of overall and potential growth are important factors for a company to consider when entering a market. Total effort in marketing mix requires accurate forecasting, as this is usually

coupled to Brand Support, Advertising and Promotion (A&P) budgets and other marketing campaigns. If a product does not reach the budgeted numbers in the forecast, alternative marketing programs need to be considered or the product re-prioritized.

2. Market Segmentation

A market segment is a group of customers, consumers, retailers, wholesalers, distributors and importers who respond in a similar way to a given set of marketing stimuli based upon their own needs, wants and demands. Market segmentation divides the total market into these various groups of potential buyers. Naturally, each segment can have contradictory or even parallel needs, characteristics and behaviors that cause us to create or develop products that can be marketed to these groups through a variety of ways also known as the marketing mix. To achieve total synergy and control over the marketing process it is essential to understand the five levels of segmentation and how they can affect an overall strategic marketing mix.

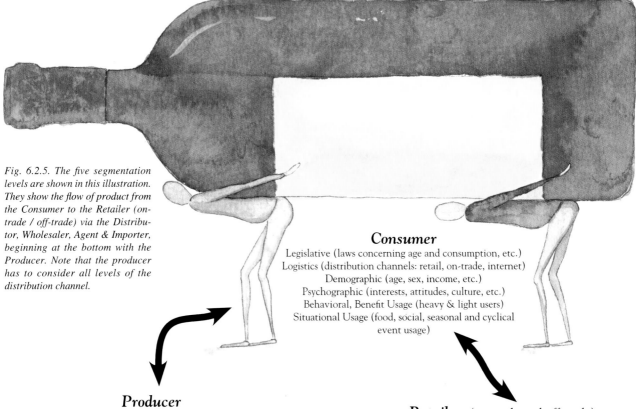

Fig. 6.2.5. The five segmentation levels are shown in this illustration. They show the flow of product from the Consumer to the Retailer (on-trade / off-trade) via the Distributor, Wholesaler, Agent & Importer, beginning at the bottom with the Producer. Note that the producer has to consider all levels of the distribution channel.

Consumer
Legislative (laws concerning age and consumption, etc.)
Logistics (distribution channels: retail, on-trade, internet)
Demographic (age, sex, income, etc.)
Psychographic (interests, attitudes, culture, etc.)
Behavioral, Benefit Usage (heavy & light users)
Situational Usage (food, social, seasonal and cyclical event usage)

Producer
Sells to: Importer, Wholesaler, Distributor & Consumer
Geographic (location)
Legislative (laws concerning age, consumption, distribution, on-trade and off-trade licenses, etc.)
Logistic (distribution channels)
Demographic (age, sex, income, etc.)
Psychographic (interests, attitudes, culture, etc.)
Behavioral, Benefit Usage (heavy & light users)
Situational Usage (food, social, seasonal and cyclical event usage)
Operating Environmental Factors:
Demographics, Operating Variables, Purchasing Variables, Situational Variables, Personal Characteristics, Consumer Trends, Personal Characteristics, Consumer Trends, Needs, Wants and Demands, Support (government export dept. if available)

Retailer (on-trade and off-trade)
Sells to: the Consumer
Geographic (location)
Legislative (laws concerning age, consumption, distribution, borders: country, state, county and city lines, on-trade and off-trade licenses, etc.)
Logistics (distribution channels: retail store, restaurant, bar, hotel room, etc.)
Demographic (age, sex, income, etc.)
Psychographic (interests, attitudes, culture, etc.)
Behavioral, Benefit Usage (heavy & light users)
Situational Usage (food, social, seasonal and cyclical event usage)

Importer / Agent
Sells to: Wholesaler, Distributor, Retailer & Consumer
Geographic (location)
Legislative (laws concerning age, consumption, distribution, on-trade and off-trade licenses, etc.)
Logistic (distribution channels)
Demographic (age, sex, income, etc.)
Psychographic (interests, attitudes, culture, etc.)
Behavioral, Benefit Usage (heavy & light users)
Situational Usage (food, social, seasonal and cyclical event usage)
Operating Environmental Factors:
Demographics, Operating Variables, Purchasing Variables, Situational Variables, Personal Characteristics, Consumer Trends, Personal Characteristics, Consumer Trends, Needs, Wants and Demands,
Support from Producer

Wholesaler / Distributor
Sells to: Retailer & Consumer
Geographic (location)
Legislative (laws concerning age, consumption, distribution, on-trade and off-trade licenses, etc.)
Logistics (distribution channels)
Demographic (age, sex, income, etc.)
Psychographic (interests, attitudes, culture, etc.)
Behavioral, Benefit Usage (heavy & light users)
Situational Usage (food, social, seasonal and cyclical event usage)
Operating Environmental Factors:
Demographics, Operating Variables, Purchasing Variables, Situational Variables, Personal Characteristics, Consumer Trends
Support from Agent & Importer

Fig. 6.3. A temperature-controlled storage depot for wines being shipped in the Bordeaux area.

3. Market Positioning

The positioning of a wine is a balance between pricing, product differentiation and image or branding. The wine's uniqueness, competitiveness in relation to price and quality and understanding of the environmental conditions, is critical when positioning a product. Here, a clear and distinctive place, relative to the competition at all five segmentation levels, needs to be established, if positioning a wine product for volume, pricing and value perception is one of your key factors. At the higher end of the pricing scale this will naturally call for more focus on the wine's image and consistency in quality. Keep in mind that if you are a small producer you'll need to prepare for alternative production channels if too much demand is created. In addition, supplying wine at very competitive prices without securing additional quantities, according to the projected demand for that specific price bracket is very dangerous and can lead to a re-stocking dilemma. I have seen sales for out-of-stock products decrease from 5000 cases per week to less that 45 cases due to out-of-stock problems. Positioning and forecasting is therefore a strategically important function.

4. Competitive Marketing Strategies

Your company's marketing strategy would naturally depend upon its overall standing, financial stability, economies of scale and distribution channels. The larger companies have economies of scale and a distribution channel in place. Marketing and positioning strategies are often influenced by the distribution channels the company holds within various geographical regions. Strategies can vary dramatically from a total re-invention of the wheel to just copying the procedures of competitors.

There are different market positions or competitive situations that you might find yourselves in at any given time. These are known as Market Leader, Market Challenger, Market Follower, Market Nicher and Market Survivor. These positions are also fluid just like the market and if you're not vigilant, you could lose your standing very quickly as there are always challengers around the corner. Furthermore, it is possible for a company to have one or more products positioned, in various marketing environments, with different positions at the same time.

Four Ps	*Four Cs*
Product	*Customer needs & wants*
Price	*Cost to customer*
Place	*Convenience*
Promotion	*Communication*

Fig. 6.4. Shows the classic marketing descriptions for both the product and customer mix.

The Marketing Mix (The Four Ps of Marketing)

1. Product

Product is the term used for 'goods and services'. What appellation, wine brand or style will create a competitive difference? Creating brand loyalty and generating repeat customers is a driving force for all beverages. Wine production, variety, quality, design features, brand name, packaging, sizes, services, satisfaction guarantees or returns are all instruments that are carefully considered.

2. Place

Place refers to both the physical distribution channel as much as is does to the final retail outlets, where the customer actually buys the wine. Key areas such as delivery costs, allocations, depletions, inventory levels, purchase and location of Stock Keeping Units (SKU's) in the retail stores, logistics, physical deliveries, stocking of the shelves, location and accessibility of the stores and their shopping convenience are vital.

Distribution regulations and systems vary dramatically. Sweden, Finland, Norway, Canada and 19 states in the US have monopoly systems. Other more open systems like the 'Three-Tier' are used in the United States and even more liberal unrestricted systems exist in Italy, France, Spain and Germany.

Cross-border Trade

In Europe cross-border trade has become big business and many of the monopoly and high tax countries are seeing rapid growth in such sales, as consumers are flocking to neighboring, low tax regions to buy their wines.

3. Price

The channel of distribution selected has a direct impact on pricing, as this affects credit, discounting, list pricing, allowances and promotional possibilities in regard to campaigns and drives. The dominant brands or drive brands are sometimes sold at cost and/or vastly reduce profit margins. The retailer is forced to carry these products, as they are widely promoted and customers therefore seek them out and in some cases purchase something else. Antitrust regulators should actually be looking into these anti-competitive pricing strategies, see Fig. 6.6.

4. Promotion

Promotion is the 'marketing' of the wine. Focus areas for the promotion of wine are advertising, personal selling, sales, store product placement (SKU contracts where you have to purchase listings and space on the shelves in the stores) and

---

Red Wine, Soft with Berries

5708
Vosne-Romanée 1er Cru Les Petits Monts 2001

Origin: France Vosne-Romanée Premier Cru
Vineyard: Domaine Clerget

Whole bottle 750 ml
Price: 357,00 kr

Color: Light red.
Nose: Young, fruity nose with a hint of oak, raspberry, strawberry and spices.
Taste: Young, acidic, harmonious, spicy taste with a hint of oak, raspberry and strawberry.

Fullness   Astringency   Fruit Acidity

Use: Serve at circa 16°C with fatty or wild birds, pork or fried fish.
Storage Potential: Can be cellared.
Grape Type: Pinot Noir
Alcohol by Volume: 13%

Fig. 6.5. An example of a product description card issued for all products sold through the Swedish monopoly. These cards are shown in miniature at the foot of all products but can be issued at the cash register in the format shown here. For wine enthusiasts, tasters, clubs and for those wishing to match wine to their food this is an outstanding service and benefit not yet replicated in the world today.

---

publicity through magazines, movies, television, wine festivals and other events.

Wine-Tasting Rooms & Wine Clubs are booming industry in many countries, wine-tasting clubs and wine-tasting rooms at or near to wine regions. Wine-tasting clubs are excellent marketing avenues, allowing the wholesalers and producers another channel to help pull out product. These are also good educational vehicles for trading-up customers to the quality

A WINE'S TRUE VALUE =	Actual Value + Perceptual Value + Achieved Brand Equity
	Quality + Satisfaction + Brand Loyalty
	Quality + Situational environment + Historical signification

Fig. 6.6. A wine's true value in relation to its quality, brand and situational environment..

level. A presentation of the wine is very important too. In Fig. 6.5. you can see an example of how Systembolaget in Sweden presents all wines, beers and spirits on their shelves. Product presentation is by far one of the most successful ways to show a quality product.

A Wine's True Value

The importance of grading a wine's quality and affixing prices to it is not new. The majority of consumers and buyers alike, make their purchasing decisions based upon a number of variables and values, such as quality, price, brand name and situation (Fig. 6.6).

There are three levels of value: actual, perceived and achieved brand equity. Wine brands that have achieved various levels of awareness in the public domain can benefit from a certain added value. The environment and situation that the wine is consumed in also affect the valuation process

and finally the actual quality to price ratio for all wines in a blind and neutral setting as depicted in the price to quality ratios presented in Fig. 6.9 to 6.31.

A brand has also a value and this value is based upon awareness, consistency and the repeat satisfaction achieved by the consumer when using it. Indeed this satisfaction is naturally coupled to the purchaser's situational environment and economic freedom at both time of purchase and consumption.

Quality to Price Ratios

All products have a value that needs to be measured against something. The market naturally regulates prices to an extent, but both the wholesale and retail consumers need a more consistent tool to use. In the following pages a number of graphs related to the quality and price of wines will be presented. They are the first of their kind and have been gathered and adjusted after many years of experience.

Fig. 6.7. A buying trip to Bordeaux. During these trips the buyer evaluates the quality of the wine and then compares it to the wholesale and retail selling prices. Staying competitive is vital and understanding the wine to price ratio scales provided in this book are very important. Keep in mind that it is not just the buyer or retailer that should understand these pricing ratios but also the consumer. Knowing that you've purchased a price-worthy wine adds to your enjoyment.

United States Market & Prices

1. Understanding the US Market
Understanding the distribution system in the United States is not the easiest in the world. It is extremely large, very complicated and it is like doing business in 50 different countries. I explain below the basic make-up of the market, as this will help you to understand what governs the wholesalers.

2. Control or Monopoly State
Control or monopoly states are states which have governments involved in the sale and/or distribution of alcohol beverages. In the United States there are 19 control states or rather 18 states and 1 county (Montgomery County, Maryland). Their operating guidelines are not the same and they vary from state to state. In some instances they operate as sole wholesalers and in others as retailers. In most cases the wholesale of spirits is controlled by the states but in some instances wine too. In 12 of the 18 states they have control over the retail sales as well.

3. Open or License States
There are 32 Open or License states in which the government is not actively involved in the distribution of alcohol beverages. Nevertheless, they still control and issue licenses to private citizens and companies who want to actively work in the distribution process, whether as manufacturers, importers, wholesalers or retailers. There are a number of restrictions in some Open or License States, such as the number of stores that can be owned or operated by a corporation or individual. This restriction was imposed to prevent powerful corporations from dominating the market and to encourage smaller 'Mom & Pop' enterprises.

Nevertheless, I must admit that Beverages & More, Total Beverages and other beverage chains have fantastic portfolios, which in some cases have an in-house portfolio that exceed 8,000 wines. Not even Systembolaget, a state-controlled retailer in Sweden, which prides itself on its large product portfolio can compete.

4. Reciprocity State
There are 14 Reciprocity states. These states have passed a law, which allows for direct shipments of wine to consumers into another state that has passed the same law. For example, a Californian winery may ship to New York consumers and the New York winery to consumers in California.

5. Direct Shipping
Direct shipping laws (36 states) allow direct shipment of wine to consumers. Even though there is a three-tier system this law allows producers to by-pass the wholesale and retail tiers. 14 of these are the reciprocity states and another 22 states allow for direct shipping via a permit systems or granted regulatory approval. In order for consumers to order wines directly into their home state certain conditions apply, such as obtaining a permit, payment of taxes, reporting on quantities, limited quantities, acceptance of jurisdiction, etc.

6. Three-Tier System
The three-tier system in the United States has its positive and negative aspects as do all systems. The positive aspects of this system are that it allows for more employment opportunities in the beverage and transportation sectors.

The three tiers are independent of one another and one cannot operate one in the domain of the other. The three levels are: a) Producer and/or importer, b) Distributor and/or importer and c) Retailer.

These tiers remain intact even in the control states (19 monopolies controlled each by their respective state governments and their association). Each state has a registered importer, distributor and retailer, in the case of the control states the retailers are the state

Fig. 6.8.

governments instead of private companies. In some states private persons may apply to sell alcohol on behalf of the state and in this instance they would receive an exclusive operating area.

a) Producer and/or Importer

The vineyard, which is the producer, is responsible for all aspects of quality and production and it can also import other products into the US. This means that a vineyard can import its own or even a competitor's products for resale to the off-trade (a distributor and retailer) and the on-trade (a restaurant, club or other establishments that have an alcohol license to serve alcohol).

Sales activities are also part of vineyard owners' responsibilities. In this respect they need to locate and sell their products to distributors in other states. So, most vineyards have a local and national sales force to sell, monitor depletions and replenishments and make marketing plans for the brands and ranges as well as for creating a relationship with not only the distributor but also the retailer. This has naturally led to the creation of a sales force with a primary focus to assist the distributor in making retail (off-trade) and restaurant (on-trade) sales calls.

This is a very costly and in my opinion negative aspect of the three-tier system. In order to finance this, prices must rise. I feel that the distributors have become far too complacent in their positions, even though it is their responsibility to sell and distribute their portfolios to their customers in the on- and off-trade. In many cases this complacency has led to the creation of a number of dinosaurs that are antiquated, inefficient and unproductive partners in the wine trade. Hopefully, the market economy will regulate itself, but I feel that an update in legislation to enhance instead of impeding competition needs to take place. The original purpose of the three-tier system no longer exists. If the vineyard has to sell for the distributor, something has gone wrong. Wine in the US should not be more expensive than in monopoly countries, which is the case today.

b) Distributor and/or Importer

Under the three-tier system the product must pass through a distributors doors. Unfortunately, this creates a slight complacency leading to a less efficient distribution system. This is especially true when a distributor is in control of an entire area or state. This inefficency subsequently leads to higher prices. In Sweden, for example, a case of wine can be shipped from Malmö (in the south) to Kiruna (in the north), a distance of 2,200 km (1,428 miles), say from Florida to Chicago, for 29.00 Kronor ($3.40) per case with a next day delivery, if ordered before 12:00 midday.

Ten years ago there were about 800 large distributors in the US and today that has dwindled to around a mere 400. Unfortunately, this prevents many good artisan wineries from listing their products with distributors, as they have become overburdened with literally, thousands of brands in their portfolios'.

c) Retailer

The retailer or restaurateur is the contact point between the consumer and the producer. They are, in my opinion, responsible for educating and guiding the public through the wonderful and exciting world of wine, varieties, styles and regions. An educated and happy customer is a repeat customer.

There are a number of excellent chains in California and the east coast that offer a very good range of wines from all regions of the world. I am very impressed to see such large portfolios in retail outlets and my hopes for the three-tier system in self-regulating itself has been revitalized.

You might ask how they achieved this? Well, they contracted directly with a number of international wholesalers and distributors and simply ordered the products, paid a small fee to the US importer (an associate) and their distributor and took matters into their own hands, an excellent initiative.

In summary, each entity sits on a vital part of the distribution channel. The original intention was certainly to produce a stable system for the collection of taxes and to prevent monopolies from establishing themselves. The tax objective has been achieved but what about the oligopolies of the distribution system? No system is perfect but it has to improve continuously.

7. Other Regulations

There are literally hundreds of other laws that could affect the consumers' portfolio choice. Laws also exist for exclusive Franchises, Exclusive Territories, Primary Source and many more. There are many restrictions in regard to the marketing and promotion of beverages.

8. Pricing & Brand Portfolios

Prices are very competitive and in most cases product portfolio diversity is large. Even in California, which is a major wine-producing state, you can find large portfolios of brands from around the world. I have tried to make a note of this as in many other wine-producing countries around the world you'll find that the domestic market dominates brand portfolio diversity.

US Price to Points Value Graphs for Red Wines

Red Wine Price Point Scale:

The prices range from $3.49 for a 70/75-point wine up to $395 for a 96/100-point wine. Red wine prices in the US are very competitive at the $4.99 to $8.50 range and the consumer gets plenty of wine for money.

There seems to be a huge gap on the medium-priced ($13.50 - $17.90) range. This is unfortunate as many very good wines found around the world can be found in the category.

Points	Price	Points	Price
70-75	$3,49	88	$12,60
75-78	$3,69	88-89	$13,50
78-81	$3,99	89	$14,00
81-83	$4,49	89-90	$17,99
83-84	$4,99	90	$23,00
84	$5,69	90-91	$33,00
84-85	$6,49	91	$45,00
85	$7,39	91-92	$65,00
85-86	$8,50	92-94	$90,00
86	$9,29	94-95	$120,00
86-87	$10,00	95-96	$190,00
87	$11,20	96-100	$395,00
87-88	$11,80		

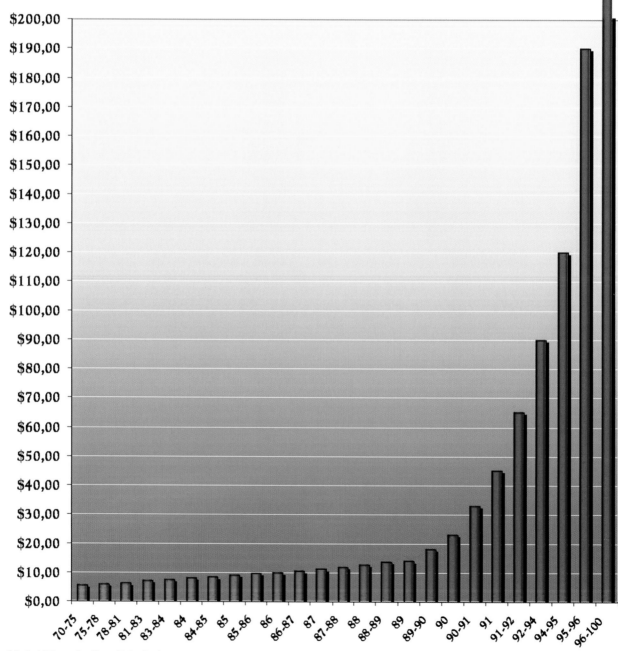

Fig. 6.9. Red Wine – Quality to Price Scale.

US Price to Points Value Graphs for White Wines

White Wine Price Point Scale:

The prices range from $2.99 for a 70/75-point wine up to $120 for a 96/100-point wine. White wine prices in the US are very competitive at the $4.00 to $11.50 range and the consumer gets plenty of wine for money.

As with red wines, there seems to be another huge gap for white wines in the medium to medium plus ($15.50 - $33.00) price level. This is unfortunate as many very good wines found around the world can be found in the category.

Points	Price	Points	Price
70-75	$2,99	91	$23,00
75-78	$3,25	91-92	$33,00
78-81	$3,50	92-94	$45,00
81-83	$3,75	94-95	$65,00
83-84	$4,00	95-96	$90,00
84	$4,25	96-100	$120,00
85	$5,25		
86	$6,25		
87	$7,25		
88	$9,00		
89	$11,50		
90	$15,00		

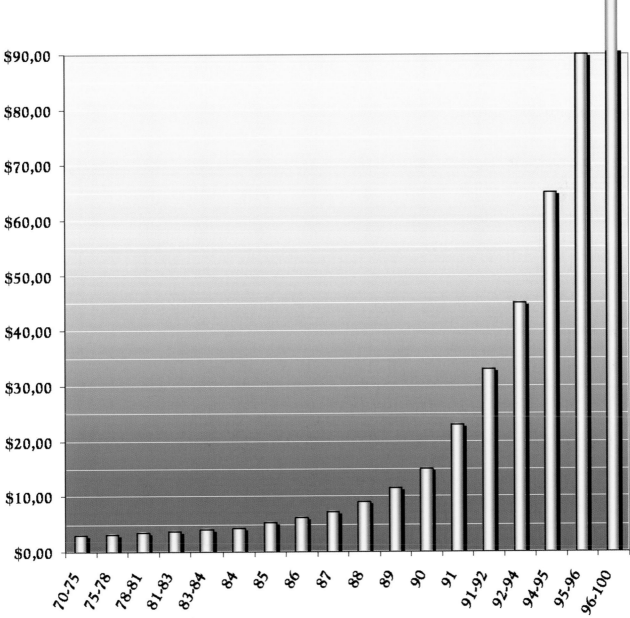

Fig. 6.10. White Wine – Quality to Price Scale.

US Price to Points Value Graphs for Champagne & Sparkling Wines

Champagne & Sparkling Wine Price Point Scale:

The prices range from $3.50 for a 70/75-point wine up to $235 for a 96/100-point wine. Sparkling prices in the US are very competitive at the premium $85.00 to $223.00 range and the consumer gets plenty of wine for money.

There seems to be a rather large gap for Champagne and sparkling wines in the medium plus ($25.00 - $70.00) range.

Points	Price	Points	Price
70-75	$3,50	89	$35,00
75-78	$4,30	90	$50,00
78-81	$4,50	91	$72,00
81-83	$5,50	91-92	$85,00
84	$7,00	92-94	$95,00
85	$10,50	94-95	$110,00
86	$12,00	95-96	$150,00
87	$18,00	96-100	$235,00
88	$25,00		

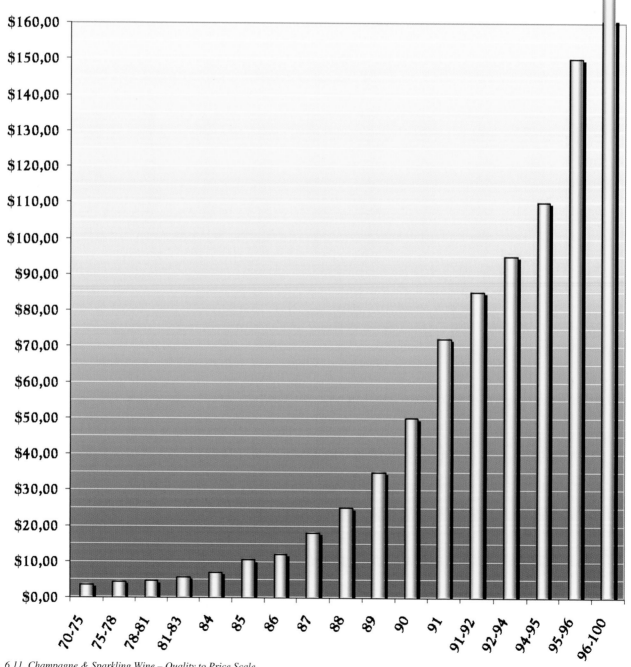

Fig. 6.11. Champagne & Sparkling Wine – Quality to Price Scale.

US Price to Points Value Graphs for Sweet Wines

Sweet Wine Price Point Scale:

The prices range from $4.00 for a 75-point wine up to $550 for a 96/100-point wine. Sweet wine prices in the US are reasonably good the $20.00 to $90.00 range and the consumer can get good quality wine for money.

Premium sweet wines are very expensive and the choice is unfortunately limited.

Points	Price	Points	Price
70-75	$4,00	90	$65,00
75-78	$7,00	91	$80,00
78-81	$9,00	92	$90,00
81-83	$11,00	93	$110,00
84	$13,00	94	$175,00
85	$15,00	95-96	$300,00
86	$20,00	96-100	$550,00
87	$25,00		
88	$30,00		
89	$35,00		

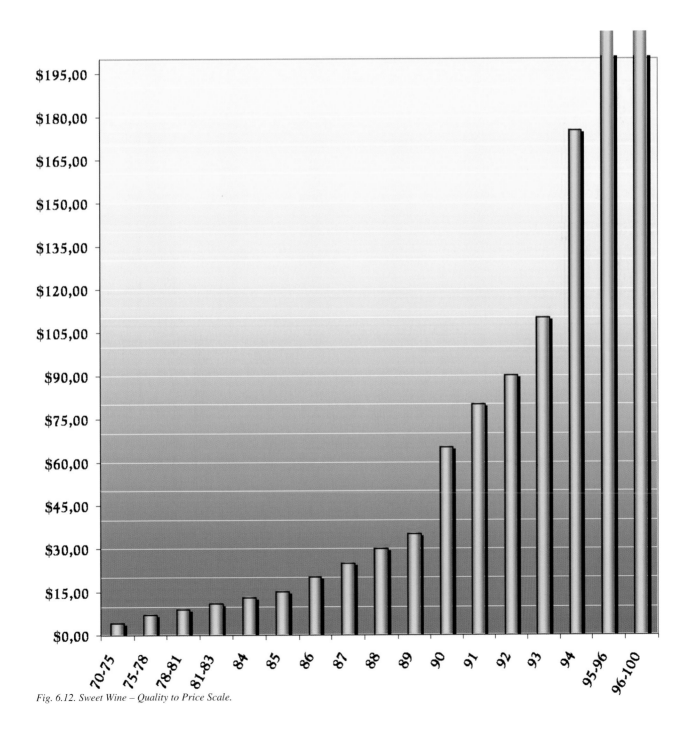

Fig. 6.12. Sweet Wine – Quality to Price Scale.

US Price to Points Value Graphs for Port Wines

Port Wine Price Point Scale:

The price ranges from $8.00 for a 82-point wine up to $450 for a 96/100-point wine. There are many medium quality port wines on the market and this seems to be a public favorite. Prices are exceptionally good in for port in the $63.00 - $68.00 price ranges.

Points	Price	Points	Price
82	$8,00	90-91	$68,00
83	$9,00	91	$75,00
84	$10,00	91-92	$99,00
85	$13,00	92-94	$152,00
86	$18,00	94-95	$175,00
87	$25,00	95-96	$275,00
88	$40,00	96-100	$450,00
89	$55,00		
90	$63,00		

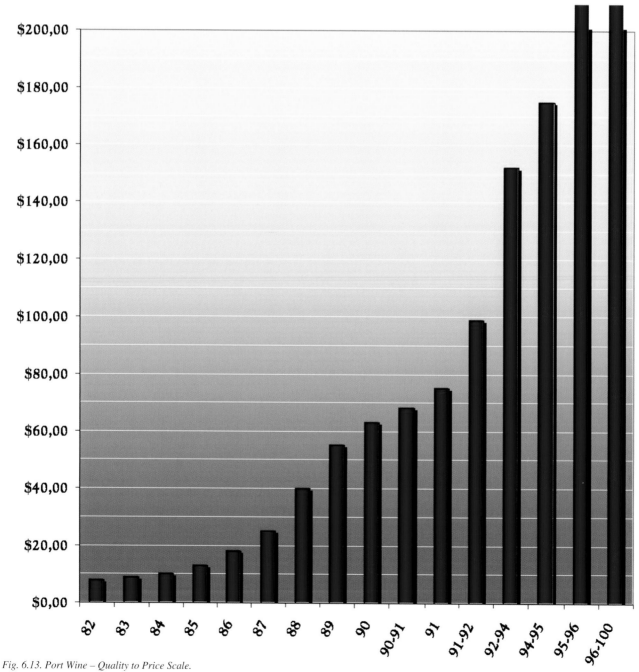

Fig. 6.13. Port Wine – Quality to Price Scale.

United Kingdom Market & Prices

Easy Access with High Alcohol Taxes

The UK market is relatively open with few regulations that can impede a good wine forward. The distribution channels are mature and well-developed. Current trends show that 'off-trade' sales are growing faster than 'on-trade'. The reason: Firstly, consumers can order online and buy direct. Secondly, wholesalers are not required to have a license, if they purchase from an importer with a license and their sales channels have helped to grow home consumption. Thirdly, retailers are offering a better selection of drinks at cheaper prices and finally, more entertaining at home. Due to high tax rates, cross-border trade to Calais, France is growing rapidly.

1. Retail

Supermarkets are becoming a main distribution channel for wines. Three supermarkets, namely Waitrose, Sainsbury's and Tesco's, are leading the way with larger, more descriptive presentations of their wines; unfortunately, the ratio of fruit-driven wines in relation to style-driven is a lot higher and represents a more volume-driven concept instead of quality. The ethical responsibility of educating and trading up general customers is therefore reduced dramatically.

Specialist 'off-licences', also called liquor stores or bottle shops have well-stocked portfolios with good balance between style- and fruit- driven wines. Though one aspect that keeps bothering me is the lack of product character descriptions. The UK wine trade is by far the most knowledgeable in the world and the only reason, I can find, for the lack of descriptive character information could be that the sales staff want to make personal contact with the customer.

The average supermarket sales price is still below £3.99 and 90 percent of sales are below £5. The £4.99 to £5.99 price range is showing the greatest growth and is up by 20 percent in 2004.

2. On-trade

France is still the number one country in the on-trade with about 33 percent, Australia 16 percent, Italy 15 percent, South Africa about 10 percent and the US 6 percent of this market. Nevertheless, US wines grew by around 25 percent in 2004. European wines were struggling to hold onto their 59 percent

of the on-trade sector in 2004. It will be interesting to see what happens in 2005.

As with the US market, the importance and domination of major brands is growing. They have 19 percent of the market and grew in 2003 by 64 percent, which is not a good development for small wineries.

One of the most important trade shows in the industry is the annual International Wine & Spirits Fair held in London. www.londonwinefair.com.

3. Government regulations and Web Site Links:
Info UK Government– www.ukonline.gov.uk
EU Customs– www.europa.eu.int/comm/taxation_cutoms/customs/customs.htm
HM Customs and Excise– www.hmce.gov.uk
UK Statistics– www.statistics.gov.uk
Info European Union–
www.europa.eu.int/index-en.htm

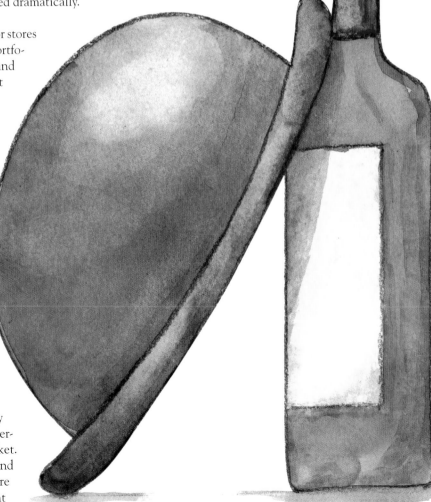

Fig. 6.14.

United Kingdom Price to Points Value Graphs for Red Wines

Red Wine Price Point Scale:

The prices range from £2.99 for a 70/75-point wine up to £260 for a 96/100-point wine. The off-trade accounts for 90% of all red wines sold in the UK under £5.25.

Due the high alcohol medium-priced wines in the £15 range are of good value.

Points	Price	Points	Price
70-75	£2,99	88	£11,99
75-78	£3,19	88-89	£13,69
78-81	£3,49	89	£14,99
81-83	£3,99	89-90	£16,99
83-84	£4,15	90	£18,99
84	£4,39	90-91	£25,00
84-85	£5,25	91	£33,00
85	£5,89	91-92	£47,00
85-86	£7,35	92-94	£65,00
86	£8,00	94-95	£89,00
86-87	£9,00	95-96	£149,00
87	£9,99	96-100	£260,00
87-88	£10,99		

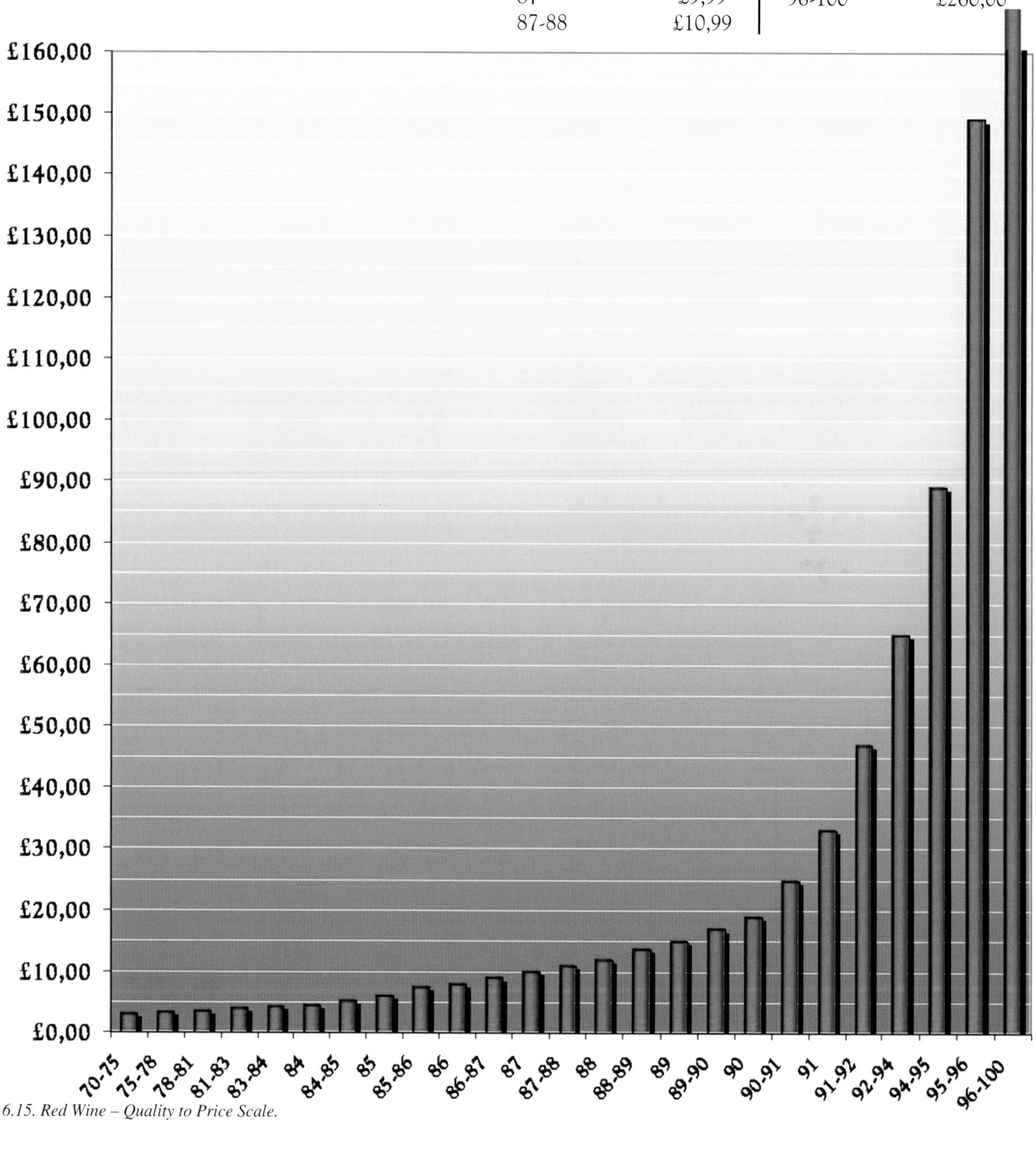

Fig. 6.15. Red Wine – Quality to Price Scale.

United Kingdom Price to Points Value Graphs for White Wines

White Wine Price Point Scale:

The prices range from £2.99 for a 70/75-point wine up to £145 for a 96/100-point wine.

Good values are found in medium-priced wines around the £13 range. The under £5 category seems to have the largest growth rate, while French wines still dominate the on-trade with about 34% .

Points	Price	Points	Price
70-75	£2,99	90	£18,00
75-78	£3,25	91	£27,00
78-81	£3,50	91-92	£36,00
81-83	£3,75	92-94	£55,00
83-84	£4,00	94-95	£85,00
84	£4,25	95-96	£105,00
85	£5,00	96-100	£145,00
86	£6,00		
87	£7,25		
88	£9,00		
89	£13,00		

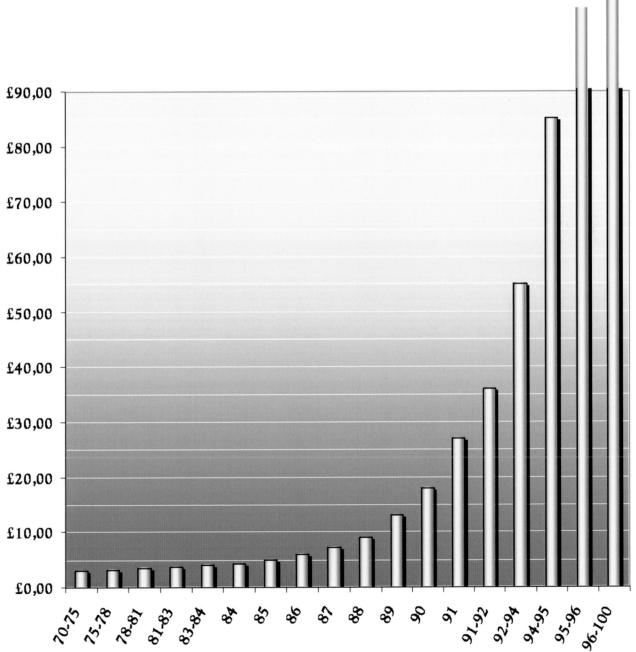

Fig. 6.16. White Wine – Quality to Price Scale.

United Kingdom Price to Points Value Graphs for Champagne and Sparkling

Champagne & Sparkling Wine Price Point Scale:

The prices range from £3.99 for a 70/75-point wine up to £225 for a 96/100-point wine.

Champagne has always been and will always be a favorite in the UK. There are literally hundreds of brands to choose from and the best values can be found between £23 to £31.

Points	Price	Points	Price
70-75	£3,99	90	£31,00
75-78	£4,19	91	£38,00
78-81	£4,29	91-92	£49,00
81-83	£5,49	92-94	£65,00
84	£6,79	94-95	£89,00
85	£7,89	95-96	£159,00
86	£8,99	96-100	£225,00
87	£11,99		
88	£15,00		
89	£23,50		

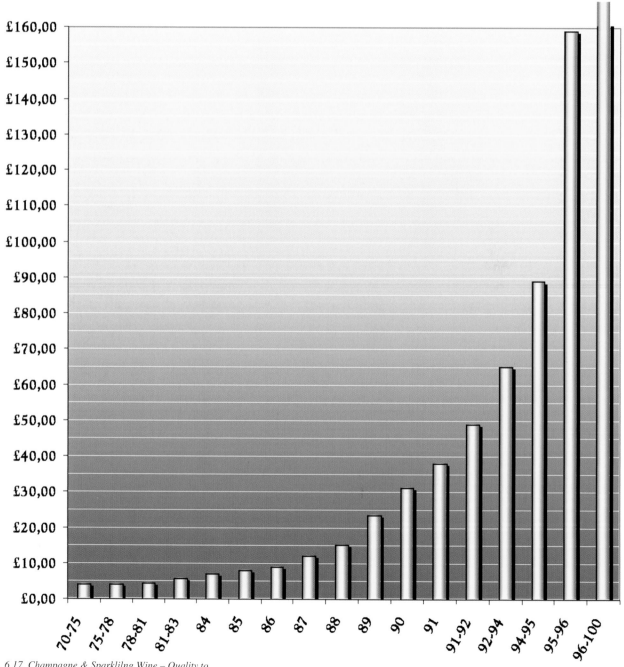

Fig. 6.17. Champagne & Sparklilng Wine – Quality to

United Kingdom Price to Points Value Graphs for Sweet Wines

Sweet White Wine Price Point Scale:

The prices range from £5.59 for a 70/75-point wine up to £329 for a 96/100-point wine.

Another favorite in the UK, sweet wines, have declined in the past couple of years but a rebound is showing strong results. Excellent deals can be found around £30 and over £180.

Points	Price	Points	Price
70-75	£5,59	89	£34,00
75-78	£6,39	90	£45,00
78-81	£8,49	91	£50,00
81-83	£9,39	92	£75,00
84	£12,69	93	£99,00
85	£15,79	94	£150,00
86	£19,00	95-96	£249,00
87	£22,00	96-100	£329,00
88	£29,00		

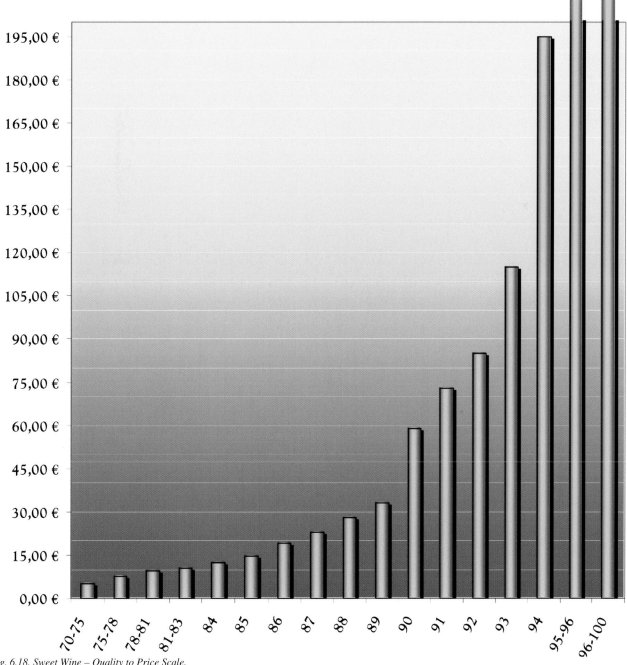

Fig. 6.18. Sweet Wine – Quality to Price Scale.

United Kingdom Price to Points Value Graphs for Port Wines

Port Wine Price Point Scale:

The prices range from £7.00 for a 70/75-point wine up to £135 for a 96/100-point wine.

Some of the best Port selections can be found in the UK. Many good values and all price points is an indication that the UK market will always remain solid 'Port Country'.

Points	Price	Points	Price
82	£7,00	90	£32,00
83	£9,90	90-91	£37,00
84	£11,00	91	£42,00
85	£13,49	91-92	£50,00
86	£15,50	92-94	£67,00
87	£18,00	94-95	£89,00
88	£24,00	95-96	£115,00
89	£28,00	96-100	£135,00

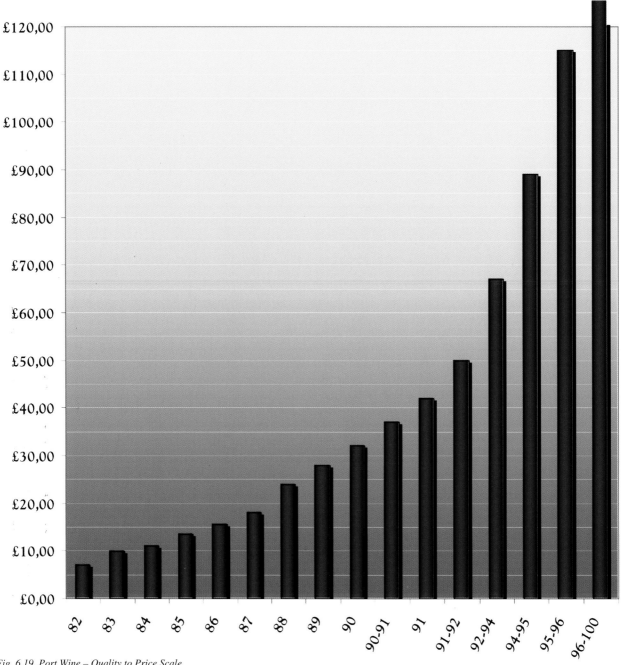

Fig. 6.19. Port Wine – Quality to Price Scale.

French, German, Italian and Spanish Market & Prices

1. Unrestricted Systems

Italy, Spain, Germany and France are by far the most liberal countries, when it comes to taxes and distribution of wine products within the European Union. Their taxes are virtually nothing in relation to other neighbors and monopoly countries. Their regulations are at a minimum as compared to the three-tier system found in the US. Furthermore, they all have good wine value below the medium plus to premium price ranges.

2. France

Unlike other regulated countries the French food retail system is comprised of six categories: hard-discounters, (Leader Price, Franprix, Lidl), supermarkets (Carefoure), hypermarkets (Carefoure), city centre stores and department stores. Traditional outlets including 'magasins de proximité' or neighbourhood stores and specialised food stores. These stores account for about 25% of alcohol sales.

In France the wine tax in only 1%. The French are also very good at marketing their wines by emphasizing the social use for their products and creating brand loyalty. Foreign imports are a miserable 3% of the market and, although I love French wines, I would also like to see more foreign varieties. Competition is good.

3. Spain

The on-trade is the key to distribution in Spain. Quality wine accounts for 70% of the total wine sales, sparkling wine for 50% and table wine for 45%. The reason for this is that most Spaniards like to entertain outside of the home. The vast majority of the on-trade purchase their wines from specialist distributors. A good development is that Spain is now importing about 5% of its sales from other wine-producing countries and this seems to be progessing too. Spain has an open market so wines can be sold and distributed through most distribution channels.

Supermarkets account for about 58% of retail sales. Their margins are very low and the customer receives very good value. Good quality international wines can be found at top end supermarkets, whilst a limited range of table wines can be found in lower-end supermarkets. Spanish retailers: specialist outlets (vinotecas), mainstream wine retailers (bodegas), department stores - El Corte Inglés.

4. Italy

The trends in the wine sector show some promise. While the popularity of high quality products seems to be growing, the "tetra-brick" is by far the most dominant product group. It has become the preferred packaging for many social occasions and at home. A sad development, I might add. The on-trade is still a traditional table wine battleground and has many good wines in the €8-€15 range. Unfortunately, there are very few international wines to choose from.

5. Germany

The sixth largest producer of wine in the world and the third largest exporter of wine; moreover, it is the fourth largest wine market in the world. 80% of German wine imports come from Italy, France and Spain and the rest of the world split the remaining 20%. Germany is the largest market for sparkling wines in the world, with a per capita consumption of just above 4.5 liters in 2004.

Distribution is open and wines can be purchased both on-line, in supermarkets and specialty stores.

Fig. 6.20.

French, German, Italian and Spanish
Price to Points Value Graphs for Red Wines

Red Wine Price Point Scale:

The prices range from $2.30 for a 70/75-point wine up to $350 for a 96/100-point wine. German consumers have increased their consumption of red wines dramatically and already make up 59% of the total wine market. Imported red wine accounts for three-quarters of the total red wine purchased by German consumers.

Very good values are to be found under €18 in all regions. Top quality red over €200 are not as competitive.

Points	Price	Points	Price
70-75	2,30	88	8,50
75-78	2,40	88-89	9,00
78-81	2,50	89	9,50
81-83	3,00	89-90	14,00
83-84	3,30	90	18,00
84	3,60	90-91	27,00
84-85	3,90	91	33,00
85	4,30	91-92	60,00
85-86	4,70	92-94	75,00
86	5,00	94-95	115,00
86-87	7,00	95-96	200,00
87	7,50	96-100	350,00
87-88	8,00		

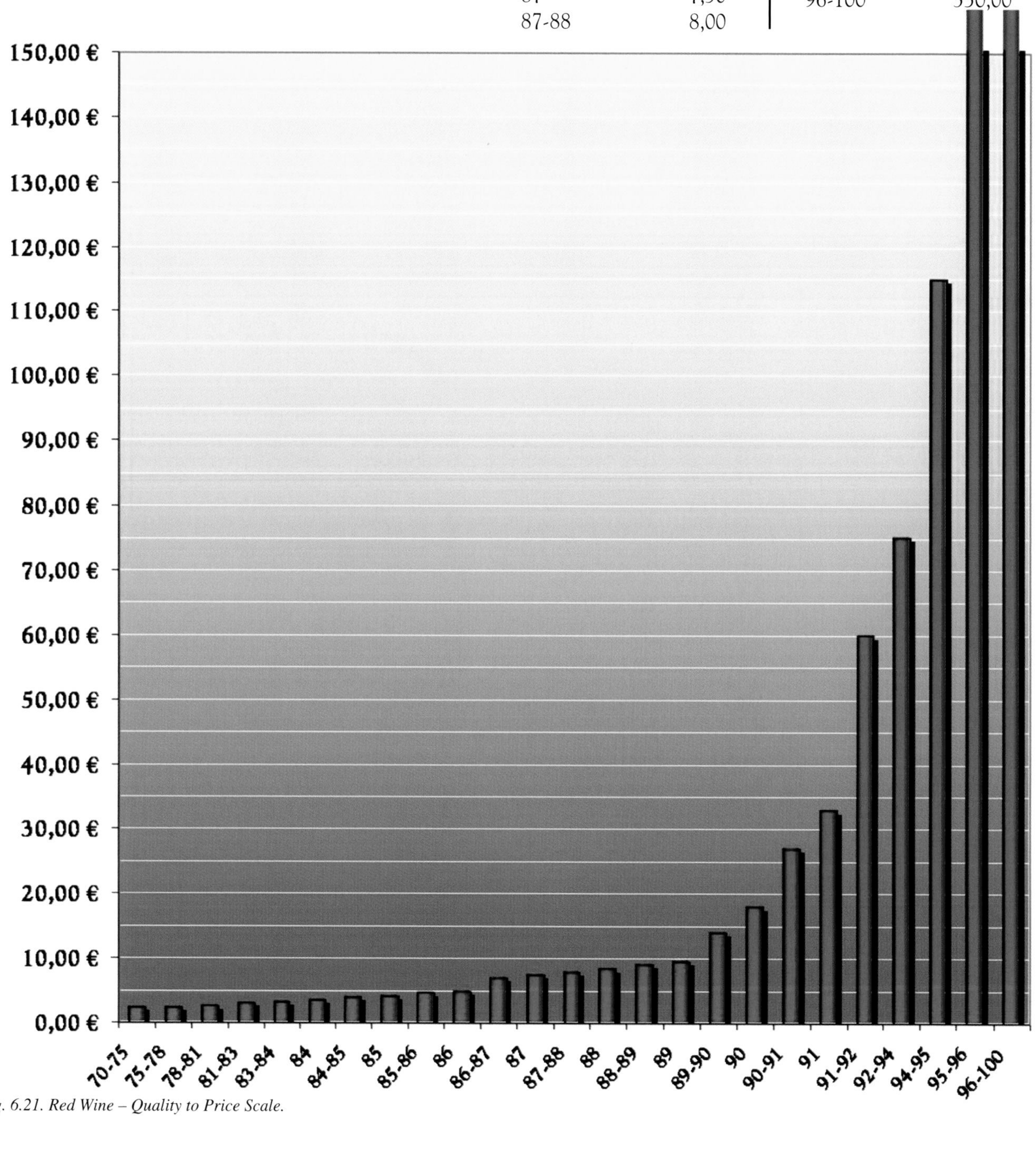

Fig. 6.21. Red Wine – Quality to Price Scale.

French, German, Italian and Spanish
Price to Points Value Graphs for White Wines

White Wine Price Point Scale:

The prices range from $2.20 for a 70/75-point wine up to $105 for a 96/100-point wine.

All regions have advantageously priced local wines up to €12.50, thereafter they are not too competitive with the exception of Germany.

Points	Price	Points	Price
70-75	2,20	90	12,50
75-78	2,40	91	17,00
78-81	2,80	91-92	27,00
81-83	3,20	92-94	36,00
83-84	3,60	94-95	55,00
84	4,00	95-96	81,00
85	4,50	96-100	105,00
86	5,20		
87	6,00		
88	7,00		
89	9,00		
Points	Price		

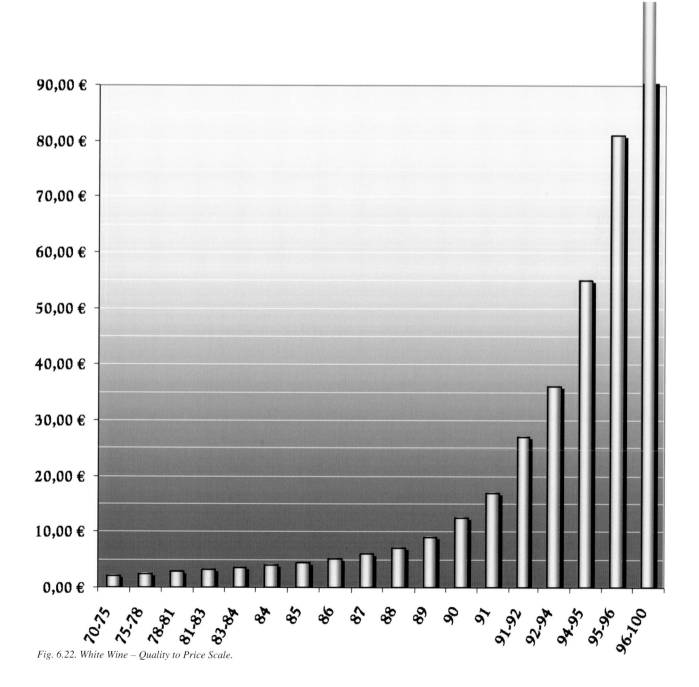

Fig. 6.22. White Wine – Quality to Price Scale.

French, German, Italian and Spanish
Price to Points Value Graphs for Champagne, Cava and Sparkling Wines

Champagne, Cava & Sparkling Wine Price Point Scale:

The prices range from $2.50 for a 70/75-point wine up to $250 for a 96/100-point wine.

Germany is by far the leader when it comes to price-worthy sparkling wines. Germany has the largest sparkling wine market in the world with a per capita consumption of over 4.5 liters per person. Nevertheless, France is not far behind, followed by Spain and then Italy. Good values across all pricing ranges.

Points	Price	Points	Price
70-75	2,50	90	47,00
75-78	3,00	91	59,00
78-81	4,00	91-92	72,00
81-83	5,00	92-94	85,00
84	6,20	94-95	99,00
85	7,50	95-96	170,00
86	12,00	96-100	250,00
87	18,00		
88	25,00		
89	35,00		

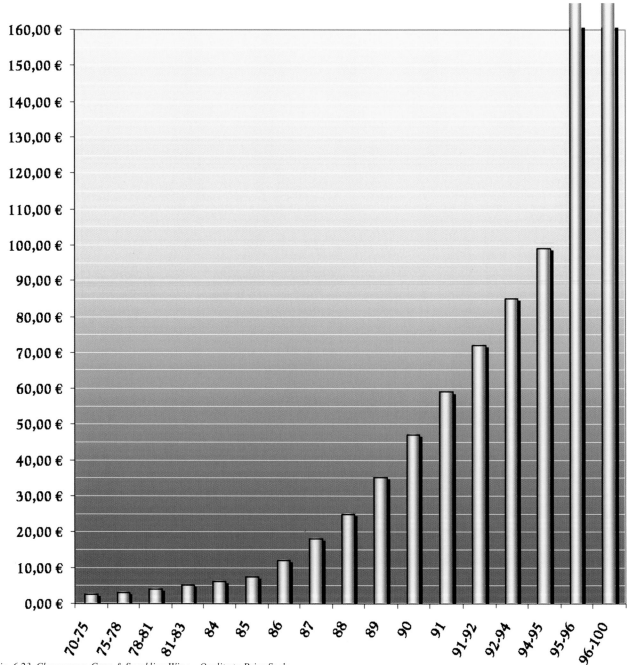

Fig. 6.23. Champagne, Cava & Sparkling Wine – Quality to Price Scale.

French, German, Italian and Spanish
Price to Points Value Graphs for Sweet Wines

Sweet White Wine Price Point Scale:

The prices range from $5.00 for a 70/75-point wine up to $500 for a 96/100-point wine.

Germany is the most competitive for wines under €10, but, Italy and Spain are more competitive in the medium €14-€19 priced wines, while France dominates value in the premium €73 price category.

Points	Price	Points	Price
70-75	5,00	89	33,00
75-78	7,50	90	59,00
78-81	9,50	91	73,00
81-83	10,50	92	85,00
84	12,49	93	115,00
85	14,50	94	195,00
86	19,00	95-96	290,00
87	23,00	96-100	500,00
88	28,00		

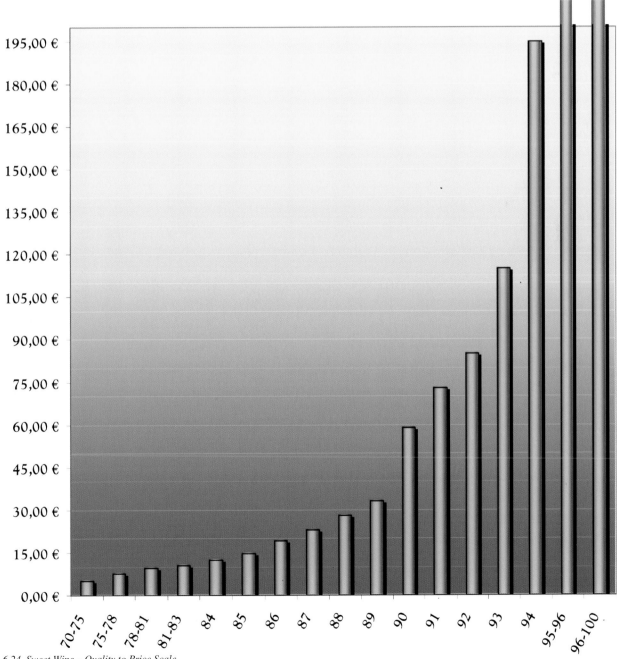

Fig. 6.24. Sweet Wine – Quality to Price Scale.

French, German, Italian and Spanish
Price to Points Value Graphs for Fortified Wines

Port Wine Price Point Scale:

The prices range from $6.00 for a 70/75-point wine up to $215 for a 96/100-point wine.

Spain consistently dominates all price sectors this category. The reason must be its geographical connection with Portugal.

Points	Price	Points	Price
82	6,00	90	55,00
83	7,50	90-91	64,00
84	9,75	91	71,00
85	11,00	91-92	85,00
86	16,00	92-94	97,00
87	21,00	94-95	121,00
88	32,00	95-96	147,00
89	44,00	96-100	215,00

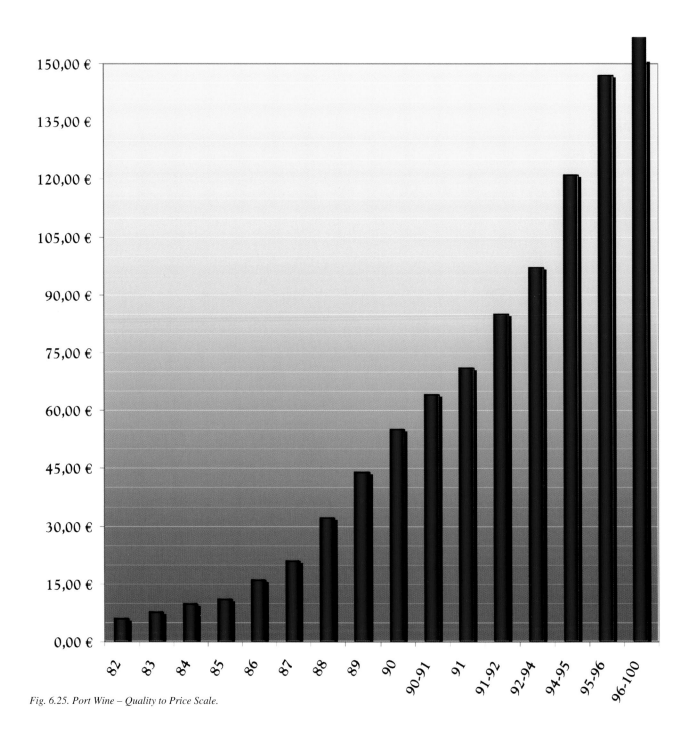

Fig. 6.25. Port Wine – Quality to Price Scale.

Swedish Market & Prices

1. Monopoly State

The Swedish state monopoly is called Systembolaget AB and is responsible for all sales of alcohol beverages over 3.5% alcohol by volume to the public. Systembolaget cannot import directly but must purchase its products through registered importers. All importers receive a detailed list of products to be purchased on a monthly basis. These lists are provided in a yearly plan and adjusted on a monthly and semi-annual basis.

All importers have the right to submit wines that they feel fit into the beverage category. Those products considered acceptable by the monopoly will then be tested in a blind tasting conducted by the buyers at Systembolaget. The winner or the beverage with the best quality 'wine to price ratio' will be purchased and listed either throughout the country or in a smaller number of specialized stores in relation to the price level and sales statistics of each geographical region. Price levels then become of vital importance. All products except those winning the tasting are excluded. The importer has the opportunity to submit the wine to market testing. If this proves to be a seller, the product is accepted into the portfolio and listed according to its price level. The waiting period for this test listing is over two years. So patience is a virtue?

There is another list called an 'order list', which is a list of products available through Systembolaget. This list encompasses other wines and products available from various importers and can be ordered in by the consumer. The only problem with this is that the consumer must be patient and plan instead of buying impulsively. Systembolaget has today about 450 basic wine brands, sold in all stores nationwide with some selected stores strategically placed throughout the country. These stores have over 1200 products on the shelves. Together with the order list this gives the consumer the possibility to order over 6000 different brands, a good service by any means.

I don't believe in letting loose the oligopolies, as they would dominate the retail industry just like Systembolaget, but a system which allows for a maximum of two stores per individual or company, such as in New York State, these companies could then compete against be noted that the registered importers have the right to sell their products to the on-trade (licensed restaurants and hotels).

Unfortunately, the state has not overlooked this either. In order to dominate the import side too, the state owns its own import and manufacturing company called Vin & Sprit. Vin & Sprit is the most dominant importer and producer in Sweden with a number of vineyards around the world, not to forget the Absolute product range which it produces and distributes. This leads to stiff competition for the remaining 420 importers.

2. Customer Service

The public might not have an open system, but one area in Sweden that is far ahead of the competition is customer service. A knowledgeable workforce, very good product character descriptions and internet stock levels for wines available in each of their stores.

Systembolaget seems to believe, as I, that a well-educated public will learn to appreciate wine for its quality, trade-up and would therefore be less likely to abuse wine. I believe that product information and education is the way to compete.

N.B.: kr = Swedish Crowns in the following price graphs.

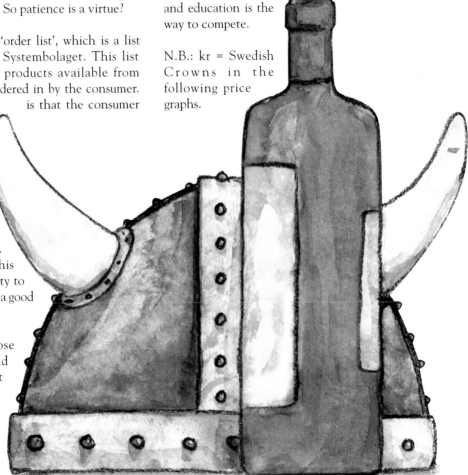

Fig. 6.26.

Swedish Price to Points Value Graphs for Red Wines

Red Wine Price Point Scale:

The prices range from 42.75 kr for a 70/75-point wine up to 2,962.50 kr for a 96/100-point wine.

Red wines dominate with about 80% of the sales. This percentage is reduced slightly during the summer. Wines under 80.00 kr are not of good value as compared to Denmark and Germany (cross-border sales), but they are very competitive in the price ranges from 101.00 kr and up. One reason for this is that Systembolaget has a fixed mark-up of 21% and wines at these levels become very competitive.

Points	Price	Points	Price
70-75	42,75 kr	88	94,50 kr
75-78	45,00 kr	88-89	101,25 kr
78-81	47,25 kr	89	105,00 kr
81-83	52,50 kr	89-90	134,93 kr
83-84	56,25 kr	90	172,50 kr
84	60,00 kr	90-91	247,50 kr
84-85	63,75 kr	91	337,50 kr
85	67,50 kr	91-92	487,50 kr
85-86	71,25 kr	92-94	675,00 kr
86	75,00 kr	94-95	900,00 kr
86-87	79,50 kr	95-96	1 425,00 kr
87	84,00 kr	96-100	2 962,50 kr
87-88	88,50 kr		

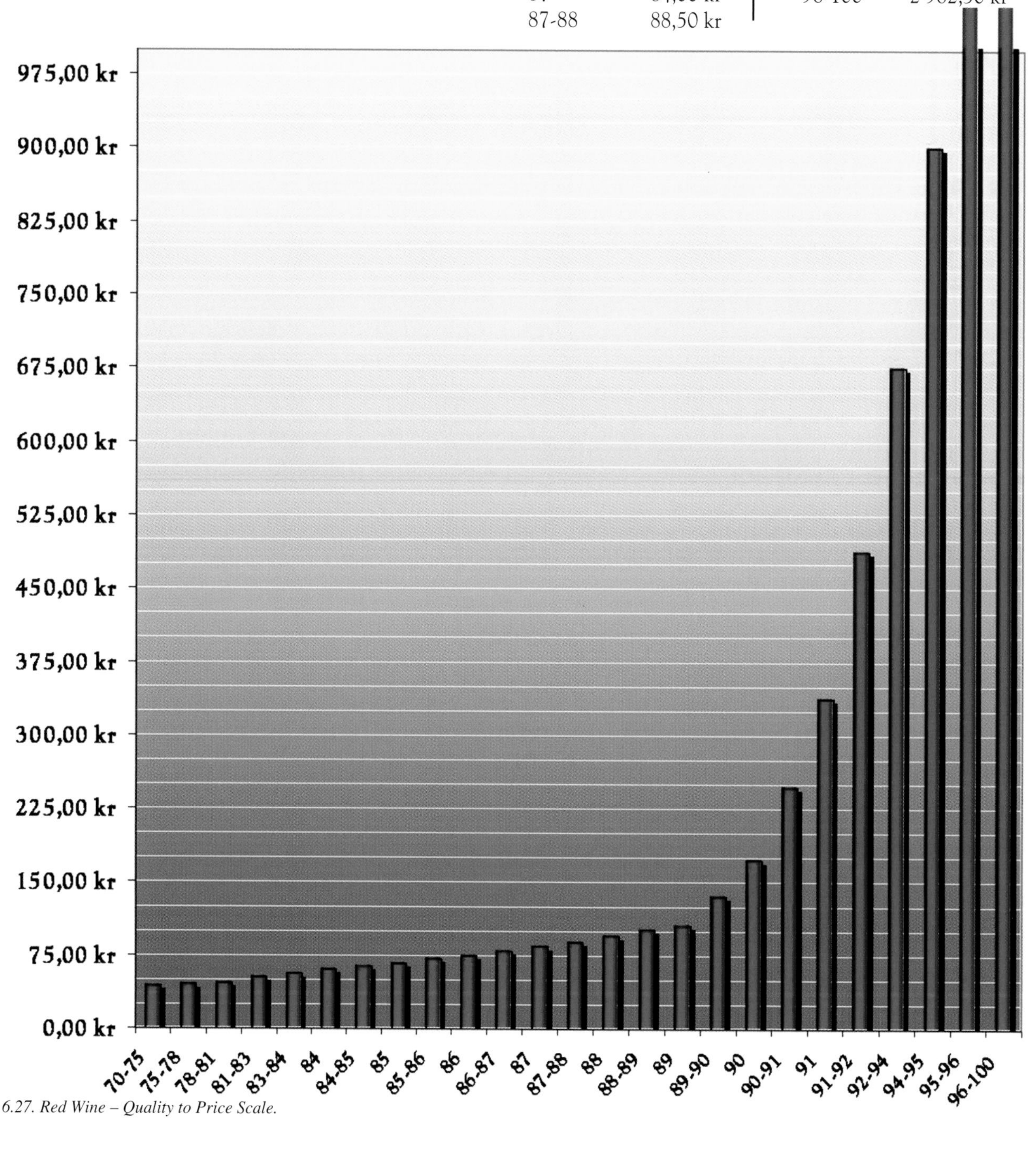

Fig. 6.27. Red Wine – Quality to Price Scale.

Swedish Price to Points Value Graphs for White Wines

White Wine Price Point Scale:

The prices range from 43.00 kr for a 70/75-point wine up to 1,200.00 kr for a 96/100-point wine.

Wines under 70.00 kr are not of good value as compared to the cross-border wines in Denmark and Germany; nevertheless, they are very competitive in the price ranges from 99.00 kr and up. One reason for this is that Systembolaget has a fixed mark-up of 21% and wines at these levels become very competitive.

Points	Price	Points	Price
70-75	43,00 kr	90	125,00 kr
75-78	46,00 kr	91	172,00 kr
78-81	49,00 kr	91-92	285,00 kr
81-83	52,00 kr	92-94	375,00 kr
83-84	55,00 kr	94-95	600,00 kr
84	58,00 kr	95-96	900,00 kr
85	62,00 kr	96-100	1 200,00 kr
86	68,00 kr		
87	75,00 kr		
88	85,00 kr		
89	99,00 kr		

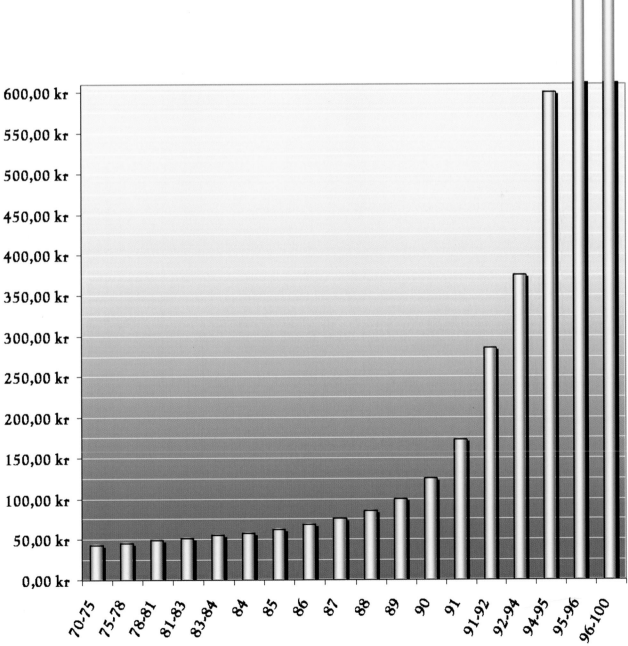

Fig.6.28. White Wine – Quality to Price Scale.

Swedish Price to Points Value Graphs for Champagne & Sparkling Wines

Champagne & Sparkling Wine Price Point Scale:

The prices range from 45.00 kr for a 70/75-point wine up to 2,100.00 kr for a 96/100-point wine.

Although there is a limited variety of Champagne and sparkling wines at Systembolaget, I feel too few, the prices are very good between 187.00 kr and 350.00. Premium brands are not competitive.

Points	Price	Points	Price
70-75	45,00 kr	90	475,00 kr
75-78	51,00 kr	91	540,00 kr
78-81	55,00 kr	91-92	635,00 kr
81-83	65,00 kr	92-94	750,00 kr
84	78,00 kr	94-95	925,00 kr
85	90,00 kr	95-96	1 600,00 kr
86	135,00 kr	96-100	2 100,00 kr
87	187,00 kr		
88	250,00 kr		
89	350,00 kr		

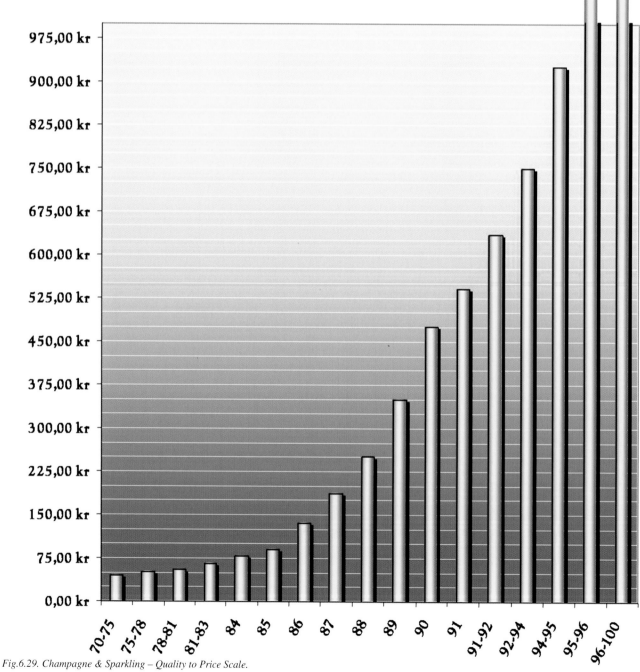

Fig.6.29. Champagne & Sparkling – Quality to Price Scale.

Swedish Price to Points Value Graphs for Sweet Wines

Sweet Wine Price Point Scale:

The prices range from 55.00 kr for a 70/75-point wine up to 3,600.00 kr for a 96/100-point wine.

A limited portfolio of sweet wines has led to a category of wines that is not too competitive. All price levels show a competitive weakness.

Points	Price	Points	Price
70-75	55,00 kr	90	475,00 kr
75-78	59,00 kr	91	550,00 kr
78-81	69,00 kr	92	675,00 kr
81-83	75,00 kr	93	825,00 kr
84	89,00 kr	94	1 312,00 kr
85	115,00 kr	95-96	2 550,00 kr
86	175,00 kr	96-100	3 600,00 kr
87	220,00 kr		
88	269,00 kr		
89	399,00 kr		

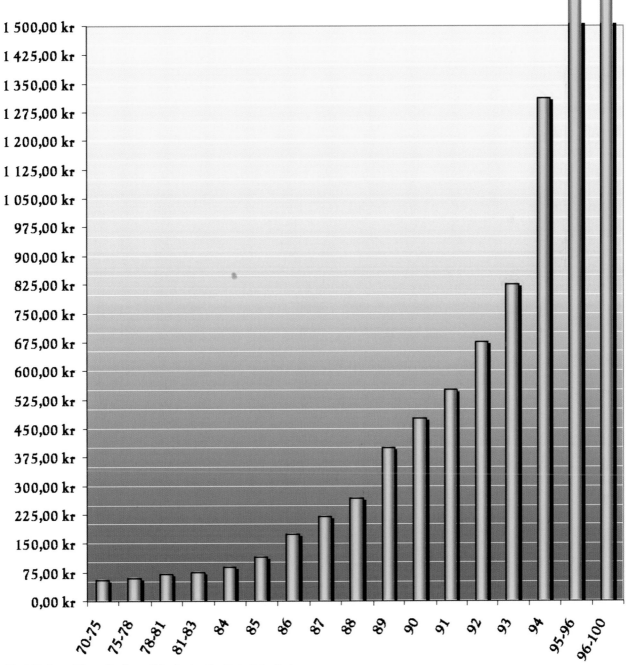

Fig.6.30. Sweet Wine – Quality to Price Scale - Quality to Price Scale.

Swedish Price to Points Value Graphs for Port Wines

Port Wine Price Point Scale:

The prices range from 69.00 kr for a 70/75-point wine up to 3,3750.50 kr for a 96/100-point wine.

Yet another category that has suffered from a loss in portfolio variety. Systembolaget used to have a very good brand portfolio and the reduction has led to less of a competitive pricing structure. The alcohol tax is also higher for fortified wine.

Points	Price	Points	Price
82	69,00 kr	90	450,00 kr
83	75,00 kr	90-91	562,00 kr
84	97,00 kr	91	725,00 kr
85	135,00 kr	91-92	875,00 kr
86	187,00 kr	92-94	1 150,00 kr
87	245,00 kr	94-95	1 312,00 kr
88	315,00 kr	95-96	1 875,00 kr
89	412,00 kr	96-100	3 375,00 kr

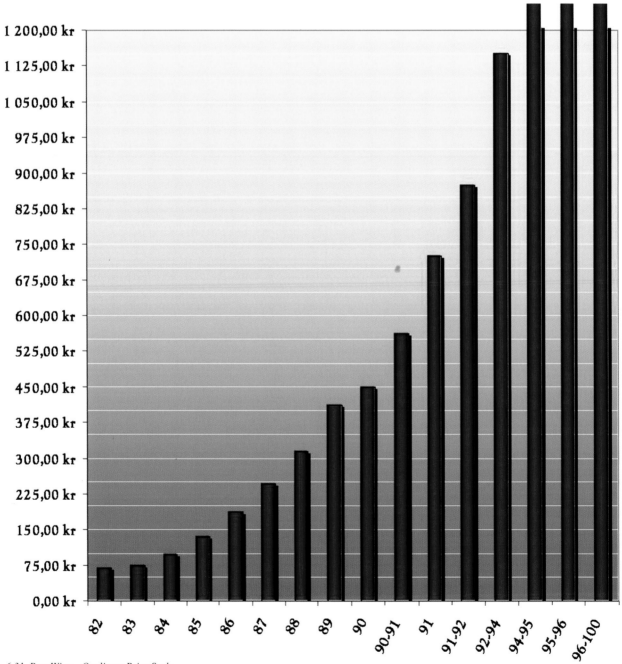

Fig. 6.31. Port Wine – Quality to Price Scale.

Chapter 7

Grape Varieties, Oak & Additives

Although there are thousands of grape varieties to choose from, 30 of the most well-known have been selected, and each one will be covered in detail in this chapter. I am fully aware that there are many other important varieties, some of which will appear in future publications.

Nevertheless, I hope that you will get enough information about each of the grape varieties discussed. For each of them I will give you some background to the grape, its origin, the various styles and whether or not it is used in a blend as well as the grape's phenology and wine-tasting characteristics for red and white wines. At the bottom of each page a character summary is provided along with tactile sensory graphs, which help you to identify the variety, decide on storage potential, grape typicity and how to match it with food or cheese.

Each of the grapes discussed have their own unique characteristics, which I call 'trademark characters'. These

characters are usually present, unless the climate conditions were adverse and/or something went wrong in the winemaking process.

The aim of this chapter is to show the benefits of each variety. By understanding these benefits you may gradually increase your appreciation for the grape and be able to combine it appropriately with various kinds of foods and in different social situations.

The end of this chapter is dedicated to discussing the purpose, use and effects of oak in wine and winemaking. This will help you understand the various characteristics caused by the oak itself as well as the differences between European and American oak.

The following is a list of the 30 grapes for which you'll find a full description:

Red Grapes	White Grapes
Barbera	Aligoté
Cabernet Franc	Chardonnay
Cabernet Sauvignon	Chenin Blanc
Cinsaut	Gewürztraminer
Gamay	Grüner Veltliner
Grenache	Macabeo
Malbec	Muscat à Petit Grains
Merlot	Muscadet
Nebbiolo	Pinot Blanc
Pinot Noir	Pinot Gris
Sangiovese	Riesling
Syrah	Sauvignon Blanc
Tempranillo	Sémillon
Pinotage	Trebbiano
Zinfandel	Viognier

Fig. 7.1. The 30 grapes mentioned in this figure, 15 red and 15 white, are described in this chapter.

Barbera

Barbera is the most widely planted grape variety in the world. In both Italy and California it is regarded as a valued grape, as it thrives in warm climates but, more importantly, also produces high acidic wines with low tannin content. Being usually a good complement to food, it is considered a good average table wine.

Synonyms: Barbera Sards, Perricone and Pignatello on Sardinia.

Areas Found:
Barbera has its roots in Italy with the north Italian districts Barbera d'Alba, Barbera d'Asti and Barbera del Monferrato but is also found in Argentina and South Africa and, most importantly, in California's San Joaquin Valley, where it is responsible for about 13% of the state's total grape production. Barbera is grown throughout southern Italy as well and is the most planted grape variety, closely followed by Sangiovese.

Wine Styles and Blends:
Found as a single varietal but more often today used as a blended wine in warmer climates, where the grape's high acid levels help to lift the other heavier varieties that tend to suffer from poor acidity if picked too late.

Grape Physiology:
Vigour: Very vigorous. It produces high yields of about 70 hl/ha. Grows well on sandy, fine and poor soils.

Phenology: Ripens in late-season, so it is a good grape for warm weather climates were summers are relatively hot. At full maturity the average sugar content is from 22° to 23.5° Brix / Balling (total dissolved compounds in grape juice and sugar concentration) and total titratable acid of 6 to 7.5 g/l.

Berries: Medium in size, with a thin skin. The berry has an off-round shape grape with a bluish / violet / pink-red color.

Diseases: Susceptible to leafroll, rot and Pierce's disease.

Sensory Characteristics:
Appearance:
In young wines, Barbera has a deep purple hue with a pinkish hue towards the rim-proper. In warmer climates, such as in southern Italy and central California, Barbera has a tighter gradient but changes hue a lot quicker. In 85-point wines it has a light to medium purple/ruby-red hue when young, and the wine starts to change color already after the 2nd to 3rd year. Good mature wines develop an orange brick-colored rim already around their 5th to 6th year.

The Nose:
Barbera has a fruity acid character of cherry, strawberry and even some blackcurrant and raspberry when young. Can be aged in oak.

The Palate:
Known for its high acid content Barbera has usually very little but soft 'fine tannins' and balanced as per the ratio chart (3/10 for tannin and 8/10 for acid). The alcohol levels range from 11% to 12.5%. A volatile aroma of plums is usually evident in the aftertaste.

Excellent Food Combinations:
Barbera combines perfectly with fatty or creamy foods. It can also be served with light meat dishes and even a variety of shell-fish, fish and chicken, pâté and quiche plates.

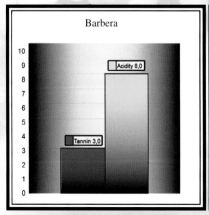

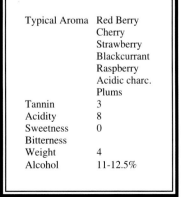

Typical Aroma	Red Berry
	Cherry
	Strawberry
	Blackcurrant
	Raspberry
	Acidic charc.
	Plums
Tannin	3
Acidity	8
Sweetness	0
Bitterness	
Weight	4
Alcohol	11-12.5%

Fig. 7.2. Barbera Tannin to Acid sensory ratios.   Fig. 7.3. Barbera sensory summary.

Cabernet Franc

There are not too many wines bottled using 100% Cabernet Franc, the most famous being Château Haut-Brion and Château Cheval Blanc in St. Emilion, which is one of the five first growths from Bordeaux.

Synonyms: Breton, Carmenet, Bouchet, Gross-Bouchet, Grosse-Vidure, Bouchy, Noir-Dur, Méssange Rouge, Trouchet Noir, Bordo and Cabernet Frank.

Areas Found:
Cabernet Franc is the third most popular grape variety in the Bordeaux region but is also grown in the Loire Valley in France and found in California, Washington State oregon, South Africa, Australia, New Zealand, Chile, Argentina and in some isolated areas of Spain and Italy.

Wine Styles and Blends:
It comprises about 6-8% of the Bordeaux blend and its major purpose is aromatics and softness. It is mainly a blended variety of Cabernet Sauvignon, Merlot and Petit Verdot.

Grape Physiology:
Vigour: Very productive with good yields exceeding that of its cousin Cabernet Sauvignon.

Phenology: Ripens in early late-season and prior to Cabernet Sauvignon. At full maturity the average sugar content is from 23° to 24.5° Brix / Balling (total dissolved compounds in grape juice and sugar concentration) and total titratable acid of 5.5 to 7 g/l.

Berries: Larger than Cabernet Sauvignon in size, with a thick skin and good tannin (pigments). The berries are round in shape with a blue-black color. They have cylindrical and conical cluster bunches.

Diseases: Susceptible to powdery mildew.

Sensory Characteristics:
Appearance:
Cabernet Franc has a relative dark gradient and deep blue-black color when young but tends to change color rather early. In very good wines this change in color starts way before Cabernet Sauvignon at about its 5th year.

Excellent first class wines and blends will only start to change color after the 6th to 7th years but will develop an orange brick-colored rim in about their 8th to 10th year.

The Nose:
Cabernet Franc is full of blackberries, mint, green olives, nutmeg, ripe plums and violets. You may even find some strawberry-like characteristics. Trademark characters are violets, mint and ripe plums.

The Palate:
The acidity and balance as per ratio chart (5.2/10 for tannin and 6/10 for acid). Cabernet Franc can produce wines with a complex and elegant balance and can compete with the best of wines. It has good fruit, acid and tannin balance ratios displaying more acidity than tannin under normal fermentation conditions. The alcohol levels range from as little as 11.5% to 13.5%.

Excellent Food Combinations:
From colder climates like the Loire Valley, it is best suited to lighter meat dishes, quiches, smoked or fried fish dishes and even salads. For a more full-bodied Cabernet Franc taste a good cut of beef or even lamb and a cheese variety plate.

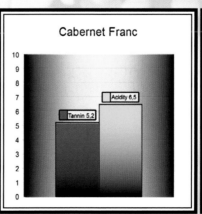

Fig. 7.4. Cabernet Franc Tannin to Acid sensory ratios.

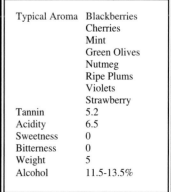

Typical Aroma	Blackberries
	Cherries
	Mint
	Green Olives
	Nutmeg
	Ripe Plums
	Violets
	Strawberry
Tannin	5.2
Acidity	6.5
Sweetness	0
Bitterness	0
Weight	5
Alcohol	11.5-13.5%

Fig. 7.5. Cabernet Franc sensory summary.

Cabernet Sauvignon

Cabernet Sauvignon is the 'King' of grapes and can be found in vineyards and store shelves throughout the world. Without refute being the most popular red grape variety in the world, it can be grown in a number of soil types from the preferred well-drained gravel soils of Bordeaux to the over-fertile soils, which produce uneven fruit at harvest.

Synonyms: Petit-Cabernet, Vidure, Petite-Vidure, Bouchet, Bouche, Petit-Bouchet, Sauvignon Rouge.

Areas Found: Originally from Bordeaux the grape is grown around the world and in almost all wine-producing regions.

Wine Styles and Blends:
A single varietal or can be blended. The Classic Bordeaux blend includes Cabernet Franc, Merlot, Petit Verdot and even Malbec. Other varieties known to be blended with Cabernet Sauvignon are Sangiovese, Nebbiolo, Shiraz, Tempranillo, Tinto Barocca, Zinfandel, Mourvèdre and even Pinot Noir.

Grape Physiology:
Vigour: Excellent vigour, but if the soil is too fertile uneven berry growth can be found.

Phenology: Ripens in late season, so it can be prone to weather fluctuations. At full maturity the average sugar content is from 23.5° to 25° Brix / Balling (total dissolved compounds in grape juice and sugar concentration) and a total titratable acid of 6 to 7 g/l.

Berries: Small, round and very dark. The skin is tough and thick, producing lots of phenols and deeply colored wines. The pips are rather large.

Diseases: Susceptible to downy and powdery mildew. Because of its thick skin it has a strong resistance to botrytis infection. This is not to say that it cannot be infected with botrytis.

Sensory Characteristics:
Appearance:
In good young wines, Cabernet Sauvignon displays a dark, deep tone with a tight gradient from the bowl to rim. Bluish-purple-red in young wines, this hue gradually starts to change color around the 3rd -4th year. Good mature wines develop an orange brick-colored rim in about their 6th to 8th year. Classic wines begin to change color only around the 8th year and obtains a brick-red hue at about their 12th to 15th year.

The Nose:
Young wines display ripe blackcurrants combined with cedar wood, pencil shavings and other dark berries. As the wine matures, so do the aromas too. Oak-matured wines offer a slightly spicy character of cigar box, vanilla of oak, tobacco and a mixture of dark and red berries. The signature trait of blackcurrants still remains a major component. The new world styles often present a mint/ eucalyptus nose in addition to the above characters.

The Palate:
The taste will have a substantial backbone of tannin and acid in young wines but are usually balanced as per the ratio chart. The Cabernet Sauvignon variety can produce complex wines with a lingering length. When young, they are mouth-puckering, but with enough fruit to allow the tannins to mellow in time. A lesser Cabernet Sauvignon can be a little stalky. The alcohol levels range from 11% to 15%. If matured in oak, the after-taste is in most cases long.

Excellent Food Combinations:
Various meat dishes with reduced sauces. Young fruit-driven wines should be served with heavier meat dishes, while mature wines go better with gourmet cooking, beef or wild dishes.

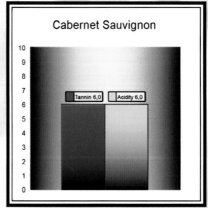

Fig. 7.6. Cabernet Sauvignon Tannin to Acid sensory ratios.

Typical Aroma	
	Blackcurrant
	Blue Berries
	Dark Berries
	Mint
oak -	Cedar wood
oak -	Tobacco
oak -	Coffee
Tannin	5 to 8
Acidity	5 to 8
Sweetness	0
Bitterness	0 to 2
Weight	4 to 9
Alcohol	11-15%

Fig. 7.7. Cabernet Sauvignon sensory summary.

Cinsaut

This is one of the important blending grapes in the world today. It can be grown as a bush wine, where it produces good wines with a meaty backbone of dried fruits. It is an exceptionally good blender with a potential of very high sugar levels.

Synonyms: Cinsault, Plant d'Arles, Bourdales, Milhau, Morterille Noir, Picardan Noir, Espagne, Calabre, Petaire, Malaga, Hermitage and Blue Imperial.

Areas Found: Cinsaut is found in France in the Midi, Provence, Rhône and Languedoc-Rousillon, North Africa, Australia, Italy, Spain but is at its best in South Africa. It is still the third most planted grape in South Africa after Chenin Blanc and Palomino.

Wine Styles and Blends:

Cinsaut has a meaty, fleshy, dried fruit, jam-type style with low tannin extraction and high acidity. It can be found as a single variety but today more than ever it is blended with Cabernet Sauvignon, Shiraz, Grenache and is naturally one of the 13 grape varieties of the famous Châteauneuf-du-Pape. The best rosé wines are usually produced from the Cinsaut grape.

Grape Physiology:

Vigour: Moderate to low. Cinsaut yields about 40 hl/ha for well made wines and slightly more when used in bulk blended wines. Cinsaut grows well on most types of soils.

Phenology: Ripens in late mid-season. It is an excellent hot weather grape. At full maturity the average sugar content is from 22° to 26° Brix / Balling (total dissolved compounds in grape juice and sugar concentration) and total titratable acid of 5 to 7 g/l.

Berries: Large and oval in size, it is one of the largest grapes grown with a very thick skin. The berry has a slight off-round shape grape with a dark blue color.

Diseases: Susceptible to powdery mildew and downy mildew.

Sensory Characteristics:

Appearance:

Color ranges dramatically as it can produce everything from rosé and full-bodied wines to ports. In good reds with 88 points the wines have a bluish/ruby-red hue, medium tone and spread gradient. Cinsaut starts to change color early in its 3rd to 4th year. Good mature wines develop an orange brick-colored rim in about their 6th to 7th year.

The Nose:

Cinsaut has a very fruity nose, which comes from its thick skins and high sugar content. These characters are usually associated with jam, stewed dried fruit and even nuances of plums and strawberry jam.

The Palate:

You would normally assume that a grape with very thick skins like Cinsaut would also produce very tannin-rich, astringent, wines. This is not the case with Cinsaut. It has soft 'fine tannins' with a good acidity and are balanced as per the ratio chart above (3.5/10 for tannin and 6.3/10 for acid). The alcohol levels range from 10.5% to 12.5%.

Excellent Food Combinations:

Summertime, lunch or an early dinner and a Cinsaut rosé, need I say more.

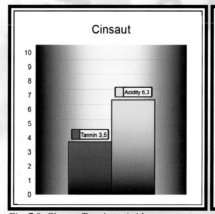

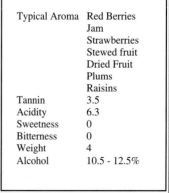

Typical Aroma	Red Berries
	Jam
	Strawberries
	Stewed fruit
	Dried Fruit
	Plums
	Raisins
Tannin	3.5
Acidity	6.3
Sweetness	0
Bitterness	0
Weight	4
Alcohol	10.5 - 12.5%

Fig. 7.8. Cinsaut Tannin to Acid sensory ratios.

Fig. 7.9. Cinsaut sensory summary.

Gamay

If someone mentions Beaujolais, you automatically remember the Gamay grape. Before you judge any wine, it is important to consider its compatibility with the situation. Beaujolais has in the past couple of years received a reputation as a simple table wine. If you are in the dead of winter and the temperature is below zero, you don't normally drink a light- to medium-bodied red wine with high acidity and low tannin ratios, but rather a full-bodied heavily extracted wine.

Synonyms: Gamay Noir à Jus Blanc, Petit Gamai, Gamay Rond, Bourguignon Noir.

Areas Found: 98% of the Beaujolais district in France is planted with the Gamay grape, which is also found in Loire, northern Rhône as well as in Switzerland, Spain and the US.

Wine Styles and Blends:

Beaujolais Nouveau is famous throughout the world for its young, very fruity, newly vinified grapes. It is made for drinking during the warmer days of summer, when an acidic but fruity alternative to white wine is needed. Whole bunches of grapes are placed into an anaerobic, oxygen-free vat, where they undergo carbonic maceration. Carbonic maceration is an intercellular fermentation within the grape producing up to 3-4% alcohol by volume. The must is then inoculated with yeast and a normal fermentation process begins. This process produces very fruity characters in the wine with little tannin. Gamay can also be blended with Pinot Noir. Many rosé wines are made from the Gamay grape.

Grape Physiology:

Vigour: Moderately vigorous. It produces yields of about 50 hl/ha. Grows well on a sandy-clay topsoil over granite.

Phenology: Ripens in early mid-season. At full maturity the average sugar content is from 19° to 21.5° Brix / Balling (total dissolved compounds in grape juice and sugar concentration) and total titratable acid of 6 to 7 g/l.

Berries: Small to medium in size, with a thin skin. The berry is round in shape with a purple-bluish-black color.

Diseases: Susceptible to Grey Rot.

Sensory Characteristics:

Appearance:

The thin skin has a low tannin pigment concentration, which results in a light, pale, red wine. A large, wide gradient is also noticeable. The hue is usually blue-purple with a light gradient tone. A young wine would start to change color after only the 1st year. Heavily macerated Gamay grapes will show a darker tone and changes in about their 2nd year. They develop an orange brick-colored rim around their 3rd to 4th year.

The Nose:

Gamay has a very young, red berry, fruity nose with some hints of bananas, pears, caramel, strawberries, bubblegum and floral characters.

The Palate:

Known for its good acidity, Gamay usually displays soft 'fine tannins' and is balanced as per the ratio chart above (2/10 for tannin and 5.5/10 for acid). The alcohol levels range from 11% to 13%.

Excellent Food Combinations:

Gamay goes very well with a variety of fish dishes, light meats, pizza and barbeques, not to mention a myriad of cheese from goat's, sheep's and cow's milk.

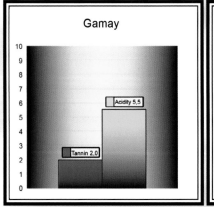

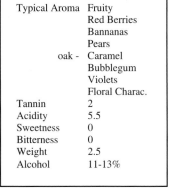

Typical Aroma	Fruity
	Red Berries
	Bannanas
	Pears
oak -	Caramel
	Bubblegum
	Violets
	Floral Charac.
Tannin	2
Acidity	5.5
Sweetness	0
Bitterness	0
Weight	2.5
Alcohol	11-13%

Fig. 7.10. Gamay Tannin to Acid sensory ratios.   Fig. 7.11. Gamay sensory summary.

Grenache

Grenache, the work horse of blends in Spain and the Rhône Valley, is one of the most widely planted grapes in the world and is responsible for a large proportion of production and therefore an important grape to discuss. Both red and white varieties exist. The white is called Grenache Blanc and the red Grenache Noir or simply Grenache.

Synonyms: 'Garnacho' exists as a name primarily in Navarra, but 'Garnacha' is the common name in the rest of Spain. Other synonyms: Lladoner, Tinto, Tinto Aragones, Granaccia, Carignan Rosso, Rousillon Tinto, Grenacha, Alicante, Carignane Rousse and others.

Areas Found: Grenache is found in most growing regions from Chile, Argentina, South Africa, Australia, US, Algeria, Spain, France, Italy to Hungary.

Wine Styles and Blends:
Found as a blended variety, very seldom as a single variety. In Rhône it can represent as much as 60% of a blend and in Rioja and Navarra in Spain it can reach up to 80%. It is usually blended with Tempranillo, Syrah, Cabernet Sauvignon, Nebbiolo and others.

Grape Physiology:
Vigour: Very productive. Grenache grows well in warm climatic conditions and various soil types. The long growing season produces high sugar levels with low acid and tannin.

Phenology: Ripens in late season but buds early. At full maturity the average sugar content is from 24° to 27° Brix / Balling (total dissolved compounds in grape juice and sugar concentration) and total titratable acid of 4.5 to 6 g/l.

Berries: Small in size, with a medium to thick skin with lower anthocyan (pigments) levels resulting in poorer hues. The berry has an off-round, oval shape grape with a blackish color.

Diseases: Susceptible to downy mildew, botrytis (bunch rot), moths, insects and birds because of the overly fruity grape with high sugar levels and low acid and tannin content.

Sensory Characteristics:
Appearance:
Grenache is paler than most wines. It is usually blended; therefore, in a young Rioja wine it will have a medium to light tone with a ruby-red hue and a moderate gradient. The wines start to change color after the 3rd year. In blends with Syrah from Rhône with 89/90 points the wines are almost black, but a rim color of blue-purple-red can be found. The wines start to change color after the 5th year in southern Rhône. Good mature wines develop an orange brick-colored rim in about their 8th to 10th year.

The Nose:
Grenache is responsible for the fruitiness and 'flesh' in the wine. It has lots of ripe dark berries with lavender, red berries, plums and rosemary characteristics. Trademark characters would be lavender, rosemary and other spices.

The Palate:
The acidity and balance as per the ratio chart (3.3/10 for tannin and 5/10 for acid). Grenache can produce very alcoholic, rich wines with some of the highest alcohol levels possible, using normal yeast and under normal fermentation conditions. The alcohol levels range from as little as 12.5% but can reach as high as 16%.

Excellent Food Combinations:
This would naturally depend upon the blend and whether or not one is in Rioja or Rhône.

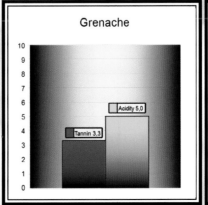

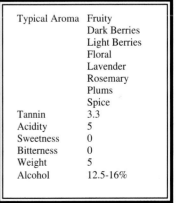

Typical Aroma	Fruity
	Dark Berries
	Light Berries
	Floral
	Lavender
	Rosemary
	Plums
	Spice
Tannin	3.3
Acidity	5
Sweetness	0
Bitterness	0
Weight	5
Alcohol	12.5-16%

Fig. 7.12. Grenache Tannin to Acid sensory ratios.   *Fig. 7.13. Grenache sensory summary.*

Malbec

Malbec, known throughout the world, is actually a synonym for Côt. It is traditionally one of the grapes approved in the Bordeaux blend and used in very small quantities. Although not grown extensively, this grape does have good potential, if handled correctly.

Synonyms: Malbeck, Noir de Pressac, Pressac, Auxerrois, Cahors, Pied Rouge, Jacobain and Grifforin.

Areas Found: Malbec has gained a reputation for quality Cahors in the southwest of France but is also found in small quantities in the Bordeaux blend. In Côte de Bourg and Côte de Blaye it is grown and blended in much larger proportions, compared to the left bank of the Gironde. It is the third largest grown variety in Argentina, where it produces some good full-bodied wines. It is also found in South Africa, Chile, Australia and California.

Wine Styles and Blends:
Found as a single variety and a blend, Malbec produces very fruity wines. As a single variety it provides full-bodied, coarser and greener wine styles almost like a Merlot, but with more tannin. Malbec is usually blended with Cabernet Sauvignon, Merlot, Petit Verdot, Tannat, Gamay, Cabernet Franc.

Grape Physiology:
Vigour: Moderate. It produces yields of about 45 hl/ha. Grows well on gravel with good drainage.

Phenology: Ripens in mid-season, so it is a good grape for cooler weather climates, where summers are shorter. At full maturity the average sugar content is from 22.5° to 24.5° Brix / Balling (total dissolved compounds in grape juice and sugar concentration) and total titratable acid of 5.6 to 7.2 g/l.

Berries: Small to medium in size and with a thick skin. The berry is round in shape with a bluish-black color.

Diseases: Susceptible to a number of diseases, frost, rot and poor berry set.

Sensory Characteristics:
Appearance:
Malbec has a dark red hue, almost black which comes from its thick, pigment-rich skin. The tone gradient is very tight but tends to change hue rather early in comparison with its color. A young wine would start to change color after the 5th to 6th year. Good mature wines develop an orange brick-colored rim already around their 8th-9th year.

The Nose:
Malbec is very fruity with characteristics such as blackberry, mulberry, plum, prune, blackcurrant, liquorices and even hints of eucalyptus on occasion. It is usually aged in oak.

The Palate:
Known for its backbone of tannin, Malbec usually displays hard 'coarse tannins' and is balanced as per the ratio chart above (7.5/10 for tannin and 6/10 for acid). The alcohol levels range from 12% to 14%.

Excellent Food Combinations:
Best suited to spicy meat dishes, stews, pizza and many other daily home-made dishes.

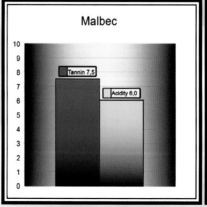

Typical Aroma	Blackberry
	Mulberry
	Plum
	Prune
	Blackcurrant
	Liquorice
	Eucalyptus
Tannin	7.5
Acidity	6
Sweetness	0
Bitterness	0
Weight	7
Alcohol	12-14%

Fig. 7.14. Malbec Tannin to Acid sensory ratios.   Fig. 7.15. Malbec sensory summary.

Merlot

If Cabernet Sauvignon is the 'King' of grapes then Merlot must be the 'Queen'. It can produce up to 70 hectoliters per hectar, but higher quality vineyards do a 'green harvest' pruning away of about 50% of the yield. At harvest this relates to about a 30% reduction during the summer so as to concentrate fruit quality. Most Bordeaux Châteaux feel that a quality harvest is optimized at around 35-39 hl/ha. *Synonyms:* Crabutet, Bigney, Vitraille, Merlau, Sémillon Rouge and Médoc Noir.

Areas Found: Originally from Bordeaux the grape is grown around the world and in almost all wine-producing regions. It is the most planted variety in the Bordeaux region and the third largest variety in France. Château Pétrus in Pomerol can demand the highest prices in the world for a Merlot-wine.

Wine Styles and Blends:
Found as a single varietal or can be blended. The Classic Bordeaux blend includes Merlot with Cabernet Sauvignon, Cabernet Franc, Petit Verdot and even Malbec. Other varieties known to be blended with Merlot are Grenache, Sangiovese, Shiraz and Tempranillo.

Grape Physiology:
Vigour: Medium to good but Merlot is sensitive to both dry weather and rain. Moderate to high yields.

Phenology: Ripens in mid-season so can be prone to weather fluctuations. At full maturity the sugar is from 23° to 24.5° Brix / Balling and total titratable acid of 6 to 7 g/l.

Berries: Medium size, round, blackish color and thin skinned.

Diseases: Susceptible to botrytis and downy mildew. Because of its thin skin it has a low resistance to botrytis infection if planted in fertile soils and if temperature and humidity conditions are less advantageous.

Sensory Characteristics:
Appearance:
In good young wines, Merlot displays a deep tone with a tight gradient from the bowl to rim. In 89/90-point wines it has a dark bluish-purple-red hue in young wines and gradually starts to change color around the 3rd to 4th year. Good mature wines develop an orange brick-colored rim in about their 8th to 10th year. Classic wines only begin to change color around the 8th year and brick-red hue at about their 12th to 15th year.

The Nose:
Fruitcake and more fruitcake is what you should be looking for in Merlot. It has a smooth, heavy, fruity nose of mixed spices with characters such as plums, currants and raisins. With some ageing you'll find vegetable, barnyard, mushrooms and hay tones. In oak-matured wines you can find characters of cigar box, vanilla, chocolate and tobacco. The signature trait of plums still remains a major component. New world styles have a mint/eucalyptus nose in addition to the above characters.

The Palate:
In Bordeaux wines, the taste will have a substantial backbone of tannin when young and high acid, usually balanced as per the ratio chart above (5/10 for tannin and 6.5/10 for acid). Merlot has softer, sweeter, warmer characters on the palate. It can produce complex wines with a very good length. Alcohol levels from 11% - 14%.

Excellent Food Combinations:
Matches very well with dark meat dishes but also with duck, goose and turkey. Young fruit-driven wines should be served with meat dishes, while mature wines go better with gourmet cooking, heavier meats or wild dishes.

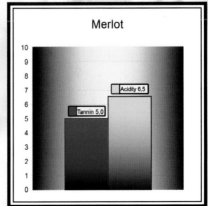

Typical Aroma	Dark Berries
	Plums
	Heavy Fruit
	Mixed Spices
oak -	Tobacco
oak -	Cedar
	Raspberry
	Cherry
	Currants
Tannin	5
Acidity	6.5
Sweetness	0
Bitterness	Can be burnt
Weight	7 to 9
Alcohol	11-14%

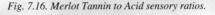

Fig. 7.16. Merlot Tannin to Acid sensory ratios.   *Fig. 7.17. Merlot sensory summary.*

Nebbiolo

In Italy, Nebbiolo is the 'King' of grapes. Nebbiolo produces full-bodied wines that can be cellared for many decades and in par with the best wines in the world. It was the first candidate to be considered for the Denominazione d'Origine Controllata e Garantita (D.O.C.G.) designation in 1963.

Synonyms:
Spanna, Spana, Pugnet, Picotener, Nebbiolo Canavesano and Chiavennasca.

Areas Found:
Nebbiolo's home is Piedmont in northwest Italy but it can be found in other areas in Italy too. It is also found in the USA, Chile, Argentina and South Africa.

Wine Styles and Blends:
Usually found as a single varietal. There are two distinct styles of Nebbiolo. To try to convince one or the other about which style is better is just like trying to argue with winemakers in Chablis in regard to whether they should or should not use oak barrels during maturation. Nebbiolo's two styles have anything to do with oak barrels, as is Chablis, but instead oxidative and anaerobic winemaking procedures. The old style uses oxidative techniques when producing their wines, while the newer avoids it. I like them both.

Grape Physiology:
Vigour: Very productive and can grow almost anywhere but does well in the calcareous soils of Piedmont. Good yields about 55 hl/ha.

Phenology: Ripens in late mid-season. At full maturity the average sugar content is from 23° to 25° Brix / Balling (total dissolved compounds in grape juice and sugar concentration) and total titratable acid of 6 to 7 g/l.

Berries: Small in size with a very thick skin and excellent phenolic qualities. The berries are round in shape and the grape has a blue-black color.

Diseases: Due to its very thick skin and small berries it is resistant to almost all parasites and infections but susceptible to odium.

Sensory Characteristics:
Appearance:
Nebbiolo has a tight gradient and a very dark, deep blue-black color when young. The oxidative tends to change color rather early at about its 5th year but the anaerobic style begins to change at around the 8 to 10 year mark.

The Nose:
Nebbiolo offers an orgy of aromas which include plums, tar, cherries, violets, liquorices, mushrooms, blackberries, black-pepper and mint. Trademark characters would be plums, tar, violets and mint.

The Palate:
The tannin to acidity balanced as per the ratio chart above (10/10 for tannin and 7/10 for acid). Nebbiolo is by far one of the world's mighty full-bodied wines. Nebbiolo produces wines with complexity and elegance and has excellent fruit, acid and tannin balance ratios. The alcohol levels range from as little as 12.5% to 14.5%.

Excellent Food Combinations:
Older wines (about 20 years) should be served with a cheese and dried meat plate. Younger wines should be accompanied by game or beef.

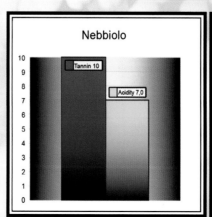

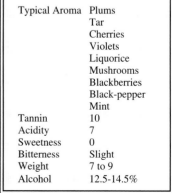

Typical Aroma	Plums
	Tar
	Cherries
	Violets
	Liquorice
	Mushrooms
	Blackberries
	Black-pepper
	Mint
Tannin	10
Acidity	7
Sweetness	0
Bitterness	Slight
Weight	7 to 9
Alcohol	12.5-14.5%

Fig. 7.18. Nebbiolo Tannin to Acid sensory ratios.

Fig. 7.19. Nebbiolo sensory summary.

Pinotage

Professor Perold of Stellenbosch University created the Pinotage grape variety in the 1920s, by cross-pollinating the Pinot Noir with the Cinsaut grapes. This has led to many developments and in 1966 the Pinotage Society was formed to market and promote Pinotage internationally. A success story one might say. Pinotage accounts for about 6% of all plantings in South Africa.

Synonyms:

Not yet, but I am sure some will come in time.

Areas Found:

Naturally, Pinotage is found throughout South Africa but the top qualities usually come from Stellenbosch and Paarl. The Pinotage vine has also been exported to Zimbabwe, New Zealand, Germany, Argentina, Chile, Australia and now even the US.

Wine Styles and Blends:

Usually as a single variety but is also blended with Cabernet Sauvignon, Merlot and Shiraz. It is a medium-bodied wine with good storage and quality standards.

Grape Physiology:

Vigour: Moderate to good. Pinotage yields about 55 hl/ha. Pinotage is a very versatile grape and can grow on many soil types and in varied micro-climates. It grows well on most types of soils.

Phenology: Ripens in early season. At full maturity the average sugar content is from 22° to 24° Brix / Balling (total dissolved compounds in grape juice and sugar concentration) and total titratable acid of 5 to 7.8 g/l.

Berries: Small and oval. Thick strong skins and blue-black in color

Diseases: Susceptible to powdery mildew, downy mildew and botrytis.

Sensory Characteristics:

Appearance:

In good reds with c. 88-points the wines have a bluish/purple-red hue, a medium tone and semi-tight gradient. Pinotage starts to change color rather early in their 4th to 5th year. Good mature wines develop an orange brick-colored rim in about their 6th to 7th year.

The Nose:

Pinotage has a green young type association but displays good fruit and a nose of strawberries, raspberries, spices and an earthy type character.

The Palate:

Usually a number of post-nasal volatile characteristics, are evident, such as spice, cherry and strawberry. It has medium 'fine to coarse tannins' with a good acidity and balanced as per the ratio chart above (5/10 for tannin and 7.5/10 for acid). The alcohol levels range from 11.5% to 13.5%.

Excellent Food Combinations:

Matches best with spicy foods, beef, pork chops, lamb and even a good barbeque.

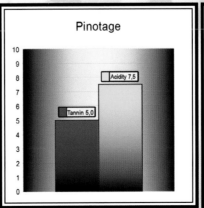

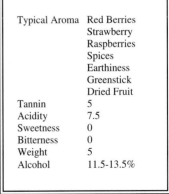

Typical Aroma	Red Berries
	Strawberry
	Raspberries
	Spices
	Earthiness
	Greenstick
	Dried Fruit
Tannin	5
Acidity	7.5
Sweetness	0
Bitterness	0
Weight	5
Alcohol	11.5-13.5%

Fig. 7.28. Pinotage Tannin to Acid sensory ratios.

Fig. 7.29. Pinotage sensory summary.

Pinot Noir

Thought to be one of the oldest grape varieties, Pinot Noir is one of the most challenging grapes to grow and can produce up to 30 hectoliters per hectar. Responds well to being planted on well-drained and calcareous soils. *Synonyms:* Pineau, Franc Pineau, Savagnin Noir, Morillon, (France); Spätburgunder, Blauburgunder, Klevener (Germany); Pinot Nero, Pignola (Italy); Nagyburgundi (Hungary).

Areas Found: The grape is at its best in Burgundy and Alsace but has established itself in many wine countries. Very good wines are now being produced in Washington State oregon and northern California in the US and South Africa, New Zealand and Germany, not to forget Chile. There are hundreds, if not thousands, of Pinot Noir clones in the world today, such as Pinot Blanc, Pinot Gris and Gamay. I would not be surprised if both Negro Amaro (Apulia, Italy) and Tempranillo (Spain) are old clones too.

Wine Styles and Blends:
Found as a single varietal or can be blended. Champagne grows more Pinot Noir than the whole of Burgundy. The reason for this is that it is one of the varieties in blended Champagne with Pinot Meunier and Chardonnay.

Grape Physiology:
Vigour: Moderate.
Phenology: Ripens in early-season, so it is a good grape for cold weather climates, where summers are relatively short. At full maturity the average sugar content is from 23° to 24° Brix / Balling (total dissolved compounds in grape juice and sugar concentration) and total titratable acid of 6 to 7 g/l.

Berries: Small in size with a thin skin. The berry is an off-round shape with a scarlet/violet/ blue color.

Diseases: Susceptible to downy mildew and weather changes. Because of its thin skin it has a low resistance.

Sensory Characteristics:
Appearance:
In young wines, Pinot Noir has a lighter tone with an extended gradient. In 89/90-point wines it has a light to medium purple/ruby-red hue in young wines and starts to change color already after the 2nd-3rd year. Good mature wines develop an orange brick-colored rim in about their 6th-8th year.

The Nose:
Pinot Noir has a wonderfully warm, spicy, red berry, strawberry, cherry, raspberry and floral character when young. Very good wines display, along with red berries, violets, a nuance of chocolate, vegetables and spices as they age. Oak characters would be evident in oak-matured wines. The signature trait of strawberries and red berries still remains a major identifying character. New world styles also have dark-berry fruit along with the above characters.

The Palate:
In northern Burgundy Pinot Noir wines can have more tannin as shown here. Usually soft 'fine tannins' and good underlying acidity and balanced as per the ratio chart above (5/10 for tannin and 7.5/10 for acid). Pinot Noir can produce very delicate and elegant wines with a very good length. Alcohol levels from 12% to 13%.

Excellent Food Combinations:
Pinot Noir can be served well with light meats, various bird dishes (goose, duck and chicken) and textured fish dishes like salmon. It is excellent with foie gras, cheese and pâté too. Although other wine professionals suggest wild deer and darker meats with a Pinot Noir, I tend not to prefer these, as I feel that other wine styles suits them better and that the marked acidity levels of Pinot Noir highlight more delicate dishes very well.

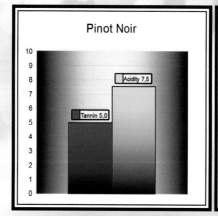

Fig. 7.20. Pinot Noir Tannin to Acid sensory ratios.

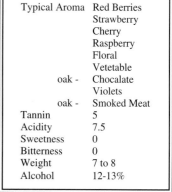

Typical Aroma	Red Berries
	Strawberry
	Cherry
	Raspberry
	Floral
	Vetegable
oak -	Chocalate
	Violets
oak -	Smoked Meat
Tannin	5
Acidity	7.5
Sweetness	0
Bitterness	0
Weight	7 to 8
Alcohol	12-13%

Fig. 7.21. Pinot Noir sensory summary.

Sangiovese

If Nebbiolo is the 'King' of grapes in Italy then Sangiovese must be the Queen. Sangiovese producers many styles from average to excellent wines. Sangiovese, Jupiter's Blood, is Italy's most widely planted grape variety. **Synonyms:** Sangiovese Grosso: Dolce, Sangiovese Gentile, Sangiovese Toscano, Calabrese, Sanvicetro, Prugnolo (Montepulciano), Brunello (Montalcino). Sangiovese Piccolo: Sangiovese di Romagna, San Gioveto, Sangiovese del Verrucchio.

Areas Found:

Sangiovese is found throughout the winemaking world today. In Italy Sangiovese Piccolo is found in the southern regions and Sangiovese Grosso in north and central Italy (Tuscany; Chianti Classico, Vino Nobile di Montepuciano, Brunello di Montalcino, etc.). Also found in the US, Chile, Argentina and South Africa.

Wine Styles and Blends:

Sangiovese is found as a single varietal and blend. As a single variety it producers elegant wines, which are just perfect matches with food, antipasto and cheese. Sangiovese is blended mainly with Cabernet Sauvignon but also Merlot, Caniolo, Colorino, Mammolo. Interestingly enough, two white varieties, Malvasia and Trebbiano, are also blended into the reds. Sangiovese Piccolo is usually responsible for the myriad of table wines and Sangiovese Grosso for the more classical style.

Grape Physiology:

Vigour: Average. Needs well-drained soils to produce good quality, otherwise ripening is uneven. Sangiovese prefers a calcareous clay type soil base. Moderate yields of about 60 hl/ha.

Phenology: Ripens in late mid-season. At full maturity the average sugar content is from 23° to 24° Brix / Balling (total dissolved compounds in grape juice and sugar concentration) and TA of 5.5 to 7.2 g/l.

Berries: Small if Piccolo and large if Grosso. Grosso has thick skins and Piccolo thin and they produce good phenolic qualities. The berries are round in shape and the grape has a reddish-blue-black color.

Diseases: Sangiovese Grosso has good resistant capabilities, but Sangiovese Piccolo with the thinner skin can be susceptible to rot.

Sensory Characteristics:
Appearance:

Better clones of Sangiovese have a deeper color and a tighter gradient. Sangiovese is usually lighter in tone than a Cabernet Sauvignon. The color starts to change early at about its 4th to 5th year and can result in an orangey-brick-red hue already in the 8th year.

The Nose:

Sangiovese has a warm spicy nose with cherries, red berries, nuts, cloves and a slit mint character. Trademark characters would be cherries and spiciness.

The Palate:

The tannin to acidity balanced as per the ratio chart above (6/10 for tannin and 8/10 for acid). Sangiovese is a very good example of a medium- to full-bodied wine. They can produce wines with a lot of finesse and complexity. The alcohol levels range from as little as 12 % to 13.5%.

Excellent Food Combinations:

The balance of high acidity to tannin and the cherry, red berry characters help Sangiovese to be one of the best food to wine matches. It serves very well with veal, lamb and cheese plates, not to mention, various antipasto dishes.

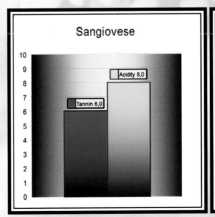

Fig. 7.22. Sangiovese Tannin to Acid sensory ratios.

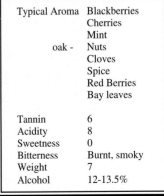

Typical Aroma	Blackberries
	Cherries
	Mint
oak -	Nuts
	Cloves
	Spice
	Red Berries
	Bay leaves
Tannin	6
Acidity	8
Sweetness	0
Bitterness	Burnt, smoky
Weight	7
Alcohol	12-13.5%

Fig. 7.23. Sangiovese sensory summary.

Syrah / Shiraz

One of the oldest and noblest of grape varieties. This grape grows best in poor soil, gravel, granite and even high temperatures. Full-bodied wines with powerful characteristics these wines are in high demand throughout the world and in most fashionable restaurants. **Synonyms:** Shiraz is almost as common as Syrah. Shiras, Sirac, Syra, Syrac, Sirah, Petite Syrah, Marsanne Noir, Serine, Balsamnina.

Areas Found: Syrah has its origin in Persia (Iran) some 14,000 years ago and is one of the oldest grape known. The high quality wines gained their reputation from France's Northern Rhône region: Cornas, Côte-Rôtie, Crozes-Hermitage, Hermitage, Saint-Joseph and even Gigondas. Australia is also well known for its contribution to this famous grape with many fine vintages but now even South Africa and the USA are hot on their heels. It is also produced in Argentina, Chile and New Zealand.

Wine Styles and Blends:
Found as a single varietal or can be blended. If not a single variety it is usually blended with Grenache, Cinsault, Cabernet Sauvignon, Merlot and in Southern Rhône twelve other grapes which make up the blend of a typical Châteauneuf-du-Pape.

Grape Physiology:
Vigour: Very Good. Syrah grows well in various climatic conditions and soil types.

Phenology: Ripens in mid-season so it is a good grape for cold weather climates where summers are relatively short. At full maturity the average sugar content is from 24° to 25° Brix / Balling (total dissolved compounds in grape juice and sugar concentration) and total titratable acid of 6 to 7 g/l.

Berries: Small to medium in size, with a thick skin. The berry is off-round to oval shape with a blue-black color.

Diseases: Because of its thick skin it has an unusually high resistance to diseases.

Sensory Characteristics:

Appearance:
In young wines, Syrah has a very dark to black tone with a very tight gradient. In 89/90-point wines it is almost black but a rim color of blue-purple-red can be found. The wines start to change color after the 5th year, but in Rhône this can take another 2 to 3 years. Good mature wines develop an orange brick-colored rim in about their 12th year.

The Nose:
Gamy, meaty, leather, mixed spices, black-pepper (trademark), dark berries, tar, rubber, blackcurrants and earthy are some of the characters found in young Syrah wines. In mature 90-point wines these powerful characters blend together to form an elegance of power and finesse.

The Palate:
In northern Rhône, Syrah wines can have more of a heavy backbone of tannin, as shown above. Syrah wines from Southern Rhône, Australia, South Africa are usually softer 'fine tannins' and good underlying acidity and balanced as per the ratio chart above (8.55/10 for tannin and 6/10 for acid). Syrah can produce alcoholic rich wines with an unusual elegance and very good length. The alcohol levels range from 12.5% to 14.5%.

Excellent Food Combinations:
Syrah demands a rich powerful dish of beef or wild meat, such as venison, boar or Chateaubriand with reduced sauces. It is also excellent with some aromatic cheeses.

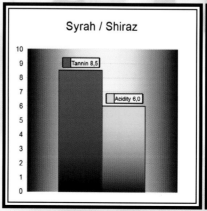

Fig. 7.24. Syrah Tannin to Acid sensory ratios.

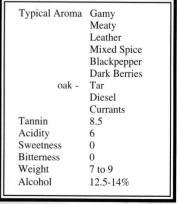

Typical Aroma	Gamy
	Meaty
	Leather
	Mixed Spice
	Blackpepper
	Dark Berries
oak -	Tar
	Diesel
	Currants
Tannin	8.5
Acidity	6
Sweetness	0
Bitterness	0
Weight	7 to 9
Alcohol	12.5-14%

Fig. 7.25. Syrah sensory summary.

Tempranillo

One of the noble grape varieties in the world. Tempranillo is Spain's most grown grape variety, which produces high quality wines of various styles. It is the major grape in the Rioja blend and has many simularities to Pinot Noir and Cabernet Franc. **Synonyms:** Ull de Llebre, Ojo de Liebe, Cencibel, Tinto Fino, Tinto Madrid, Tempranilla, Tempranillo de la Rioga, Grenache de Logrono, Tinto del Pais, Tinot Roriz and Tinot de Toro.

Areas Found:
Tempranillo was originally brought to Santiago de Compostela, Spain, by French pilgrims in northern France. Tempranillo's home is Rioja, but it is also grown in Portugal in large volumes and is known as Tinot Roriz. It is one of the grapes in Port and also found in Argentina, Chile and even South Africa.

Wine Styles and Blends:
Found as a single varietal and often in a blend. A 100% Tempranillo is very similar in characteristics to Pinot Noir. It is usually blended with Granacha or Cabernet Sauvignon in Rioja. Well-made Rioja wines containing Tempranillo can be aged for well over 30 years. The use of American oak barrels is standard in Rioja and French in Penedes.

Grape Physiology:
Vigour: Low vigour and yields bout 35 hl/ha. Grows well on calcareous soils.

Phenology: Ripens in mid-season, so it is a good grape for cold weather climates where summers are relatively short. At full maturity the average sugar content is from 21° to 24° Brix / Balling (total dissolved compounds in grape juice and sugar concentration) and TA of 6 to 7 g/l.

Berries: Medium in size with a thin to medium skins. The berry has a slight off-round shape with a bluish to black color.

Diseases: Susceptible to powdery mildew and downy mildew.

Sensory Characteristics:
Appearance:
In young wines, Tempranillo has a tight

gradient almost identical to a heavy macerated Pinot Noir from Fixin in northern Burgundy. Tempranillo tends to hold its tone and hue for at least 5 to 6 years. In 89/90-point wines it has a deep to dark, bluish-ruby-red hue, which in young wines starts to change in their 5th to 6th year. Good mature wines develop an orange brick-colored rim in about their 10th to 12th year.

The Nose:
If in Rioja and aged in American oak, the wine will have a warm, fruity, creamy-type character with hints of strawberry, dill, cherry, butter and spice. In wines aged in French oak the warm creaminess disappears but all the other characters remain. The trademark characteristics for Tempranillo are vanilla and dill.

The Palate:
If heavily macerated the wines could have an equal balance of tannin to acid but under normal conditions Tempranillo produces more acid than tannin. Usually medium 'fine tannins' with a good acidity and balanced as per the ratio chart above (5/10 for tannin and 7/10 for acid). Tempranillo can produce very delicate and elegant wines with a very good length. The alcohol levels range from 11% to 13.5%.

Excellent Food Combinations:
Aged Tempranillo should be served with elegant dishes as aged Bordeaux and Burgundy. Young wines go well with beef and lamb.

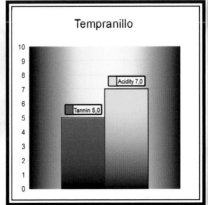

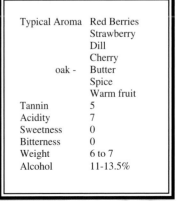

Typical Aroma	Red Berries
	Strawberry
	Dill
	Cherry
oak -	Butter
	Spice
	Warm fruit
Tannin	5
Acidity	7
Sweetness	0
Bitterness	0
Weight	6 to 7
Alcohol	11-13.5%

Fig. 7.26. Tempranillo Tannin to Acid sensory ratios.   *Fig. 7.27. Tempranillo sensory summary.*

Zinfandel

Ask an Italian and he'll tell you that Zinfandel is actually the Primitivo variety grown in southern Italy. Ask an American and they'll say California. Origin aside, Zinfandel is a winemaker's dream, it is very versitile grape and one which can produce many different styles from white and light roses to sparkling, full-bodied red wines and even Port. Zinfandel is also affectionately called just Zin. **Synonyms:** Primitivo, Primativo (Italy). **Areas Found:** Zinfandel in found in small plantings in South Africa, Chile, Argentina and Australia and in a larger use in the Puglia region.

Wine Styles and Blends:
Found as a single varietal or can be blended. If not a single variety, it blends with Syrah, Cabernet Sauvignon, Merlot and sometimes Grenache. Zinfandel comes in many styles, one of which is White Zinfandel which is fruity flavored (rose – ranges from a light to dark pink). Found also as a sparkling wine and can vary considerably in residual sugar. Fortified wine, a port style of usually very good quality and light, medium and full-bodied red wines too.

Grape Physiology:
Vigour: Very Good. Zinfandel grows well in warm but not too hot climatic conditions and various soil types.

Phenology: Ripens in mid to late-season. The only problem is that it ripens unevenly, which can cause problems during harvesting. At full maturity the average sugar content is from 24° to 26° Brix / Balling (total dissolved compounds in grape juice and sugar concentration) and total titratable acid of 5.5 to 7 g/l.

Berries: Small in size, with a medium to thick skin. The berry is off-round to oval in shape with a blue-black color.

Diseases: Susceptible bunch rot if irrigated. Otherwise, due to its thick skin, it has high resistance to diseases.

Sensory Characteristics:
Appearance:
In young quality wines, Zinfandel has a very dark to black tone with a very tight gradient. In 89/90-point wines it is almost black with a rim color of blue-purple-red. The wines start to change color after the 3rd year in central California, but in Napa and Sonoma Valleys this color change can take another 2-3 years. Good mature wines develop an orange brick-colored rim in about their 8th year.

The Nose:
Blackberries, black cherries, ginger, rose-hip, cloves, mixed spices, dark berries, tar, rubber, black-currants are some of the typical characters found in good quality zinfandels. Trademark identifying characters are ginger and cloves with a slight greenstick aroma. In mature 90-point wines these powerful characters blend together to form an elegance of power and finesse.

The Palate:
In northern California the wines can have slightly more tannin and acidity than in the central region. The acidity is in balance with tannin as per the ratio chart above (6/10 for tannin and 7/10 for acid). Zinfandel can produce high alcohol wines with an unusual elegance and very good length. The alcohol levels range from 12.5% to 15%.

Excellent Food Combinations:
The spread of wine styles available from Zinfandel also provide good possibilities for combining Zinfandel with various foods. Top class red wines need to be consumed with red or wild meats.

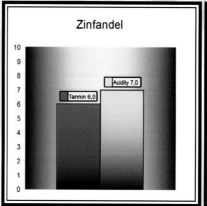

Fig. 7.30. Zinfandel Tannin to Acid sensory ratios.

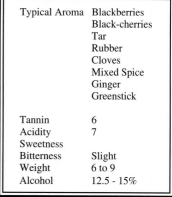

Typical Aroma	Blackberries
	Black-cherries
	Tar
	Rubber
	Cloves
	Mixed Spice
	Ginger
	Greenstick
Tannin	6
Acidity	7
Sweetness	
Bitterness	Slight
Weight	6 to 9
Alcohol	12.5 - 15%

Fig. 7.31. Zinfandel sensory summary.

Aligoté

Aligoté does not have the reputation of the Chardonnay grape, but it can produce some very good wines, resembling something between a dry un-oaked (un-wooded) Chablis and a Pinot Blanc, but with slightly more acidity. **Synonyms:** Bourgogne Aligoté, Chaudenet, Giboudot Blanc, Griset Blanc, Plant Gris and Troyen. **Areas Found:** With its home in Burgundy, France, Aligoté has spread to California, Australia, South Africa, Bulgaria, Hungary and most of the former east European states, where it was very popular.

Wine Styles and Blends:
In most cases Aligoté is found as a single variety, but it can be used as a good blending wine due to its high acidity. In the majority of cases it is vinified and matured in steel, but on occasion it meets some oak. It is at its best in Côte d'Or, where about 1/3 of France's plantings can be found. In Bulgaria and Hungary you'll be able to find Aligoté as a sparkling wine, a medium-bodied wine with good acidity.

Grape Physiology:
Vigour: Very good. Yields about 60 hl/ha. It thrives on a variety of soil types.

Phenology: Ripens in late early mid-season, so it is well adapted to cooler climate conditions. At full maturity the average sugar content is from 20° to 24° Brix/Balling and total acid of 7 to 8 g/l.

Berries: Small to medium in size, with a medium skin thickness, the berries are round with a medium pale-green color.

Diseases: Resistant to many insects but susceptible to Downey mildew.

Sensory Characteristics:
Appearance: Varies from pale-yellow to a straw-yellow hue with a greenish tint when young, with and without carbonation. It has a wide gradient. Initial changes in the hue can be detected in the 3rd year proceeding to light amber by the 4th to 5th year.

The Nose: Trademark characters are marked by young acidic citrus fruit such as Granny Smith apples, grapefruit and oranges and can show a slight oxidative nuttiness with almonds. Oaked Aligoté-wines have a slightly heavier nose with a yeastiness and more nutty almond characters as well as a slight creamy vanilla of oak.

The Palate: Unoaked Aligoté-wines are dry, fresh and similar in style to light to medium-bodied unoaked Chardonnay. A semi-sweet version can be found in east Europe.

Dry no-oak sensory ratios:
Acidity **7.5**, Fullness **4**, *Sweetness* **1**, *Bitterness* **1**.
Alcohol Levels. 11.5-12.5%

Dry oak aged sensory ratios:
Acidity **7**, Fullness **5.2**, *Sweetness* **2**, *Bitterness* **1**.
Abv. 11.5-12.8%

Sparkling sensory ratios:
Acidity **7**, Fullness **5.5**, *Sweetness* **3**, *Bitterness* **1**.
Abv. 11.5-12%

Excellent Food Combinations:
A perfect table wine, Aligoté can complement the majority of fish dishes, light meat and matured cheeses.

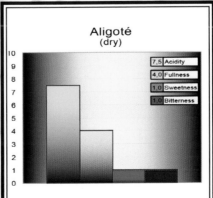

Typical Aroma	Citrus
	GS Apples
	Grapefruit
	Oranges
oak -	Nuttiness
oak -	Almonds
	Yeast
Tannin	1
Acidity	7 to 7.5
Sweetness	1 to 3
Bitterness	1
Weight	4 to 5.5
Alcohol	11.5-12.5%

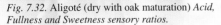

Fig. 7.32. Aligoté (dry with oak maturation) *Acid, Fullness and Sweetness sensory ratios.*   *Fig. 7.32.5.* Aligoté (dry no oak maturation) *Acid, Fullness and Sweetness sensory ratios.*   *Fig. 7.33.* Aligoté *sensory summary.*

Chardonnay

If the 'King' of black grapes is Cabernet Sauvignon then the 'King' of white grapes is without a doubt Chardonnay.

Synonyms: Pinot Chardonnay, Chardennet, Chaudenay, Pinot Blanc à Cramant, Epinette, Arnaison, Rousseau, Rousssot, Mâconnais, Petite Sainte-Marie, Melon d'Arbois, Petit Chatey, Aubaine, Gelber Weissburgunder, Weisser Clevner.

Areas Found: Chardonnay is everywhere but excellent in Burgundy, Napa Valley, Sonoma County, Mendocino County oregon, Washington State, Western and Southern Australia, Hawkes Bay New Zealand, Austria and Constantia South Africa. There are literally hundreds of other areas that produce very good Chardonnays.

Wine Styles and Blends:
Chardonnay is almost always a single blend, unless you consider Champagne, where it is blended with Pinot Meunier and Pinot Noir. It makes a range of wines from sweet to bone-dry with and without oak.

Grape Physiology:
Vigour: Moderate. Chardonnay yields about 55 hl/ha. Chardonnay is a very versatile grape and can grow on many soil types but not wet and too fertile. It thrives on calcareous soils and in both warm and cold climates.

Phenology: Ripens in early mid-season. At full maturity the average sugar content is from 19° to 26° Brix / Balling (total dissolved compounds in grape juice and sugar concentration) and TA of 5 to 7 g/l.

Berries: Small and round with a pale green to yellow hue and thin, tough and transparent skins.

Diseases: Susceptible to powdery mildew and botrytis.

Sensory Characteristics:
Appearance: Good, young and oaked Chardonnays with 88-points t should display an oily golden-yellow, greenish tint hue, with a deeper tone and displaying a semi-tight gradient. Good oaked Chardonnay can start to change color in their 4th to 5th year. Good mature wines develop an amber-orange colored hue after about their 8th to 10th year. Unoaked wines are usually not as viscous.

The Nose: Quite difficult to pinpoint as it is planted worldwide adapting to various climate conditions and vinification techniques: Unoaked (mainly in France); sharper acidity, spicy, citrus nose with underlying butter from the oak. Oaked (in warm climates); Chardonnay displays a richer, fuller, exotic fruity nose with pineapples, mangoes, leeches and a marked buttery nutty character.

The Palate: Young, it is easy to drink as it has an instant appeal of fruit with a marked steely acidity, if Chablis or Washington State. In warmer climates, Chardonnay will be full, ripe and rounder in character, but always having a viscous flavor of buttery Chardonnay. The flavor can sometimes be lost as the high alcohol overpowers the wine's fruitiness. Oaked; rich with creamy vanilla, oak and spice characters.

Sweet Botrytis (Austria)
Acidity **7.5**, Fullness **8**, *Sweetness* **8**. Abv. 12.8%

Excellent Food Combinations:
Chardonnay is great with fish, spicy foods, chicken, pork chops, lamb and a good barbeque.

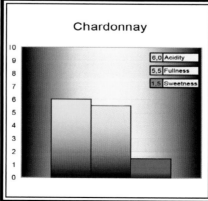

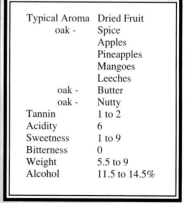

Typical Aroma	Dried Fruit
oak -	Spice
	Apples
	Pineapples
	Mangoes
	Leeches
oak -	Butter
oak -	Nutty
Tannin	1 to 2
Acidity	6
Sweetness	1 to 9
Bitterness	0
Weight	5.5 to 9
Alcohol	11.5 to 14.5%

Fig. 7.34. Chardonnay (oak maturation) Acid, Fullness and Sweetness sensory ratios.

Fig. 7.34.5. Chardonnay (no oak maturation) Acid, Fullness and Sweetness sensory ratios.

Fig. 7.35. Chardonnay sensory summary.

Chenin Blanc

Chenin Blanc is the most characteristic grape variety of the central Loire Valley in France. It acquired its name from Mont-Chenin in the Touraine district around the fifteenth century. **Synonyms:** Blanc d'Anjou, Confort, Pineau d' Anjou, Pineau de Briollay, Pineau de la Loire, Pineau de Savennières and Steen.

Areas Found: Originally the best examples came from the Central Loire Valley in France, but today 23% of South Africa's vineyards are planted with Steen (Chenin Blanc) along with the US, New Zealand, Australia, Chile, Argentina and Italy.

Wine Styles and Blends:
Chenin Blanc was traditionally an unoaked grape variety, but in South Africa there are excellent oak-aged wines. It varies in style from bone-dry to sweet wines, white port, sherry, sparkling and even brandy. It is in the majority of cases a single variety but, due to its high acidity, it can be blended with Chardonnay or Sauvignon Blanc.

Grape Physiology:
Vigour: Very vigorous. Yields about 45 hl/ha. It is very versatile on many soil types and climate conditions.

Phenology: Ripens in mid-season. At full maturity the average sugar content of 19°-25° Brix / Balling and TA of 6.8 - 8 g/l.

Berries: Small, oval, rich, green hue and thin skin.
Diseases: Very susceptible to botrytis infection and also Powdery mildew and Downey mildew.
Sensory Characteristics:

Appearance: A light, pale, green-yellow to green-golden, color when young, with and without carbonation. It has a wide gradient with initial change in hue at the 4th year, proceeding to light amber by the 7th year. **Oaked** Chenin Blanc-wines are more viscous than non-wood-aged, they show a greenish straw-yellow hue when young and change color in their 4th to 5th year. Good mature wines develop a light amber hue after their 8th to 10th year.

The Nose: Trademark characters such as fresh citrus, grassy characters are found in dry wines, whereas the sweet wines offer a honeyed, apricot, peachy character always followed with a firm backbone of acidity; therefore, they can live for forty years or more. Unoaked wines have a sharper citrus nose than oaked, richer, as above, with weight and vanilla of oak.

The Palate: Unoaked wines have very high acidity levels. Dry wines are clean, uncomplicated with mineral and apply characters in the aftertaste. Sweet botrytis wines are fruity, encompassing apricots, honey, peaches and spice.

Dry un-oaked sensory ratios:
> Acidity **9.5**, Fullness **3**, Sweetness **1**, Abv. 11.5-12.5%

Dry oak aged sensory ratios:
> Acidity **9.5**, Fullness **4**, Sweetness **2**, Abv. 12.5-14%

Sweet botrytis oak aged sensory ratios:
> Acidity **8**, Fullness **5**, Sweetness **7**, Abv. 11.5-13%

Excellent Food Combinations:
Poached fish and delicate fish dishes in butter. Cheese plates with French artisan country cheeses like Epoisses and Comté are perfect combinations.

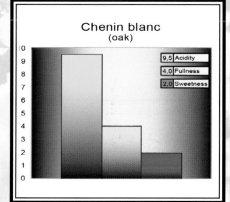

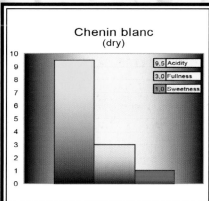

Typical Aroma	Citrus
	Peachy
	Apricot
oak -	Honey
	Acidic
	Grassy
	Melon
	Floral
	Slight Spice
Tannin	1
Acidity	9.5
Sweetness	1 to 8
Bitterness	0
Weight	3 to 5
Alcohol	11 to 14%

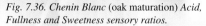

Fig. 7.36. Chenin Blanc (oak maturation) Acid, Fullness and Sweetness sensory ratios.   *Fig. 7.36.5. Chenin Blanc (no oak maturation) Acid, Fullness and Sweetness sensory ratios.*   *Fig. 7.37. Chenin Blanc sensory summary.*

Gewürztraminer

Gewürztraminer or Traminer is a pink-skinned grape variety originally from Germany where 'Gewürz' means spice. **Synonyms**: Traminer, Rotclevner, Savagnin Rosé, Gris Rouge, Clevner, Tramini, Heida and many other synonyms. **Areas Found**: Originally from the Pfalz region in Germany, the Gewürztraminer was introduced into Alsace after 1871 and can now be found in South Africa, Australia, New Zealand, Austria, California, Hungary, The Czech Republic, Romania, Italy and Switzerland. The wineries in Alsace produce the quality that all Gewürztraminers should be judged against.

Wine Styles and Blends:

Produces very aromatic wines, often described as spicy, but their complex bouquet can range from grapey-muskiness to a pungency-like pepper. It is at its best in Alsace, but the Austrians also make excellent sweet botrytis, which can last for 50 years or more. In Alsace they are almost perfect due to their rich, dry and sweet, aromatic, perfumed nose offering a complex and balanced wine . Usually only found as a single variety.

Grape Physiology:

Vigour: Moderate vigour. Yields about 50 hl/ha. It thrives on deep loam, clay type soils with a good mineral content.
Phenology: Ripens in mid-season. At maturity the average sugar is 20°-26° Brix/Balling and TA of 5-7.5 g/l.

Berries: Medium in size and oval. They have a pinkishred-copper hue and are used for white winemaking. Gewürztraminer has a medium skin thickness.

Diseases: Susceptible to noble rot (Botrytis cinerea).

Sensory Characteristics:
Appearance: Can range from a light copper to a deep yellow hue and very viscous. It has a medium to tight gradient. Initial changes in the hue are from the 3rd year proceeding to a darker copper -orange-amber hue by the 5th to 6th year. When maturated in oak it appears to be even more viscous and has a slightly darker gradient.

The Nose: Trademark characteristics for an Alsace Gewürztraminers are heady, weighty wines with exotic flavors of leeches, roses orange blossom orange peel, mixed spice and perfume. A spicy richness with a hit of marmalade-toffee, apricot, honey and smoky like characters. Oaked wines display characteristics as above with cream and vanilla.

The Palate: These wines can be both dry and sweet. High alcohol, full-bodied palate, sweet with a spicy character. Low in acidity. When dry, they are honeyed and powerful. Also described as impressive in their flavor concentration, but can just as easily be too heavy; potent wines lacking in acidity, sluggish and clinging on the palate, rather sipped than drunk.

Dry with oak sensory ratios:

Acidity **5.5**, Fullness **6**, *Sweetness* **1**, Bitterness **3**, Abv. 11.5-13.5%

Sweet with oak aged sensory ratios:

Acidity **5.8**, Fullness **6.8**, *Sweetness* **7**, Bitterness **3**, Abv. 12.5-14.5%

Excellent Food Combinations:

Perfect match for smoked salmon, grilled fish, spicy foods and even curry. A good Munster or Epoisses cheese along with some smoked meats is just wonderful with Gewürztraminer.

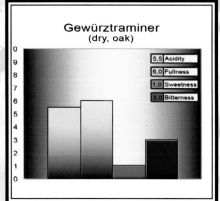

Fig. 7.38. Gewürztraminer (oak maturation) Acid, Fullness and Sweetness sensory ratios.

Fig. 7.38.5. Gewürztraminer (sweet with oak maturation) sensory ratios.

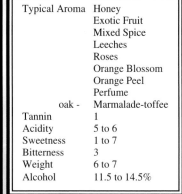

Typical Aroma	Honey
	Exotic Fruit
	Mixed Spice
	Leeches
	Roses
	Orange Blossom
	Orange Peel
	Perfume
oak -	Marmalade-toffee
Tannin	1
Acidity	5 to 6
Sweetness	1 to 7
Bitterness	3
Weight	6 to 7
Alcohol	11.5 to 14.5%

Fig. 7.39. Gewürztraminer sensory summary.

Grüner Veltliner

Grüner Veltliner is the most widely planted white variety in Austria and can give the Alsace wines a very good running for their money. They are complex in character with good citrus, spicy, fruity characters with high acidity levels. **Synonyms:** Grünmuskateller, Veltlini, Weissgipfler, Mouhardrebe, Manhardsrebe, Zleni Veltlinac, Veltlini and Grüner.

Areas Found: Its home being originally in Austria, Grüner Veltliner, provides excellent charismatic white wines. It can also be found in Hungary, the Czech Republic, Slovakia and Slovenia.

Wine Styles and Blends:
The Grüner Veltliner grape produces very good single variety wines and is also used as a blend on occasion with Chardonnay and Riesling. Depending upon the vineyard's style, a slight prickle of carbonic acid (CO_2) can sometimes be present in the wine.

Grape Physiology:
Vigour: Very good. Yields about 90 hl/ha. It thrives on a variety of soil types.

Phenology: Ripens in mid- to late season. At full maturity the average sugar content is from 19° to 23° Brix/Balling and total acid of 7 to 9 g/l.

Berries: Medium in size. The berries have a tough medium skin thickness.

Diseases: Resistant to many insects but susceptible to peronospera.

Sensory Characteristics:
Appearance: A greenish tint, pale-yellow hue with and without a slight carbonation. Viscous wines with a light to medium tone. Initial changes in the hue can be detected in the 4th year proceeding to light amber by the 6th to 7th year.

The Nose: Trademark characters are marked by a spicy, floral rose, fruity, citrus and mineral aroma with velvety acidic tones.

Grüner Veltliner which has undergone some oak maturation, usually 9-12 months, has an additional discrete smoky aroma with tones of apples, apricots, mango, honey, peaches and vanilla characters.

The Palate: Oaked wines are dry with low residual sugar and high acidity levels, but with a good viscous weight. The wines contain high acid with a medium to full-body displaying some good volatile aromatics. There can be a slight bitterness in the aftertaste.

Dry no-oak sensory ratios:
 Acidity 8, *Fullness* **5.5**, *Sweetness* **1**, *Bitterness* **0.5**, *Abv.*11.5-12.5%
Dry oak aged sensory ratios:
 Acidity 8, *Fullness* **7**, *Sweetness* **1**, *Bitterness* **0.5**, *Abv.* 12-12.8%

Excellent Food Combinations:
Excellent when served with shell-fish and other fish dishes. Complements many aromatic cheeses matured (aged 18 months or longer) with the exception of blue cheese.

Fig. 7.40. Grüner Veltliner (oak maturation) Acid, Fullness and Sweetness sensory ratios.

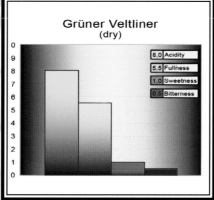

Fig. 7.40.5. Grüner Veltliner Acid, Fullness and Sweetness sensory ratios.

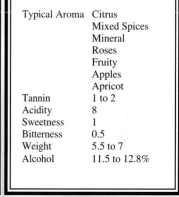

Typical Aroma	Citrus
	Mixed Spices
	Mineral
	Roses
	Fruity
	Apples
	Apricot
Tannin	1 to 2
Acidity	8
Sweetness	1
Bitterness	0.5
Weight	5.5 to 7
Alcohol	11.5 to 12.8%

Fig. 7.41. Grüner Veltliner sensory summary

Macabeo / Viura

Macabeo is the most widely planted white variety in Spain and the primary white grape in the Rioja region. **Synonyms:** Macabeu, Lardot and Alcanol. **Areas Found**: Its home being Spain, Viura can also be found in Languedoc-Rousillon in south France and Portugal.

Wine Styles and Blends:
The Viura grape produces both very good single varieties and is also used as a blend in both white, red and sparkling wines. The blend percentage in Spanish sparkling wines (CAVA) is usually 40/40/20 with the Viura or Macabeo, Parellada and Xarello varieities. They make a full range of sparkling wines from bone-dry to sweet and rosé. Dry steel-fermented wines usually range from dry to semi-dry and oaked or wooded wines, matured in oak, are usually dry. The Viura grape is known to be blended with Tempranillo (red), Malvasia, Chardonnay and even Sauvignon Blanc. Macabeo is a medium-bodied wine with high acidity.

Grape Physiology:
Vigour: Very good. Yields about 70 hl/ha. It thrives on a variety of soil types.

Phenology: Ripens in late season. At full maturity the average sugar content is from 19° to 23° Brix/Balling and total acid of 7 to 9 g/l.

Berries: Medium in size. The berries have a tough medium skin thickness.

Diseases: Resistant to many insects but susceptible to Downey mildew.

Sensory Characteristics:
Appearance: A greenish tint, pale-yellow, viscous with and without carbonation. It has a medium gradient. Initial changes in the hue can be detected in the 3rd year proceeding to light orangey-amber by the 4th to 5th year.

The Nose: Trademark characters are marked by a floral medium to compound aroma with citrus, apples, tropical fruit and velvety acidic tones.

Oaked Viura wines have an additional discrete smoky aroma with tones of citrus, apricots, banana, vanilla and earthy characters.

The Palate: Unoaked wines are mainly dry but can also be found with various residual sugar levels from dry to sweet. In most cases you'll come across a dry Viura with high acidity levels, medium-bodied with some volatile aromatics. There is a slight bitterness in the aftertaste.

Dry no-oak sensory ratios:
    Acidity **5-9**, Fullness **4**, Sweetness **1-4**, Bitterness **0.5**, Abv.11-12.5%
Dry oak aged sensory ratios:
    Acidity **7-9**, Fullness **6-7**, Sweetness **1-2**, Abv. 11.5-13.5%
Sparkling sensory ratios:
    Acidity **9**, Fullness **4-7**, Sweetness **1-9**, Bitterniess **0**, Abv. 11.5-12.5%

Excellent Food Combinations:
Excellent when served with shell-fish and other fish dishes. Complements a matured (aged 18 months) Manchego, which is an artisan sheep-cheese made in Spain.

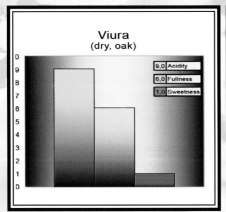

Fig. 7.42. Macabeo / Viura (oak maturation) Acid, Fullness and Sweetness sensory ratios.

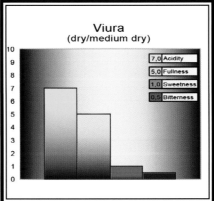

Fig. 7.42.5. Macabeo / Viura Acid, Fullness and SweetAness sensory ratios.

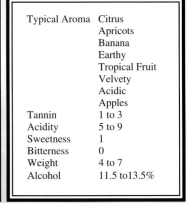

Typical Aroma	Citrus
	Apricots
	Banana
	Earthy
	Tropical Fruit
	Velvety
	Acidic
	Apples
Tannin	1 to 3
Acidity	5 to 9
Sweetness	1
Bitterness	0
Weight	4 to 7
Alcohol	11.5 to13.5%

Fig. 7.43. Macabeo sensory summary.

Muscadet

When you hear the term 'sur lie', one automatically thinks of a Muscadet. **Synonyms:** Melon de Bourgogne is the actual name, whereas Muscadet, a synonym, has become more known. Other synonyms are Gamay Blanc à Feuilles Rondes, Gros Auxerrois, Lyonnaise Blanche, Weisserburgunder and Pinot Blanc surprisingly in California. **Areas Found:** Centered around Nantes on the seaboard of the Loire River in western France, Muscadet is produced in one of three appellations: Muscadet AC, Muscadet de Sèvre-et-Maine AC and Muscadet des Côteaux de la Loire. It can also be found in California and in some experimental phases in South Africa.

Wine Styles and Blends:

The Melon de Bourgogne produces very good single varieties and is not normally used in a blend. Muscadet AC usually provides an average white table wine with marked acidity, while Muscadet de Sèvre-et-Maine AC produces the vast majority of wines in the region, about 80%, in a 'sur lie' or on the lees style. This style is where the wines, while ageing in oak barrels, are allowed to be kept on the spent (dead) yeast cells and other grape skin matter without being racked-off or filtered. These wines are considered to have more flavor with softer and creamier characteristics. Muscadet des Côteaux de la Loire also produce 'sur lie' wines. Wine produced on their lees can age for many years.

Grape Physiology:

Vigour: Good. Yields about 60 hl/ha. It thrives on schistose or granite and deep fertile soils.

Phenology: Ripens in mid-season. At full maturity the average sugar content is from 19° to 22° Brix/Balling and total acid of 6 to 8 g/l.

Berries: Small to medium in size. The berries have a tough medium skin thickness.

Diseases: Susceptible to Botrytis, black rot, peronospera.

Sensory Characteristics:

Appearance: A greenish tint, very pale-yellow hue when young and not very viscous. A light tone, wide gradient and initial changes in hue in the 3rd year proceeding to light orangey-amber by the 4th to 5th year.

The Nose: Trademark characters are marked by a citrus, apple and almond tone. Muscadet oaked 'sur lie' has a wonderful yeast, citrus, gooseberry, almond on occasion even nettles. It can also show discrete smoky and earthy characters.

The Palate: Unoaked wines are mainly dry but can also be found with various residual sugar levels from dry to semi-dry. In most cases you'll come across a dry wine with high acidity levels, medium-bodied with some volatile aromatics.

Dry no-oak sensory ratios:
> *Acidity* **9**, *Fullness* **2**, *Sweetness* **1**, Abv. 11-12%

Dry oak aged "sur lie" sensory ratios:
> *Acidity* **9**, *Fullness* **4**, *Sweetness* **1**, Abv. 11.5-12.3%

Excellent Food Combinations:

Excellent when served with shell-fish and most other fish dishes. Complements matured cow- and goat-cheeses.

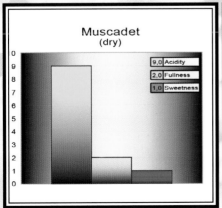

Fig. 7.46. Muscadet (no oak) Acid, Fullness and Sweetness sensory ratios.

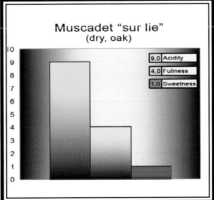

Fig. 7.46.5. Muscadet "sur lie" (no oak) Acid, Fullness and Sweetness sensory ratios.

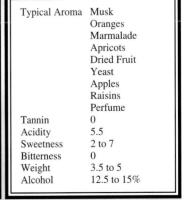

Fig. 7.47. Muscadet sensory summary.

Typical Aroma	Musk
	Oranges
	Marmalade
	Apricots
	Dried Fruit
	Yeast
	Apples
	Raisins
	Perfume
Tannin	0
Acidity	5.5
Sweetness	2 to 7
Bitterness	0
Weight	3.5 to 5
Alcohol	12.5 to 15%

Muscat à Petits Grains

Muscat is a group (commonly known as a family), used in general terms to describe many Muscat varieties of the species vitis vinifera, rather than a single variety. The five best known varieties are Muscat Blanc à Petits Grains (top quality sweet wines), Muscat d'Alexandrie (usually table grapes but some table wines too), Muscat Ottonel (usually dry whites), Muscat Hamburg (mainly used as table grapes) and Orange Muscat (sweet wines). **Synonyms:** Muscat Blanc, Frontignac, Moscato, Moscato Bianco, Moscato d'Asti, Muscat Canelli, Muscat Frontignac, White Muscat, White Frontignac, Brown Muscat and many other synonyms. Muscat d'Alexandrie is called Hanepoot in South Africa.

Areas Found: The Muscat family may be the oldest grape variety known. It is planted in most wine-growing regions.

Wine Styles and Blends:

Muscat Blanc à Petits Grains is easily recognizable by its perfumed musk characteristics. The wines are often sweet, frequently fortified, from 3-5% up to 15% abv, especially from the Mediterranean and Australia. Alsace as well as some producers from Languedoc-Roussillon produce a dry style . In Italy it is widely used to make sparkling wine low in alcohol. Usually only found as a single variety.

Grape Physiology:

Vigour: It varies depending upon the climate and soil types. Yields vary from 30-55 hl/ha. It thrives on fertile soils.

Phenology: Ripens in mid-season. At maturity the sugar content is 22°-26° Brix/Balling and TA is 5-7.5 g/l.

Berries: Small in size and off-round. They have a straw to golden-yellow hue and are used for white winemaking.

Diseases: Susceptible to sunburn, most diseases and pests. It seems everyone and everything like these grapes.

Sensory Characteristics:

Appearance: Can vary in color from pale, pinkish-yellow-gold to deep golden-yellow with a slight greenish tint when young. It has a medium to tight gradient. Initial changes in the hue can be detected in the 4th year proceeding to darker golden-orange-amber hue by the 7th to 8th year.

The Nose: Trademark characteristics for a fortified Muscat de Beaumes-de-Venise from southern Rhône, would show a distinctive musky aroma combined with hits of grape orange and marmalade.

The Palate: Trademark taste characteristics are high alcohol levels around 15% abv. The body (weight) is less than that of a botrytis wine from Sauternes and Austria. Muscat Blanc à Petit Grains is low in acidity and high alcohol levels compensate for this when fortified. When dry, they are honeyed and complex.

Dry sensory ratios:

Acidity **5.5**, Fullness **3.5**, Sweetness **2**, Abv. 12.5-13%

Sweet with sensory ratios:

Acidity **5.5**, Fullness **5.5**, Sweetness **7,** Abv. 14-15%

Excellent Food Combinations:

Muscat Blanc à Petit Grains is great as an appetizer by itself or with some hard matured cow or sheep-cheeses like Comté (cow), Gruyère (cow), Parmigiano Reggiano (cow) or Pecorino Sardo (ewe). Matches well to a number of delicate desserts which include chocolate.

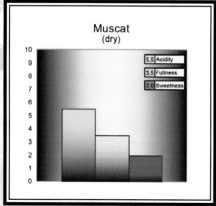

Fig. 7.44. *Muscat de Petit Grains* (dry no oak) *Acid, Fullness and Sweetness sensory ratios.*

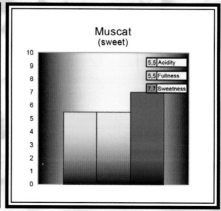

Fig. 7.44.5. *Muscat de Petit Grains Acid, Fullness and Sweetness sensory ratios.*

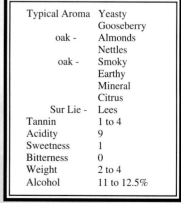

Fig. 7.45. *Muscat de Petit Grains sensory summary.*

Pinot Blanc

Pinot Blanc is not related to Chardonnay as once believed – it is part of the Pinot Noir variety of grapes. Often what is called Pinot Blanc in Australia is actually Chardonnay and some of the Pinot Blanc vines in California have been identified as Melon de Bourgogne. Pinot Blanc is being used more and more in sparkling wines throughout the world.

Synonyms: Beli Pinot, Clevner, Pinot Bianco, Pineau Blanc, Borgogno Bianco, Weissburgunder, Weiser Klevner, Weisser Ruländer and Klevanjka.

Areas Found: With its home being Burgundy in France Pinot Blanc has spread northeast Italy, South Africa, Australia, New Zealand, Chile, Argentina, US, Austria, Germany, Hungary, the Czech Republic and Slovakia.

Wine Styles and Blends:
In most cases Pinot Blanc is found as a single variety. In the majority of cases it is vinified and matured in steel but on occasion it meets some oak. It is at its best in the northeast of Italy, Alsace and California. Usually vinified dry and has also been known to be blended into sparkling wines. A medium-bodied wine with good acidity.

Grape Physiology:
Vigour: Average. Yields about 70 hl/ha. It thrives on chalky soils that run deep and that are damp.

Phenology: Ripens in late early season. At full maturity the average sugar content is from 20° to 24° Brix/Balling and total acid of 6 to 7.5 g/l.

Berries: Small to medium in size but they tend to be rather compact. The berries are round with a medium pale green. They have a medium to thick skin.

Diseases: Resistant to many insects but tend to rot due to the compactness of the berries on a bunch.

Sensory Characteristics:
Appearance: Varies from pale to straw in color when young and with and without carbonation. It has a wide gradient. Initial changes in the hue can be detected in the 3rd year, proceeding to light amber by the 5th to 6th year. Oaked; Usually fermented and aged in steel but when in oak it has a viscous appearance and is slightly more straw-yellow in color.

The Nose: Trademark characters are marked by tree fruit, floral and a slight spiciness. An Unoaked wine is usually more citrus and slightly sharper, apple and floral characters, while oaked wines have a light fresh apple aroma, with a touch of spices and yeast. Oak aged Pinot Blanc takes on a more honey character. It is richer and has some butter, possibly yeast type characters could be evident with the addition of vanilla of oak.

The Palate: Unoaked wines are dry and very similar to a light medium-bodied Chardonnay. The crispy acidity is due to the large amount of total acidity present but it can also provide a honeyed version in the US.

Dry no-oak sensory ratios:
> Acidity 6, Fullness 8, *Sweetness* 2, Abv. 9.5-12.5%

Dry oak aged sensory ratios:
> Acidity 6, Fullness 8.5, *Sweetness* 2, Abv. 12.5-14%

Sparkling sensory ratios:
> Acidity 7, Fullness 6, *Sweetness* 1, Abv. 11.5-13%

Excellent Food Combinations:
A perfect table wine, Pinot Blanc can complement the majority of fish dishes, light meat and mild cheeses.

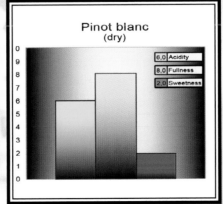

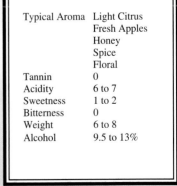

Typical Aroma	Light Citrus
	Fresh Apples
	Honey
	Spice
	Floral
Tannin	0
Acidity	6 to 7
Sweetness	1 to 2
Bitterness	0
Weight	6 to 8
Alcohol	9.5 to 13%

Fig. 7.48. Pinot Blanc (no oak) Acid, Fullness and Sweetness sensory ratios.

Fig. 7.49. Pinot Blanc sensory summary.

Pinot Gris

Pinot Gris is like Pinot Blanc a mutation of the Pinot Noir grape. *Gris* is French for 'gray'. The color of the grape can vary substantially, producing wines that range from white to slightly pink. **Synonyms:** Pinot Beurot, Pinot Burot, Tokay d'Alsace, Malvoisie, Gris Cordelier, Fauvet, Auvernat Gris, Petit Gris, Ruländer, Grauer Burgunder, Graulkevner, Grauer Riesling, Tokayer, Pinot Grigio, Tokayer, Crvena Klevanjka, Rulanda.

Areas Found: Originally from Burgundy, it is grown at its best in Alsace as well as in Austria, Germany, Hungary, Romania, USA, Australia, New Zealand, Chile, Argentina, Austria, the Czech Republic and Slovakia.

Wine Styles and Blends:
The wineries in Alsace produce the quality that all Pinot Gris should be judged against. Here they are almost perfect due to their rich, dry, delicately perfumed offering a total balance from sight to length.

Grape Physiology:
Vigour: Moderate vigour. Yields about 45 hl/ha. It thrives in chalky soils that run deep and have a high mineral content.
Phenology: Ripens in early season. At full maturity the average sugar content is from 20° to 24° Brix/Balling and total acid of 6 to 7 g/l.

Berries: Medium in size and oval. They have a yellowish-red-black hue and are used for white winemaking. Pinot Gris has a medium skin thickness.

Diseases: Resistant to many insects, pests and diseases.

Sensory Characteristics:
Appearance: Varies from pale yellow to slightly pink in color. It has a medium gradient. Initial changes in the hue can be detected in the 4th year proceeding to light orange-amber by the 5th to 6th year. When matured in oak it has a viscous appearance and a slightly darker and more yellow-straw hue.

The Nose: Trademark characters for an Alsace Pinot Gris are marked by apricot, honey, spicy, nutty-mushroom and smoky-like characters. Unoaked wines have more citrus and are slightly sharper but display good fruit characters of apricots and dried fruits. Oaked wines have in addition cream, butter and vanilla.

The Palate: Trademark taste characteristics are everything from a crisp, light and dry wine in northern Italy (Pinot Grigio), to the rich, rustic, viscous, fat, honeyed versions from France's Alsace region, but all Pinot Gris have a slight bitterness in the aftertaste.

Dry no-oak sensory ratios:
Acidity 4, Fullness 5.5, Sweetness 2.5, Bitterness 3, Abv. 9.5-12.5%
Dry oak aged sensory ratios:
Acidity 4, Fullness 6, Sweetness 3, Bitterness 3, Abv. 12.5-14%

Excellent Food Combinations:
Pinot Gris is a perfect match to goose liver, pâté, poultry and light wild dishes. Also complements artisan cheeses with some age (±18 months of storage). Salads of various sorts can also benefit from a good Pinot Gris.

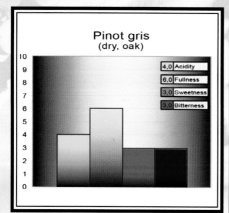

Fig. 7.50. Pinot Gris (oak maturation) Acid, Fullness and Sweetness sensory ratios.

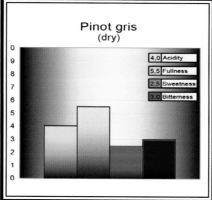

Fig. 7.50.5. Pinot Gris (no oak) Acid, Fullness and Sweetness sensory ratios.

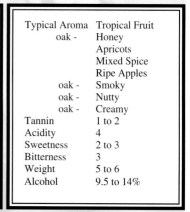

Typical Aroma	Tropical Fruit
oak -	Honey
	Apricots
	Mixed Spice
	Ripe Apples
oak -	Smoky
oak -	Nutty
oak -	Creamy
Tannin	1 to 2
Acidity	4
Sweetness	2 to 3
Bitterness	3
Weight	5 to 6
Alcohol	9.5 to 14%

Fig. 7.51. Pinot Gris sensory summary.

Riesling

Like Chenin Blanc, this is both a very versatile grape and one of the great noble varieties. **Synonyms:** Johannisberg Riesling, Rhine Riesling, Petit Rhin Riesling, Petit Riesling, Riesling Blanc, Rizling, Weisser Rielsing and White Riesling. Note that Cape Riesling is not a Riesling clone but instead Cruchen Blanc responsible for table wines. **Areas Found**: Riesling is the 2nd largest planted variety in Germany. It is responsible for fine wine production in Alsace in France and is also found in South Africa, Australia, New Zealand, Russia, Chile, Argentina, Canada and the US.

Wine Styles and Blends:

It is at its best in Alsace and Germany, producing wines that range from bone-dry to lusciously sweet but always with a wonderful crisp acidity. The Rhine Riesling, which is simply called Riesling in Germany and Alsace and White or Johannisberg Riesling in USA. In Alsace it is usually fermented dry, leaving no residual sugar, while in the best years they also make richer and sweeter Vendange Tardive and Sélection de Grains Nobles. In Germany Rieslings can make *Trocken, Halbtrocken, Kabinett, Spätlese, Auslese, Beerenauslese* and the sweetest *Trockenbeerenauslese*; naturally, they make *Eiswein* as well.

Grape Physiology:

Vigour: Moderate. Yields about 48 hl/ha. It is very versatile and can grow on many soil types but thrives on sandy loam, slate and well-drained, less fertile areas.

Phenology: Ripens in late mid-season. At maturity the sugar is 20°-23° Brix/Balling and TA of 7-9 g/l.

Berries: Small, medium in size, round with a rich, green, golden yellow hue and medium to thick skin.

Diseases: Resistant to many infections. Survive well in very low temperatures in the winter.

Sensory Characteristics:

Appearance: Pale yellow with a greenish tint when young, with and without carbonation. Wide gradient if dry and slightly tighter if sweet. Initial changes of hue in the 4th year, proceeding to light amber by the 7th year. Oaked wines are more viscous with a greenish-straw-yellow hue when young. They change color in the 4th to 5th year. Good mature wines develop a light amber hue after 10 years.

The Nose: Aromatic floral, acidic characters when young and develops with age into a unique 'diesel', 'petroleum' type aroma. Unoaked wines have sharper citrus, apple and floral characters with an acidic nose, whereas oaked wines are richer, more viscous and with oak characters.

The Palate: Unoaked Riesling d'Alsace is dry and steely and medium-bodied. In Germany, the wines are lighter and more honeyed, with delicate flavors of peaches, apricots and a mineral/slate character. In Pfalz, you'll find some of Germany's finest, fullest and broadest wines. A good Riesling will have a good balance between fruit, sweetness and acidity. Very high acidity levels whether dry or sweet. Dry wines are clean and uncomplicated. Sweet botrytis wines are fruity encompassing apricot, honey, peach and spice.

Dry no-oak sensory ratios:

Acidity **10**, Fullness **3**, *Sweetness* **1**, Abv. 9.5-12.5%

Dry oak aged sensory ratios:

Acidity **10**, Fullness **4**, *Sweetness* **2**, Abv. 12.5-14%

Sweet botrytis/Ice wine oak aged sensory ratios:

Acidity **10**, Fullness **7**, *Sweetness* **8**, Abv. 11.5-13%

Excellent Food Combinations:

Various fish dishes including grilled or baked Salmon. Cheese plates of French artisan style, such as Munster made from goat, cow or ewe are perfect combinations.

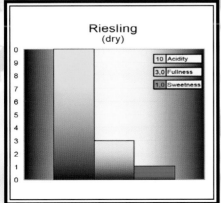

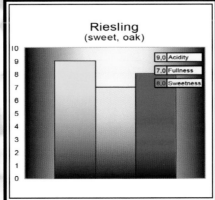

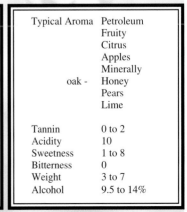

Typical Aroma	Petroleum
	Fruity
	Citrus
	Apples
	Minerally
oak -	Honey
	Pears
	Lime
Tannin	0 to 2
Acidity	10
Sweetness	1 to 8
Bitterness	0
Weight	3 to 7
Alcohol	9.5 to 14%

Fig. 7.52. Riesling (no oak maturation) *Acid, Fullness and Sweetness sensory ratios.*

Fig. 7.52.5. Riesling (sweet with oak) Acid, Fullness and Sweetness sensory ratios.

Fig. 7.53. Riesling sensory summary.

Sauvignon Blanc

Sauvignon Blanc is an aromatic variety that is generally better from cool climate vineyards. Grassy and grapefruity in cool climates; in warmer climates it is often blandly exotic. **Synonyms:** Sauvignon Jaune, Blance Fumé, Surin, Punechon, Muskat-Silvaner and Fumé Blanc. **Areas Found:** Best examples came from the Central Loire and Sancerre in France but, New Zealand, South Africa, Australia, California oregon and Washington State produces very good examples. Also found in Argentina, Chile and northeast Italy.

Wine Styles and Blends:

Sauvignon Blanc is one of the more important white grape varieties of Bordeaux, where it is found as a single variety and blended together with Muscadelle and Sémillon in both dry and sweet wine production. Sauvignon Blanc is fermented and matured in either both steel and/or oak.

Grape Physiology:

Vigour: Very vigorous. Sauvignon Blanc yields about 60 hl/ha. It is a very versatile in cool climates and thrives on soil types like chalk, gravel and sandy loam.

Phenology: Ripens in early mid-season. At full maturity the average sugar content is from 21° to 24° Brix / Balling (total dissolved compounds in grape juice and sugar concentration) and TA of 6 to 7 g/l.

Berries: Medium-small in size and oval with a distinctive grassy-herbaceous aroma. The grape has a pale, green-yellowish hue and medium tough skin.

Diseases: Susceptible to black rot and botrytis infection in overly fertile areas. Sauvignon Blanc is also susceptible to Powdery mildew and Downey mildew.

Sensory Characteristics:

Appearance: Unoaked wines have a pale, green-yellow to golden-yellow color which is typical in Loire and Bordeaux. Warmer climate Sauvignon Blanc wines are usually a little darker. Young, unoaked wines should show a greenish, pale, yellow hue with a light tight, gradient changing color only in their 3rd year and light amber in the 7th year. Sauvignon Blanc wines are viscous and with a greenish-straw-yellow hue when young and change their color in their 4th to 5th year. Good mature wines develop a light-amber color hue after about their 8th to 10th year.

The Nose: An aromatic wine with a grassy, gooseberry, blackcurrant bush and flinty tones. With age it can become vegetal, musk-like or 'catty', as in cat's pee (blackcurrant bush). Unoaked wines have sharper aromatic citrus with an acidic nose and underlying mineral characters. Oaked wines are richer with more body and vanilla.

The Palate: Young, oaked wines are fresh, crisp, green and uncomplicated and, most importantly, aromatic taste. In warm climates it has a rich, velvety character.

Unoaked wines:

> Acidity **8**, Fullness **3.5**, Sweetness **2**, Abv. 11.5-12.5%

Oak aged wines:

> Acidity **8**, Fullness **4.5-6**, Sweetness **2-8**, Abv. 12.5-14%

Excellent Food Combinations:

Shell fish, fried fish and poultry dishes. Cheese plates with French country cheeses like Munster and Epoisses are perfect complementary combinations.

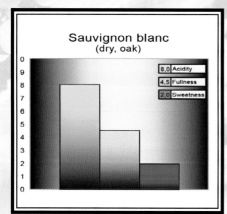

Fig. 7.54. Sauvignon Blanc (oak maturation) Acid, Fullness and Sweetness sensory ratios.

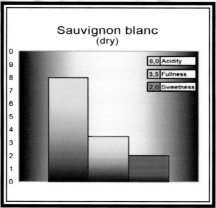

Fig. 7.54.5. Sauvignon Blanc (no oak) Acid, Fullness and Sweetness sensory ratios.

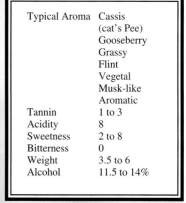

Fig. 7.55. Sauvignon Blanc sensory summary.

Typical Aroma	Cassis (cat's Pee)
	Gooseberry
	Grassy
	Flint
	Vegetal
	Musk-like
	Aromatic
Tannin	1 to 3
Acidity	8
Sweetness	2 to 8
Bitterness	0
Weight	3.5 to 6
Alcohol	11.5 to 14%

Sémillon

Sémillon a golden grape from the southwest France, is one of the unsung heroes of white grape production. As a single grape variety it is not the most elegant wine available today but as a blend it is just fantastic. **Synonyms:** Sémillon Blanc, Sémillon Muscat, Sémillon Roux, Chevrier, Colombier (not Colombar in South Africa) and Hunter River Riesling. **Areas Found:** It is one of the blended and classical grapes of Bordeaux. It is also found in the Hunter Valley in Australia, California, Washington oregon, South Africa, Chile and east Europe.

Wine Styles and Blends:
Usually blended with its traditional partners Sauvignon Blanc and Muscadelle, this golden-berried vine is the key variety of Sauternes and some of the world's longest living 'unfortified' white wines. It makes an excellent varietal dry Sémillon in the Hunter Valley, but it is best as a blend. Sweet white wines in Sauternes are combined with Sauvignon Blanc for its high acidic levels.

Grape Physiology:
Vigour: Very vigorous. Yields about 50 hl/ha. It thrives in heavy soils and over-cropping.
Phenology: Ripens in early mid-season. At full maturity the average sugar content is from 20° to 26° Brix/Balling and total acid of 5 to 7 g/l.
Berries: Medium in size and oval. They are have a yellowish-green hue and have an excellent grassy aroma when smelt. Sémillon has a medium skin thickness.
Diseases: Susceptible to grey and noble rot (Botrytis cinerea, as shown in the background).

Sensory Characteristics
Appearance: Greenish yellow-golden hue with a very viscous appearance in young wines. It has a medium to tight gradient. Initial changes in the hue can be detected in the 5th year proceeding to light-amber hue by the 8th to 10th year if a blend from Bordeaux. Oaked wines are very viscous and slightly more straw-golden-yellow in color than those without oak.

The Nose: Trademark characters for a botrytis Sémillon are apricot, honey, nuts, dried fruit and ripe citrus characters. In young dry wines a grassy citrus character can be found, but in older dry wines they develop a waxy, raisin, lanolin-type character. In sweet wines, their heavy bouquet is complex, smooth and filled with a honey-nutty character. In older sweet wines the characters develop into a softer, fuller, rounder, velvety apricot-raisin nose. Unoaked wines display apple and citrus characters with a touch of pineapple. Oaked wines also have cream, butter, vanilla and some smokiness.

The Palate: Trademark taste characteristics are grassy with low acidic levels and a lemony volatile aroma in the aftertaste.

Dry no-oak sensory ratios:
 Acidity 4, Fullness 7, Sweetness 1, Alcohol Levels. 10-12.5%
Dry oak aged sensory ratios:
 Acidity **5.5**, Fullness 6, Sweetness **2**, Abv. 12.5-13.5%
Sweet oak aged sensory ratios:
 Acidity 7, Fullness 8, Sweetness 8, Abv. 11.5-14%
Excellent Food Combinations:
A dry Sémillon is wonderful with fish and poultry such as Confit de Canard. A sweet Sémillon can be served with dessert, cheese, goose liver and Terrine.

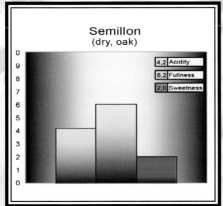

Fig. 7.56. Sémillon (dry oak maturation) *Acid, Fullness and Sweetness sensory ratios.*

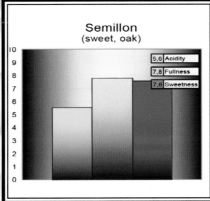

Fig. 7.56.5. Sémillon (sweet with oak) *Acid, Fullness and Sweetness sensory ratios.*

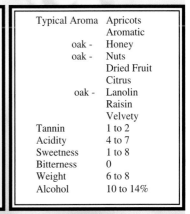

Typical Aroma	Apricots
	Aromatic
oak -	Honey
oak -	Nuts
	Dried Fruit
	Citrus
oak -	Lanolin
	Raisin
	Velvety
Tannin	1 to 2
Acidity	4 to 7
Sweetness	1 to 8
Bitterness	0
Weight	6 to 8
Alcohol	10 to 14%

Fig. 7.57. Sémillon sensory summary.

Trebbiano

Trebbiano is a very important wine grape. It is extensively planted producing more wine than any other grape variety in the world, even though the Airén, Garnacha and Rkatsiteli are planted on more acreage. It is the most common grape variety in both Italy and in France, where it is called Ugni Blanc. **Synonyms:** Greco, Rossetto, Trebianello, Buzzetto, Ugni Blanc (Cognac/Armagnac) and Clairette Ronde and Clairette Rose in other parts of France; in Portugal (Thalia) and as Saint-Emilion in the San Joaquim Valley in California. In Australia it is called White Shiraz and even White Hermitage, while in Portugal its name is Muscadet Aigre.

Areas Found: Its home being Burgundy in France, it has also spread to California, Australia, South Africa, Bulgaria, Hungary and most of the former east European states, where is was very popular. Originating in central Italy, Trebbiano has spread throughout the world. About 80% of Ugni Blanc in France is actually not used for wine but instead distilled in Brandy or Cognac.

Wine Styles and Blends:
The Trebbiano grape is most often blended with varieties exhibiting more dominant traits. It can also be found as a sparkling wine, blended, semi-sweet and single variety wine. It is known to be blended with Chardonnay, Garganega, Grechetto, Malvasia, Pinot Bianco, Pinot Grigio, Sauvignon, Verdello and other varieties that can benefit for the high acidic levels. Trebbiano is a medium-bodied wine with good acidity.

Grape Physiology:
Vigour: Very good. Yields about 50 hl/ha. It thrives on a variety of soil types.

Phenology: Ripens in late season. At full maturity the average sugar content is from 19° to 22° Brix/Balling and total acid of 7 to 9 g/l.

Berries: Small to medium in size with a tough medium skin thickness.. Due to a large number of clones, the berries can vary in color from pale-green to a pinkish-green.

Diseases: Resistant to many insects but susceptible to Downey mildew.

Sensory Characteristics:
Appearance: Greenish tint, pale-yellow when young with and without carbonation. Wide gradient with changes in the hue in the 2nd to 3rd year proceeding to light orangey-amber by the 4th to 5th year.

The Nose: acidic citrus; lemon, tart apples, such as 'Granny Smith' and hints of grapefruit or maybe almonds. All in all Trebbiano does not offer too much variety, when it comes to aroma characteristics. On occasion you might be able to find some wooded (oak) examples, which could increase the nutty almond characters and possibly a slight cream or vanilla.

The Palate: Unoaked wines produce dry, fresh and high acidity levels equivalent to something between a Sauvignon Blanc and a Chenin Blanc. Trebbiano is a light to medium-bodied with normal alcohol levels.

Dry no-oak sensory ratios:
   Acidity **9**, Fullness **6**, Sweetness **2**, Bitterness **0**, Abv. 11-12.5%
Dry oak aged sensory ratios:
   Acidity **8**, Fullness **6.5**, Sweetness **1**, Bitterness **0**, Abv. 11.5-12.8%
Sparkling sensory ratios:
   Acidity **9**, Fullness **5.5**, Sweetness **1**, Bitterness **0**, Abv. 11.5-12.5%

Excellent Food Combinations:
Trebbiano goes well with creamy matured cheeses, Pizza, barbeques in high summer.

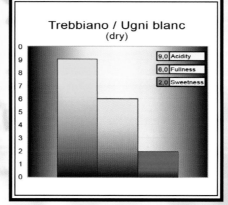

Fig. 7.58. Trebbiano Acid, Fullness and Sweetness sensory ratios.

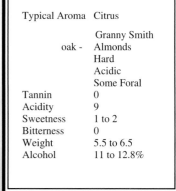

Typical Aroma	Citrus
	Granny Smith
oak -	Almonds
	Hard
	Acidic
	Some Foral
Tannin	0
Acidity	9
Sweetness	1 to 2
Bitterness	0
Weight	5.5 to 6.5
Alcohol	11 to 12.8%

Fig. 7.59. Trebbiano sensory summary.

Viognier

An esteemed white-wine grape considered very rare because of the limited acreage planted throughout the world. With its low yield and high susceptibility to vineyard diseases few wine farmers try to grow it. Viognier is very well known in the northern Rhône-wines of Château Grillet, Condrieu and Côte-Rôtie.

Synonyms:
Vionnier.

Areas Found:
There are about 38 ha in the Rhône Valley in France where some of the finest Viognier can be found. In addition there are some excellent examples coming from California namely Joseph Phelps Vineyards amongst others. Other good examples of Viognier can now be found in Australia, South Africa and Languedoc-Roussillon in the south-west of France.

Wine Styles and Blends:
Viognier is found as both a varietal and as a blend. As a varietal it is a very aromatic and floral dry white wine. As a blend it is vinified together with the syrah, a red grape, in Côte-Rôtie where it is prized for its addition of weight and violets. Viognier produces excellent wines with a long length and balance.

Grape Physiology:
Vigour: Less than average vigour. Yields only about 25 hl/ha. It thrives in sandy limestone soils with a good mineral content. It is prone unreliable ripening.

Phenology: Ripens in midseason. At full maturity the average sugar content is from 20° to 23° Brix/Balling and total acid of 5 to 7 g/l.

Berries: Medium in size and oval. They have a yellowish-red-black hue and are used for white winemaking. Viognier has a medium skin thickness.

Diseases: Resistant to many insects and pests.

Sensory Characteristics:
Appearance: Varies from pale straw to a rich, golden oily color. It has a medium to tight gradient. Initial changes in the hue can be detected in the 3rd year proceeding to golden-orange-amber by the 5th to 6th year.

The Nose: Viognier is very aromatic and shows a number of trademark characters, such as violets, peaches, apricots, apples, pears, musk and spice. Unoaked wines have more citrus and are slightly sharper but with good floral and fruit characters (peach, apricot). Oaked wines also have creamy, buttery, smoky and vanilla characters.

The Palate: *Viognier has a* typical palate that is full-bodied, rich, rustic, viscous, fat, with good 'volatile aroma' characteristics. A marked bitterness is almost always present with low acidity levels.

Dry no-oak sensory ratios:
   Acidity **3.8**, Fullness **7**, *Sweetness* **2.5**, Bitterness **4**, Abv. 12-12.5%

Dry oak aged sensory ratios:
   Acidity **4**, Fullness **8**, *Sweetness* **3**, Bitterness **4**, Abv. 12.5-13.5%

Excellent Food Combinations:
Viognier wines are best matched with charismatic, powerful fish dishes with a creamy wine sauce. In order to compete with the wine's body and character the food needs to have character too.

Typical Aroma	Aromatic
	Peachy
	Floral
	Pears
	Musk
	Tropical Fruit
	Spice
Tannin	1 to 3
Acidity	3 to 4.5
Sweetness	2.5 to 3
Bitterness	3 to 4
Weight	7 to 8
Alcohol	12 13.5%

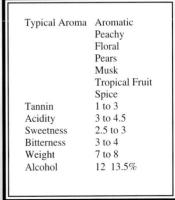

Fig. 7.60. Viognier (Dry with oak) Acid, Fullness and Sweetness sensory ratios.

Fig. 7.61. Viognier sensory summary.

Use of oak, oak barrels, tannin and other extracts

Fermentation and aging in new oak produce some of the vanilla, honey and caramel, coconut, cinnamon, cloves, toffee and my favorite coffee. Oak-fermented white wine originated in Burgundy, where it has been wide-spread for the past 30 years. Since the late 1980s this technique has been diffused throughout the wine-growing world, where the vineyards' 'first wine' typically receive a higher proportion of new-barrel fermentation.

New barrels vary dramatically in cost and the French oak barrels, which are cleaved instead of sawn like the American barrels, have traditionally been considered the most desirable, partly for their rich, mellow flavors. As a result, new French barrels cost as much as $650 per barrel, compared to $300 for an American oak barrel. The time, cost and labor factors more associated with cleaving (splitting) than sawing is the major cost differentiating factor.

Fig. 7.62. Oak barrel firing or smoking. The barrel is set upon an open fire and the insides are charred to various strengths: low, medium or heavy.

A number of flavors are determined by the species of oak, just as with the varietal differences in grapes. American oak species typically impart more intense, flavors since they have more than double the lactones that French species have. Air-drying of the staves and the level of toasting, light, medium or heavy, all play a vital role in the departing flavors too.

Wines are fermented and matured (aged) in new oak barrels, since the wine absorbs lactones, phenolic aldehydes, volatile phenols, terpenes, tannins and degradation of carbohydrates, which all result in caramelized, smoky notes, such as almonds, mocha and toffee, created by the toasting of barrel staves.

- Lactones are responsible for the oakiness of the wine and the toasting of the oak increases this coconut-like oakiness, whereas open air-drying of the staves softens these characteristics somewhat.

- Phenolic aldehydes are responsible for the vanilla characteristics derived from the oak barrels. Open-air drying and toasting also enhance these characteristics.

- Volatile phenols such as the spicy characteristics which include cloves and carnations seem to reduce with open air-drying.

- Terpenes are the natural oils found in all plants and trees. These oils are more predominate in American oak and are thought to be responsible for the butter, cream characteristics which are usually evident in wines aged in American oak.

- Tannin and other phenols provide color, astringency and help in both reducing oxidation and reduction of the wine in the barrel.

- Carbohydrates and other degraded items include furfurals which are responsible for the caramelized, bitter almond and burnt sugar, smoked meats and leather characteristics found in the wines which are derived from the toasting of barrels.

Maturation and fermentation in barrels also allow for the integration of oxygen, which gradually seeps through the staves. Some vineyards use 'micro-oxygenation' in their steel tanks. This process allows them to infuse small oxygen bubbles into the steel maturation tanks, thus creating a barrel environment. In addition to this, chips, powder and staves can be added to the fermentation and maturation process to enhance the oak characteristics.

After quality, a number of issues need to be considered by the winemaker when considering the use of oak and they are:

1. Winemaker's budget
2. Character desired (toasting requirements)
3. Origin (American or French) and type of oak (Powder, Chips, Staves, Barrels)
4. Use and length of oak during fermentation
5. Use and length of oak during maturation

Tannins occur naturally in grapes, mainly as anthocyanins, catechins and condensed tannins. Other tannins are extracted from barrels used for the wine's aging. These include hydrolyzable tannins, gallotannins and ellagitannins. They contribute to taste, providing bitter and astringent flavors. They may also eliminate excess proteins, increase and stabilize red color pigments, reduce oxidation rates, aid clarification, improve aromas and mouth-feel and supply phenolics, which contribute to positive health benefits.

Toasted Oak-Mor, Granular Oak. Info: First oak alternative that was not a by-product of barrel production. **Type:** 100% white American oak. **Form:** Granular form. **Extraction:** Very rapid. **Toast Level:** Medium level of toast. **Desired Characteristics:** Vanillin and butterscotch characters. **Use:** Added prior to fermentation and even during aging.

White Grape Skin Tannin Powder "S". **Info:** added to finished wine three weeks prior to bottling for phenolic balance. **Desired Characteristics:** phenolic balance, reduction of vegetative characters, stabilization of color in red wines and minimized the "warm" alcohol taste. **Use:** *Red Wines* - 0.2 to 1.1 gram per gallon (180 to 11.5 grams per 10 gallons). *White Wines* - 0.08 to 0.35 gram (7.5 to 35 grams per hundred gallons) .

Grape Seed Tannin, powder "PC". **Info:** Extracted from 100% white grape seeds. **Desired Characteristics:**

Oak alternatives

Fig. 7.63. Fine Oak Powder
Medium Toasts

Fig. 7.64. Medium Size
Vanilla-flavored Oak Chips

Fig. 7.65. Small Staves / Heavy Toast / Oak staves placed inside a barrel to enhance the flavour. This can help reduce the cost of purchasing new barrels annually.

Increases mid-palate body and also offers more tannic structure. *Use*: Added within three weeks of bottling and dissolves instantly. Rich in proanthocyanidin used to assist the fining of red and rose wines, stabilizing protein in whites and stabilizing color in red wines during maturation and in oak barrels. Also acts as an antioxidant and inhibits SO_2 oxidizing agents. Red Wines - 0.2 to 1.1 gram per gallon (180 to 1150 grams per thousand gallons) White Wines - 0.08 to 0.35 gram per gallon (75 to 350 grams per thousand gallons).

Other additives in wine

Tartaric Acid, powder. *Info:* Is a natural grape acid. ***Desired Characteristics:*** To increase must acidity levels in low acidic wines. Helps to lower pH levels. For wines with less than 0.5% titratable acidity will benefit from its addition. *Use:* 3.7 grams per gallon will increase acidity by 0.1%.

Citric Acid, powder. *Info:* An acid found in grapes and other fruits. Can be metabolized during fermentation, is used as a substitute for tartaric, can reduce pH levels nicely and does not disrupt tartrate stability. *Use:* 0.1 gram per gallon will help prevent iron hazes and 3.5 grams per gallon will increase the acidity by 0.1%.

Malic Acid, powder. *Info:* Tartaric and Malic acid accouint for the vast majority of acidity in grapes. *Use:* To improve acidity levels. There is a slight problem when using Malic acid as it seems to increase the pH levels in musts rather than lowering them like Citric and Tartaric acids.

Phosphoric Acid. Used to lower the pH in wines with a minimal increase in acidity levels. *Use:*Typical usage is 2 to 8 ml per gallon.

Calcium Carbonate, powder. Used to reduce acidity levels in wines. *Use:* 2.5 grams/gallon will reduce acidity by about 0.1%.

Potassium Bicarbonate, powder. Used to lower acidity levels in wine musts. *Use:* 3.4 grams per gallon will give a potential 0.1% drop in acidity.

Potassium Bitartrate, powder *(Cream of Tarter)*. It is used prior to cold stabilization and aids in the formation of tartrate crystals in wine. *Use:* 2 to 5 grams per gallon.

Ferment Yeast Nutrient and Energizer powder. Aids in the reproduction and metabolism of yeasts and to prevent stuck fermentations. *Use:* Normal use is 0.75 to 1.5 grams per gallon.

Fining Agents
A rule of thumb for all winemakers is to test a variety of fining methods and agents that can best suit your style of winemaking.

Oak Chips

Fig. 7.66. Small Size / 1/4" Granular Medium Toast

Fig. 7.67. Small Size / 1/4" Granular Heavy Toast

Fig. 7.68. Large Size / 3/4" Consistency Medium Toast

Fig. 7.69. Large Size / 3/4" Consistency Heavy Toast

Bentonite, powder. This is a clay that absorbes positively charged particles and can be used to remove many hazes. *Use:* 1 to 2 grams per gallon for finished wines. If used during fermentation you may increase the amount up to 5 grams per gallon.

Sparkolloid, powder (hot mix). Used to calrify wines. It is a n alginate-based removes many hazes. It does not require the addition of tannin. *Use:* 0.5 to 1.5 grams per gallon.

Isinglass, powder. A fining agent for whites and sparkling wines but will also remove harsh tannins in reds. *Use:* 0.01 to 0.10 gram per gallon.

Gelatin liquid. Used to reduce astringency and bitterness and to clarify red or white wines. *Use:* 0.06 ml to 0.47 ml per gallon.

Gelatin, powder. Used to clarify whites or reds and to soften tannins or remove color in reds. *Use:* 0.5 to 1.0 gram per gallon with whites and 1.0 to 2.0 grams per gallon with reds.

Potassium Caseinate, powder. Used with white wines to clarify, reduces oxidized odors and freshens the wine. It will also remove some brownish (oxidized) color pigments. *Use:* 1 to 2 grams per gallon, but can be increased to 3 grams per gallon.

Pectic and other enzymes

Enzymes are being used more and moer today by modern winemakers. Enzymes are used settling and lees compaction in juices, improvement of aroma intensity, haze prevention, higher color extraction and even color stability in red wines. They can also be used to increase the free run (juice) yield during crushing or pressing. I am almost sure thay most peptic and enzyme powders can be removed with bentonite.

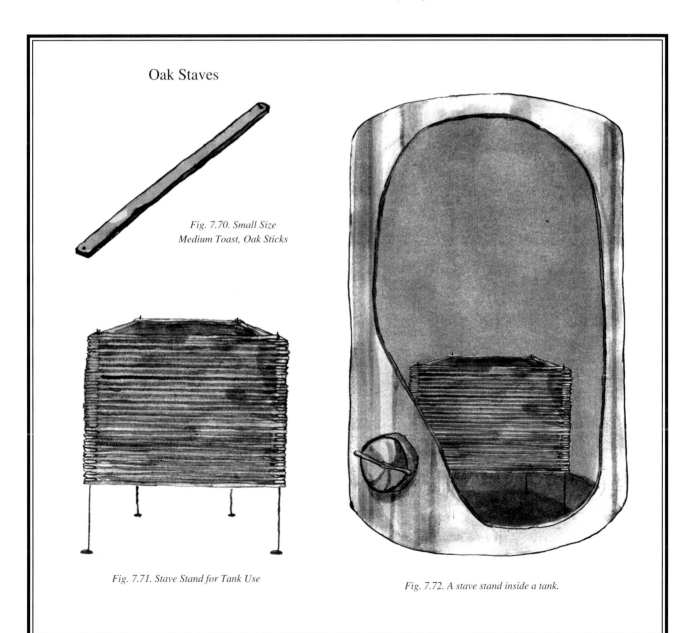

Oak Staves

Fig. 7.70. Small Size Medium Toast, Oak Sticks

Fig. 7.71. Stave Stand for Tank Use

Fig. 7.72. A stave stand inside a tank.

Glycolytic Enzyme, powder. A supplement for natural enzyme activities to release aromatic terpenols found in the grape skins and even oak barrels. Used after fermentation. *Use:* 0.07 to 0.11 gram per gallon of wine.

Rapidase, pectic enzyme powder. Improves color and polyphenol extraction during fermentation. Added during maceration of the skins. *Use:* 0.07 to 0.11 gram per gallon

Rapidase, liquid pectic enzyme. Improves juice yield and induces the settling of juices. *Use:* 12 to 24 ml per ton.

Pearex Adex, liquid pectic enzyme. Used to extract the maximum amount of sugar and juice from the grapes. *Use:* 0.5 to 1.5 ml per gallon.

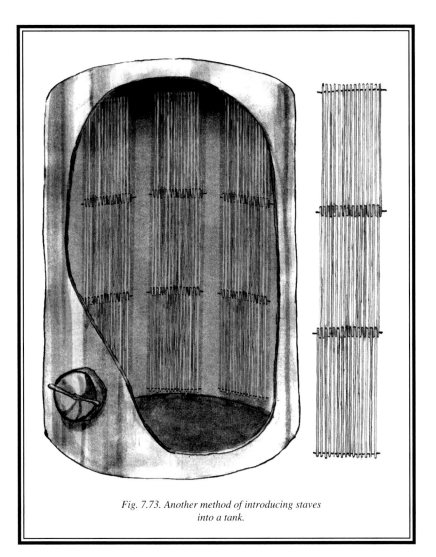

Fig. 7.73. Another method of introducing staves into a tank.

Chapter 8

Decanting and Aerating Wine

On a number of occasions I contemplated on whether or not to include this chapter in the first edition and finally, I came to the conclusion that the understanding of serving wine is quite important, especially when it comes to decanting or aerating.

The wine's current condition is by far the most important factor to take into account when contemplating on whether or not to decant the wine. Certain features are vital to keep in mind, otherwise you could damage the wine.

How do you like your wine? This is obviously a very important question to answer. Do you like it young and fruity or mature and smooth? Would you like wine to be matched with a situation or with food? Have you been storing it in your own cellar or have you just purchased it? How old is the wine? What is the style and present condition of the wine? If you have the answers to these questions then you're on the way to resolving the long debated issue of decanting.

Fig. 8.1. Perfect decanter shape with a wide base providing good air contact with the surface of the wine. On the other hand, the surface of a wine in the bottleneck is 24 mm; therefore, just uncorking a wine and leaving it in the bottle does not do very much because the space between the wine and the cork (ullage) is limited.

Some people are staunch believers that you should never decant a wine but drink it the way it is presented. In my opinion, however, the scent of a well-made wine at its top is worth its wine in gold. A wine, style or variety at its peak, where its acid, tannin, fruit, sweetness and alcohol levels are in harmony with one another is very hard to beat. You may prefer a wine at its peak, but reality does not always match preferences.

We need to know what happens to the wines when they are decanted/aerated. First we must consider the wine's temperature. The colder the wine the faster the oxygen degenerates or oxidizes the wine. If, as an example, a wine has a temperature of 0°C (32°F) it will absorb about 15mg/l,

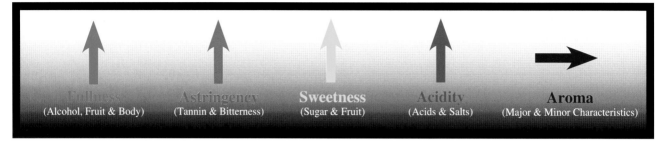

Fig. 8.2. Illustrates a full-bodied red and white wine prior to decantation. Note that the aroma in full-bodied wines can be compact, over-powerful and even closed. The reduction caused through careful aeration will help to release some captured volatile hydrogen sulfides, mercaptans and other acids.

Fig. 8.3. Illustrates what happens to the various components of a red and white wine after decantation. Oxygen increases the natural rate of reduction in wines and decanting hastens this process. When comparing Fig. 8.2 to Fig. 8.3. note that the volatile acids have deminished slightly, astringency has become smoother, there is a more distinct aroma present and the sugar remains more or less consistent but can seem a bit harder. Keep in mind that too much aeration will cause irreversable oxidation and should be avoided.

which is twice as much oxygen than if it was at 25°C (77°F). provided ascorbic acid levels are around 70 mg/l, pH between 3.1 to 3.4 and free sulfur at about 15ml/g. These are normal levels for white wines and differ slightly for the reds. Thus, temperature will affect the oxidation process.

In addition, some wines contain oxidase enzymes which cause tannin pigments (anthocyanins) to change color very quickly when exposed to air. This change in color, if oxidase enzymes are present, can occur within a couple of hours. You can actually test for these enzymes at home too. Simply take about 20 to 40 ml of the wine in a clear bottle in a warm sunny place. After a couple of hours (2 to 3) the wine will have lost its young color and changed to a brownish red. However, if a haze develops, the wine most probably has an iron haze defect and can be returned.

In short, oxygen breaks down the wine by affecting tannin, acids and fruit content. Not only red but also white wines have tannin. White wines have tannin too. In un-oaked white wines the tannin originates from the grape skins, though only for a short time period when combined with the must at crushing. Other sources of tannin are from the addition of powdered tannin or through natural oak-aging. The more oxygen that is dissolved into the wine the more rapidly the wine will change its appearance, nose and taste. By controlling the amount of oxygen that interacts with the wine one can control the wine's drinkability and present condition or at least improve on them.. Fig. 8.2 and 8.3 illustrate the

Fig. 8.4. Shows one of the better aeration devices on the market today.

effect a simple decanting can have on the wine's components.

If you have a very fruit- or tannin-rich wine and need to soften it, a simple decantation will not work if you don't decant the wine many hours beforehand. This requires a bit of planning. There are a number of aeration devices on the market today, but there is one, which I call an 'aeration funnel' seen in Fig. 8.4–8.6.

You should only aerate wines that are youthful and have plenty of tannin and fruit. Fig. 8.5 shows an aeration funnel in progress. You can see how the wine is spread out in a tulip shape creating a large surface area. This surface area mixes the wine well with oxygen. The process can be repeated a number of times depending on how closed and compact the wine is.

Old or mature wines should never be aerated, firstly, because they usually have a lot of sediment, which will only make the wine murky, secondly, as the wines are already in a mature condition, the addition of ogygen could adversely affect any subtle characterisitcs remaining. Thirdly, if the tannins have hardened, aeration will only increase this process by hastening the development of 'dead tannins' see chapter 3.

However, you can also decant older wines off their sediment. This is often done and is totally acceptable as long as you serve the wines directly afterwards. Once at a dinner at Château Lafite-Rothschild in Pauillac, Bordeaux, the sommelier decanted a magnum 1902 from its sediment, washed out the bottle, repoured the wine into the magnum and served it. Quite acceptable!

Wine at the right temperature.

If you want to hide defects in a wine, serve it cold. Temperature affects the aroma and the taste of wine. Red wines can be at room temperature or slightly cooler, but never too warm, as this increases the alcohol evaporation and creates to many volatile aromas. White wines are best served slightly cooler or chilled to about 13°C - 16°C (55°F to 60°F). If colder, you start to loose some aromatics. White sweet wines should be slightly cooler than the white dry wines but Port (Vintage and LBV), Madeira (Malmsey and Bual), Rancio and other darker fortified at the same temperature as red wines. Filling a bucket with water and ice will help to cool the wine 1°C every fifteen minutes. I do not recommend microwaving your wines to make them warmer. Yes, believe it or not, I have had reports of this too.

Fig. 8.5. The wine forms a tulip shape after being poured through the aeration funnel.

Wineglasses

Glass size is very important but generally you should not fill your glass with more wine than one fifth (1/5) to one quarter (1/4) of the glass capacity. A rule of thumb can also be to fill the glass to the widest part of the bowl in a tulip-shaped glass. The space left in the glass is called the ullage.

Wine can be enjoyed from a variety of glass types but there are also especially designed glasses that help to enhance its characteristics. The thinner glass, the smoother the wine flows onto your palate. The shape and size of the glass is important, since the aromas should be trapped in it, whilst allowing for some oxygen mix. There are a number of glass manufacturers making excellent glasses that can be used for your wine tastings. One excellent all-round glass type is the tulip shape approved by the ISO (International Standards Organization) for a wine-tasting glass.

Fig. 8.6. Leif Sahlqvist, discussing the decantation of a Gaja wine from Piemonte with the sommelier of Apotek restaurant in Reykjavik.

Fig. 8.7. A wide-based decanter with an aeration funnel.

Tasting & Grading Wine

APPEARANCE / COLOR (0-5)

Clearness:
Unclear, Clear, Cristal Clear
Protein, Salt/Calcium, Soapy, Cork, Sediment

Brightness / Luster:
Dull, Medium, Lively (Glistening)

Color (Hue):
Whites:
Greenish, Pale Yellow, Yellow, Straw, Golden, Amber
Reds:
Blue, Purple, Ruby, Orange, Brown, Brick

APPEARANCE

-1	-0.5	0	+1	+1.5	+2

COLOR

0	+1	+1.5	+2	+2.5	+3

Carbonic Acid (Bubbles):
Small / Large
None, Few, Many / Sparkle, Pearl-like

Viscosity (Oiliness):
Watery / Oily
(No legs, Thin, Thick legs)

Depth (Tone):
Light, Medium, Deep, Dark, Black

AROMA / NOSE (0-15)

Depth (Fullness):
Dumb, Little Depth, Medium, Full Aroma, Compound, Complex, Elegant

0	+1	+2	+3	+4	+5	+5.5	+6	+6.5	+7	+7.5	+8	+8.5	+9	+9.5	+10

Grape Aroma Typicity:
Not at all, Little, Acceptable, Typical

0	+1	+2	+3	+4	+5

Age Assessment:
Still-Volatile Character:
Young, Developing, Developed, Mature

Aroma Cap Difference between Still & Volatile Character:
None, Little, Good, Dramatic

Character:

Modern (New World) Style: fruit-driven, style-driven ; **Classical (Old World) Style:** fruit-driven, style-driven

Fruity, Vegetables, Earthy, Chemical, Oxidized, Woody, Caramelized, Microbiological, Floral, Spicy,

Citrus, Berry, Tropical fruit, Dried fruit, Canned/Cooked, Moldy, Petroleum, Mineral, Ester, Sulfur, Prickly, Burnt, Yeasty

Blueberry, Blackberry, Raspberry, Strawberry, Cherry, Blackcurrant, Gooseberry, Raisin, Prune, Plum, Sloe, Fig, Elderberry, Rose, Violet, Jasmine, Cinnamon, Cloves, Black / White Pepper, Mint, Allspice,	Liquorice, Leather, Cabbage, Burnt Match, Sulfur Dioxide, Vanilla, Nougat, Pine, Cedar, Oak (French /American /other), Mango, Honey, Butterscotch, Butter, Soy Sauce Chocolate, Molasses, Coffee, Cigar, Smoky, Toast,	Flor/Yeast, Sauerkraut, Sweaty, Horsey, Dates, Nuts, Grapefruit, Grapefruit Peal, Lemon, Lemon Peal, Orange, Orange Peal Apricot, Peach, Pear, Pineapple, Green Apple, Apple, Melon, Banana,	Artificial Fruit, Stalky, Stemmy, Grass/Cut Green / Red Pepper, Eucalyptus, Hay / Straw, Green Bean, Asparagus, Green / Black Olive, Tea, Artichoke, Mushroom, Musk, Tar, Plastic, Diesel, Animal, Smoked Ham	**Moldy:** Wood or Cork **Wet:** Dog, Wool or Paper Mousiness, Outhouse, Old Eggs, Acetone, Vinegar, Onion, Garlic, Dusty, Geranium, Acetic Acid, Rubber, Nail Polish Remover, Fishy, Acetaldehyde (Sherry like) New Cork (1, 2, 3, 4, 5)

Grapes:

Comments:

TASTE (0-20)

Sweetness:
Extra Dry, Dry, Medium, Semi-Sweet, Sweet

Acidity:
Low, Little, Good, High
(Tart, Marked)

Tannin:
Soft, Medium, Hard
Fine, Coarse
(Young / Mature / Dead Tannins)

} Balance White
} Balance Red

Grape Taste Typicity:
Not at all, Little, Acceptable, Typical

0	+1	+1.5	+2	+3	+3.5	+4

Alcohol Level and Balance:
Unbalanced, Acceptable, Good, Very Good

0	+1	+1.5	+2

Fruit Structure:
Thin, Medium, Intense, Complex

0	+1	+1.5	+2

Overall Balance:
Unbalanced, Acceptable, Good, V.Good, Well-balanced

0	+1	+1.5	+3	+3.5	+4	+4.5	+5

Bitterness:
None, Little, Medium, High

+1	0.5	0	-1

Body:
Thin, Light, Medium, Fullbodied,

0	+0.5	+1	+1.5	+2

Length:
Short, Medium, Long, Very Long

0	+1	+2	+2.5	+3	+3.5	+4

(10+ seconds = good, 20+ seconds = excellent)

STORAGE (0-10)

Wine Type	Combined Cellar Time + Total Potential Storage Remaining										
White Wines		1	1.5	2	3	4	5	8	10	12	15+
Red Wines	1	2	3	4	5	6	8	10	15	20	25+
Sweet Wines	2	3	4	6	8	10	15	20	25	30	35+
Fortified Wines	2	4	6	8	10	15	20	25	30	35	45+
Champagne / Sparkling	1	2	3	4	5	6	7	8	10	14	16+
Total Storage Points	**0**	**1**	**2**	**3**	**4**	**5**	**6**	**7**	**8**	**9**	**10**

Vintage / Storage Potential

Young, Developing, Developed, Mature, Undrinkable

SUMMARY

Balance:
Unbalanced, Okay, Good, Very Good, Well-balanced

Extra Points:

Quality:
Lean, Hollow, Plump, Robust
Attractive, Soft, Supple, Refined, Elegant, etc.

Attack:

Price: _____

Value:
Absolutely, Yes, Okay, No

Points 50-100:

50

+ (0-5) Color
+ (0-15) Aroma
+ (0-20) Taste and length
+ (0-10) Storage Potential
TOTAL
Bonus (Subjective Adjustment: 1, 2 or 3)

all wines begin with 50 points

Vintage:
Wine:
Vineyard:
Additional Comments:

Date of Tasting:
Article Number:
Tasting Order: 1 2 3 4 5 ( )

Index of Symbols:

Closed Aroma
Hard / Dying Tannins
Ripe Fruit
Fresh Fruit

raisins, plums, strawberry
clear character, half character, possible character

medium, long

This symbol indicates an average point score.
A variation or adjustment can be made using the +/- signs.

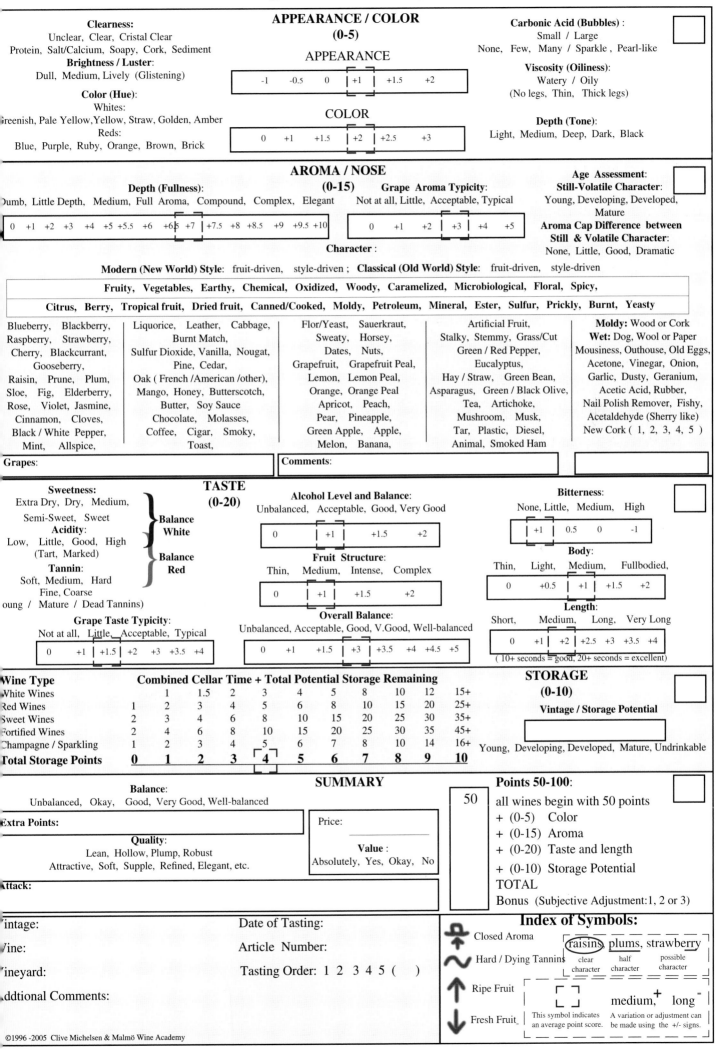

World Vintage Chart

Year	NZ Hawkes Bay	CH Maipo	AU Hunter Valley	AU South Australia	AR Mendoza	US Washington State	US Oregon	US CA (Central Valley)	US CA (North of the Bay)	SA Stellenbosch	G Mosel-Saar-Ruwer	PT Douro (Vintage Port)	IT Tuscany	IT Piedmont	SP Rioja	FR Champagne	FR Southern Rhone	FR Northern Rhone	FR Alsace	FR White Burgundy	FR Red Burgundy	FR Sweet White Bordeaux	FR Dry White Bordeaux	FR Red Bordeaux
1990	4	3	4.5	5	4.5	4	4	3	4	2	5	nv	5	5	4	5	5	5	5	4	5	5	5	5
1991	3	3	2	4	3	4	4	2.5	3.5	3.5	3	3.5	3	3	3	1.5	2	4	1	2	3	1	1.5	2
1992	3	3.5	3	3	3.5	4	4	4	4.5	4	4	4	1	2	3	2	2	2	3.5	3.5	3	0.5	2.5	2
1993	3	4	3	3	4.5	3.5	4	3.5	4	3	4	nv	4	3	3	3	3	3	4	2.5	4	0	2.5	2.5
1994	3.5	3.5	3.5	5	4	4	5	4	5	3.5	4	4.5	3	2	5	2	4	4	2.5	3	3	2	4	4
1995	3	4	3.5	3	5	3	3.5	3	4	4.5	4	nv	5	4	5	4	5	5	4.5	4.5	5	5	4	4.5
1996	3.5	4	3.5	5	5	3.5	3.5	3.5	4	2	4	nv	3	4	4	5	3	4	4	5	5	5	4	4
1997	5	4	3.5	3	3.5	3.5	3	4	5	3.5	4	4	5	5	3	2	3	4	4	4	3	4	4	3
1998	4	2	4.5	5	3	4.5	4	2	3	5	4	3.5	4	5	4	3	5	5	4	4	4	4	3.5	4
1999	4	4.5	4.5	3	4	5	5	3.5	4	4	4	nv	4	3	4	4	5	5	2.5	4	3	5	3.5	2
2000	4	3.5	3.5	3	3.5	4	4	2	5	3	3	4.5	3	4	3	2	5	4	5	3	5	4	4	5
2001	3.5	4	2	4	3.5	4	3.5	4	5	3.5	5	nv	3.5	2.5	5	nv	3.5	4	3.5	4	3	5	4	5
2002	4	3	4	3.5	4	5	4.5	4	4	3.5	3.5	nv	2	2	2.5	4	2	2	4.5	4	4	4	4	4
2003	3.5	4	4	4	4	4.5	4	4	4	4	4	nv	4.5	4.5	4	4	4	4	4	3.5	4.5	4.5	4.5	4.5

nv   non vintage
0   very bad vintage
1   bad vintage
2   average vintage
3   good vintage
4   very good vintage
5   excellent vintage

FRANCE Bordeaux: 1982, 1978, 1966, 1961, 1959, 1955, 1953, 1949, 1947, 1945, 1937, 1934
FRANCE Champagne: 1982; Rhône Reds: Southern 1983, 1981, 1978: Northern 1983, 1978
ITALY Tuscany: 1982, 1978, 1971 • Piedmont: 1982, 1978, 1971; Veneto: 1983, 1979, 1976, 1974, 1971, 1970
SPAIN Rioja: 1982, 1981, 1978 • Catalonia: 1983, 1982, 1981 Ribera del Duero: 1983, 1982, 1980, 1979
US California Cabernet: 1987, 1984, 1978; Oregon Pinot Noir: 1983, 1980
GERMANY 1983, 1976, 1975, 1971, 1964, 1959
AUSTRALIA Barossa: 1982; Coonawarra: 1982, 1980; Hunter Valley: 1983
PORTUGAL Port: 1983, 1977, 1970, 1966, 1963, 1955, 1948, 1945

Grape Character Summation Charts

Red Grape Varieties

Grape Variety	Typical Aroma	Tannin	Acidity	Sweetness	Bitterness	Weight	Alcohol
Barbera	Red Berry, Cherry, Strawberry, Blackcurrant, Raspberry, Plums, Volatility	3	8	0	0	4	11-12.5%
Cabernet Sauvignon	Blackcurrant, Chocolate, Cedar Wood, Mint, Tobacco, Coffee, Dark Berries	5 to 8	5 to 8	0	0 to 2	4 to 9	11-14%
Cabernet Franc	Blackberries, Mint, Green Olives, Nutmeg, Ripe Plums, Violets, Strawberry	5.2	6.5	0	0	5	11.5-13.5%
Cinsaut	Red Berries, Jam, Strawberries, Stewed fruit, Dried Fruit, Plums, Raisins	3.5	6.3	0	0	4	10.5-12.5%
Gamay	Fruity, Red Berries, Banana, Pears, Caramel, Bubblegum, Violets, Floral	2	5.5	0	0	2.5	11-13%
Grenache	Fruity, Dark Berries, Light Berries, Floral, Lavender, Rosemary, Plums, Spice	3.3	5	0	0	5	12.5-16%
Malbec	Blackberry, Mulberry, Plum, Prune, Blackcurrant, Liquorice, Eucalyptus	7.5	6	0	0	7	12-14%
Merlot	Dark Berries, Plums, Heavy Fruit, Mixed Spices, Tobacco, Cedar, Raspberry, Cherry, Currants	5	6.5	0	Can be burnt	7 to 9	11-14%
Nebbiolo	Plums, Tar, Cherries, Violets, Liquorice, Mushrooms, Blackberries, Black-pepper, Mint	10	7	0	0-1	7 to 9	12.5-14.5%
Pinotage	Red Berries, Strawberry, Raspberries, Spices, Earthiness, Greenstick	5	7.5	0	0	5	11.5-13.5%
Pinot Noir	Red Berries, Strawberry, Cherry, Raspberry, Floral, Vegetables, Chocolate, Violets, Smoked Meat	5	7.5	0	0	7 to 8	12-13%
Sangiovese	Blackberries, Cherries, Mint, Nuts, Cloves, Spice, Red Berries, Bayleaves	6	8	0	0-1	7	12-13.5%
Syrah/Shiraz	Gamy, Meaty, Leather, Mixed Spice, Blackpepper, Dark Berries, Tar, Rubber, Currants	8.5	6	0	0	7 to 9	12.5-14%
Tempranillo	Red Berries, Strawberry, Dill, Cherry, Butter, Spice, Warm fruit	5	7	0	0	6 to 7	11-13.5%
Zinfandel	Blackberries, Black cherries, Tar, Rubber, Cloves, Mixed Spice, Ginger, Greenstick	6	7		Slight	6 to 9	12.5-15%

White Grape Varieties

Grape Variety	Typical Aroma	Tannin	Acidity	Sweetness	Bitterness	Weight	Alcohol
Aligote	Citrus, GS Apples, Grapefruit, Oranges, Nuttiness, Almonds, Yeast	1	7 to 7.5	1 to 3	1	4 to 5.5	11.5-12.5%
Chardonnay	Dried Fruit, Spice, Apples, Pineapples, Mangoes, Leeches, Butter, Nutty	1 to 2	6	1 to 9	0	5.5 to 9	11.5-14.5%
Chenin Blanc	Citrus, Peachy, Apricot, Honey, Acidic, Grassy, Melon, Floral, Slight Spice	1	9.5	1 to 8	0	3 to 5	11-14%
Gewürztraminer	Honey, Exotic Fruit, Mixed Spice, Leeches, Roses, Floral, Orange Peel, Perfume, Marmalade-toffee	1	5 to 6	1 to 7	3	6 to 7	11.5-14.5%
Gruner Veltliner	Citrus, Mixed Spices, Mineral, Roses, Fruity, Apples, Apricot	1 to 2	8	1	0.5	5.5 to 7	11.5-12.8%
Macabeo	Citrus, Apricots, Banana, Earthy, Tropical Fruit, Velvety, Acidic, Apples	1 to 3	5 to 9	1	0	4 to 7	11.5-13.5%
Muscadet	Yeasty, Gooseberry, Almonds, Nettles, Smoky, Earthy, Mineral, Citrus, Acidic	1 to 4	9	1	0	2 to 4	11-12.5%
Muscat (d.p.g.)	Musk, Oranges, Marmalade, Apricots, Dried Fruit, Yeast, Apples, Raisins, Perfume	0	5.5	2 to 7	0	3.5 to 5	12.5-15%
Pinot Blanc	Light Citrus, Fresh Apples, Honey, Spice, Floral	0	6 to 7	1 to 2	0	6 to 8	9.5-13%
Pinot Gris	Tropical Fruit, Honey, Apricots, Mixed Spice, Ripe Apples, Smoky, Nutty, Creamy	1 to 2	4	2 to 3	3	5 to 6	9.5-14%
Riesling	Petroleum, Fruity, Citrus, Apples, Mineral, Honey, Pears, Lime	0 to 2	10	1 to 8	0	3 to 7	9.5-14%
Sauvignon Blanc	Cassis, (Cat's Pee), Gooseberry, Grassy, Flint, Vegetal, Musk-like, Aromatic	1 to 3	8	2 to 8	0	3.5 to 6	11.5-14%
Semillon	Apricots, Aromatic, Honey, Nuts, Dried Fruit, Citrus, Lanolin, Raisin, Velvety	1 to 2	4 to 7	1 to 8	0	6 to 8	10-14%
Trebbiano	Citrus, Granny Smith, Almonds, Hard, Acidic, Some floral	0	9	1 to 2	0	5.5 to 6.5	11-12.8%
Viognier	Aromatic, Peachy, Floral, Pears, Musk, Tropical Fruit, Spice	1 to 3	3 to 4.5	2.5 to 3	3 to 4	7 to 8	12-13.5%

White Grape Sensory Ratio Bars

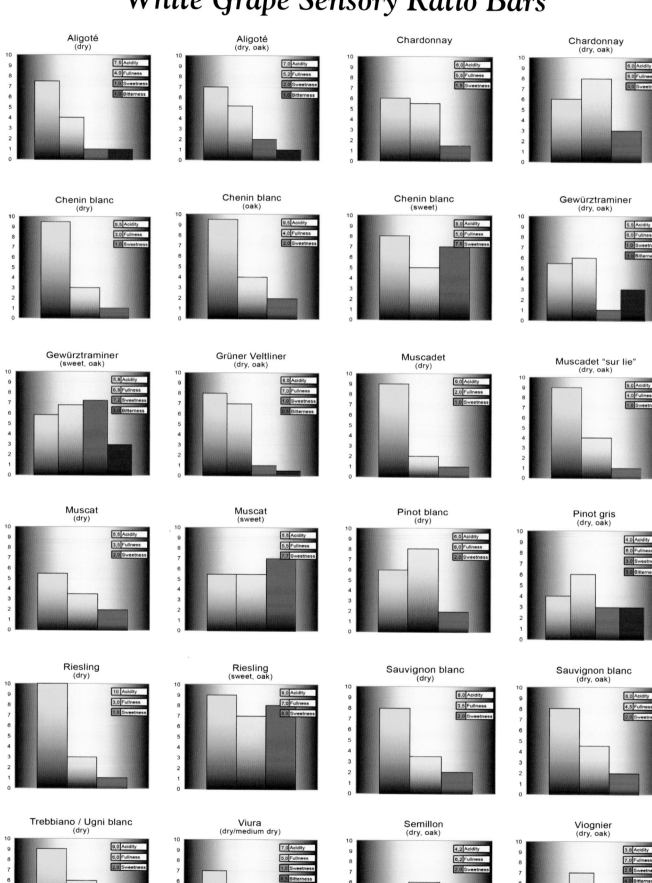

Red Grape Sensory Ratio Bars

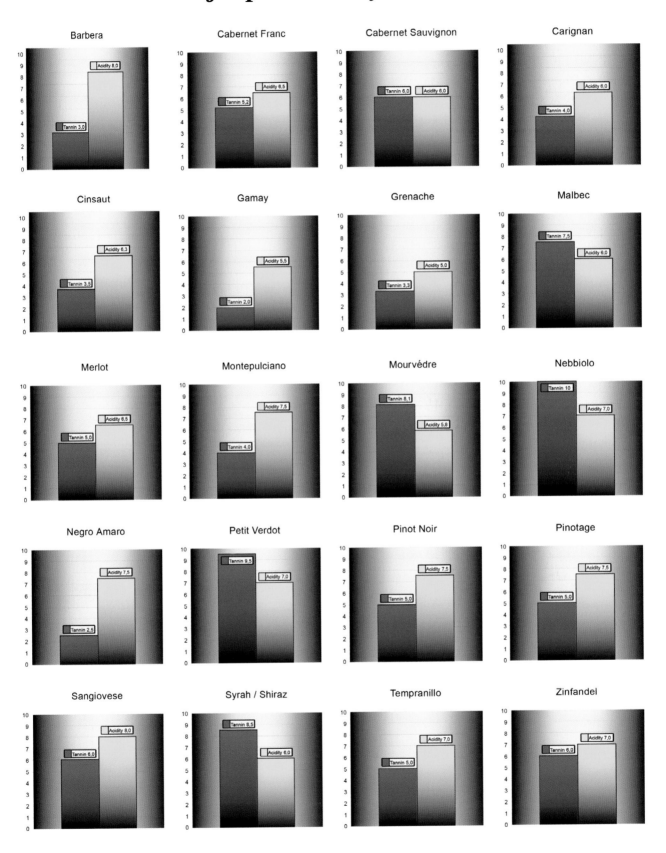

Index